The Institutional Ec
Corruption and Reform

Theory, Evidence, and Policy

Corruption has been a feature of public institutions for centuries, yet only relatively recently has it been made the subject of sustained scientific analysis. In an important contribution to this ongoing project, Johann Graf Lambsdorff shows how insights from institutional economics can be used to develop a better understanding of the institutions necessary to carry out corrupt transactions and those that are helpful in inhibiting them. He argues that rather than being deterred by penalties, corrupt actors are more influenced by other factors such as the opportunism of their criminal counterparts and the danger of acquiring a reputation of unreliability. This suggests a novel strategy for fighting corruption – the "invisible foot" – whereby the unreliability of corrupt counterparts induces honesty and good governance even in the absence of good intentions. Combining interdisciplinary theoretical research with state-of-the-art empirical investigations, this book will be an invaluable resource for researchers and policy-makers concerned with anticorruption reform.

JOHANN GRAF LAMBSDORFF is Chair in Economic Theory at the University of Passau, Germany, and Senior Research Consultant to Transparency International. He is the founder of the Corruption Perceptions Index, Which he has orchestrated since 1995.

The Institutional Economics of Corruption and Reform

Theory, Evidence, and Policy

JOHANN GRAF LAMBSDORFF

CAMBRIDGE UNIVERSITY PRESS
Cambridge, New York, Melbourne, Madrid, Cape Town, Singapore, São Paulo

Cambridge University Press
The Edinburgh Building, Cambridge CB2 8RU, UK

Published in the United States of America by Cambridge University Press, New York

www.cambridge.org
Information on this title: www.cambridge.org/9780521872751

First published 2007
Reprinted 2007
This digitally printed version 2008

A catalogue record for this publication is available from the British Library

Library of Congress Cataloguing in Publication data

Lambsdorff, Johann, Graf, 1965–
The institutional economics of corruption and reform: theory, evidence, and policy/
Johann Graf Lambsdorff.
p. cm.
Includes bibliographical references and index.

ISBN-13: 978-0-521-87275-1 (hardback)

1. Administrative agencies – Corrupt practices – Prevention. 2. Political
corruption – Prevention. 3. International finance – Corrupt practices – Prevention.
4. Institutional economics – Sociological aspects. I. Title.

JF1525.C66L36 2007
353.4′6 – dc22

2006035151

ISBN 978-0-521-87275-1 hardback
ISBN 978-0-521-06867-3 paperback

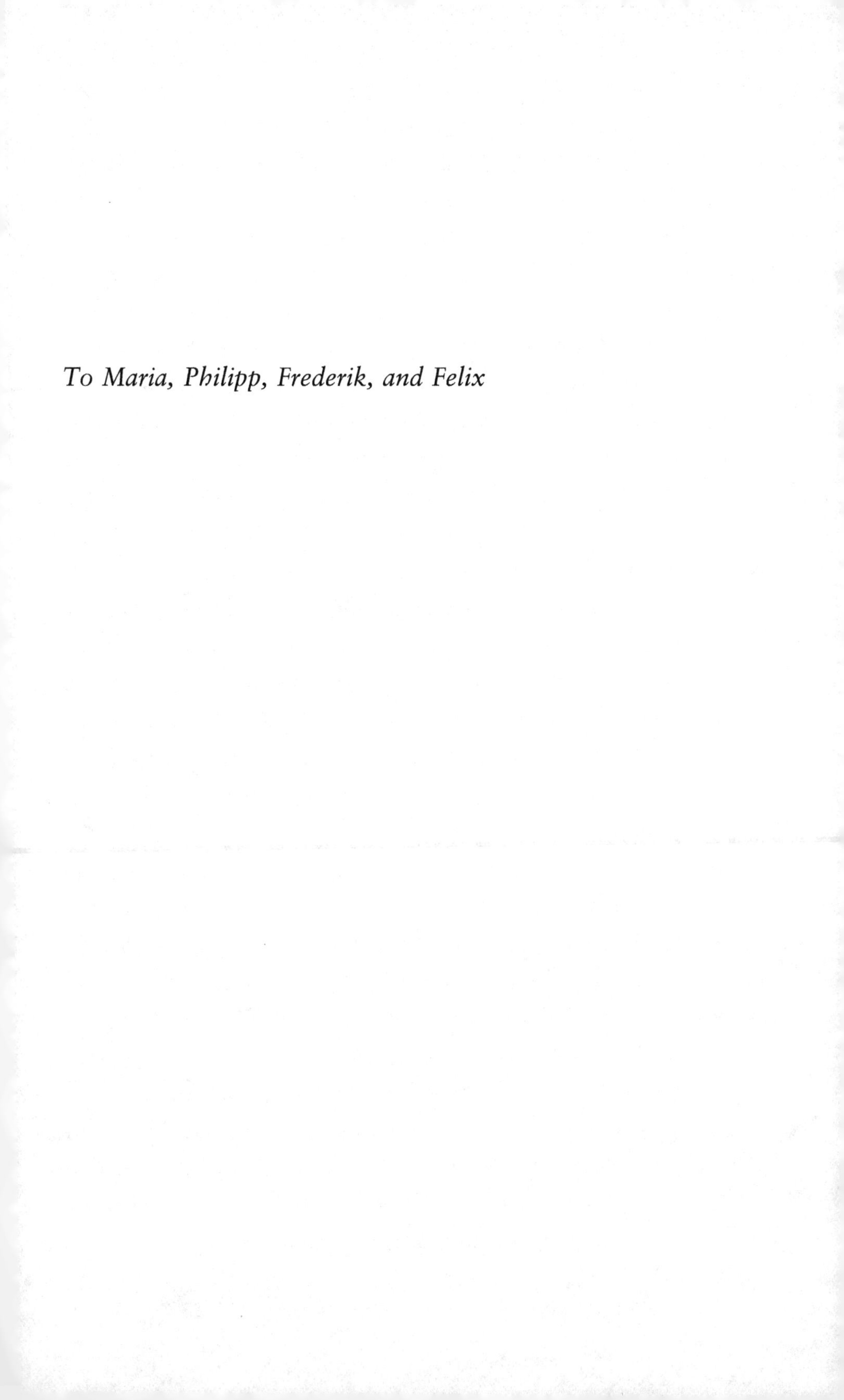

To Maria, Philipp, Frederik, and Felix

Contents

List of boxes

Acknowledgements

This book is a twelve-year project, combining research efforts since 1994. At an early stage, some parts of it became highly prominent: The Corruption Perceptions Index, which was designed in 1995 and is compiled under my leadership at the University of Passau since then, on behalf of Transparency International. This index was not predominantly designed to serve as a tool for alerting politics and the public at large. Its initial aim was to serve as a starting point for academic research. Considerable progress has been made on this front of research since then – the empirical investigations reviewed here provide evidence on this.

Many friends and colleagues have been helpful in providing critical comments. I would like to thank J. Ahrens, I. Amundsen, L. Bajec, H. Davoodi, D. della Porta, W. Easterly, B. Efron, G. Engel, O.-H. Fjeldstad, B. Frank, P. Heywood, A. K. Jain, P. Manow, P. Mauro, K. Meyer, H. Möller-deBeer, B. Mukherjee, M. Nell, G. Pfeffermann, J. Pope, S. Rose-Ackerman, M. Schinke, C. Schinke, A. Schmidt, R. Seubert, V. Tanzi, U. Teksoz, and an armada of anonymous referees. I am grateful to two anonymous referees for helping me integrate the diverse concepts presented here into a consistent book.

Some special thanks go to W. Zucchini, who was invaluable in refining the statistical methodology for the Corruption Perceptions Index and devoted much time and effort to designing appropriate algorithms. I owe many thanks to H.-J. Jarchow, who supervised my *habilitation* at the University of Göttingen. He provided me with the freedom to devote my efforts to a new area of research and supported me with his critical accuracy. Further special thanks are due to Peter Eigen. Without his organizational support through Transparency International much of my work would not have had the opportunity to reach out to a broader audience already at its early stages. Similar thanks go to Frank Vogl, Jeremy Pope, George Moody-Stuart†,

Lawrence Cockroft, and many others within Transparency International. They established a community that injects spirit into what is otherwise bloodless research. Although this book is dedicated to academic rigor I hope that some of this spirit remains.

University of Passau, October 06

A road map to this book

Those who are willing to carry out corrupt acts lose the capacity to commit to honesty. This is the core argument developed and exploited in this book. Corrupt actors can neither commit to honestly serving the public nor credibly promise reciprocity to their corrupt counterparts. This thought is at the center of understanding the disastrous economic and social consequences of corruption. At the same time, this concept deserves to be placed at the center of reform. Bribe-takers and bribe-givers have a schizophrenic relationship to honesty. They betray their superiors and the public but attempt to signal reciprocity to each other – and often fail in doing so. A strategy for reform must exploit this failure. The Achilles' heel of corrupt transactions is that a briber often does not know what he will get in return. This is a crucial weakness of those who are willing to engage in corrupt transactions. Anticorruption can therefore take the tactic of a judo-fighter – someone who exploits his opponents' weaknesses.

The power of economic thinking started with the concept of the invisible hand. Competition substituted for benevolence by guiding self-seeking actors to serve the public. With respect to fighting corruption we do not have such a powerful mechanism. If something comes close to it, it is the corrupt actor's capacity to betray each other. This betrayal is a good thing. I call this the principle of the invisible foot.[1] The willingness to take bribes works against the corrupt actors. Anticipating this, even self-seeking individuals may have reason to commit to honesty rather than seek opportunities for bribes.

This book does not provide readers with recipes on how to fight corruption. Instead of designing a toolbox it rather presents a methodological approach that, I hope, will inspire anticorruption in the

[1] This term was originally invented by Brock and Magee (1984). They used the term to indicate welfare losses arising in rent-seeking competition. My usage is different here.

future. This is repeatedly supported by cases and examples. Chapter 1 presents methodological and quantitative details. How is corruption defined, how is it measured? Why did some older guiding principles for anticorruption fail? I argue that corruption is not eliminated by fighting on a different battleground, such as reducing government, decentralizing public decision-making, privatizing public property, or enhancing competition. Corruption is a genuinely new challenge that requires novel answers. The invisible hand of competition brings about good markets but not good governance. This is shown in Chapter 1.

Chapter 2 surveys some empirical evidence on anticorruption, including its sometimes poor performance, and starts to present the core concept of this book. Having dismissed many alternative approaches to fighting corruption, the principle of the invisible foot is elaborated.

Chapters 3 and 4 explore that the corrupt actors' lack of commitment to honesty is at the core of the welfare losses of corruption. In Chapter 3, this idea is developed for bribe-taking bureaucrats. There should be no doubt that bribe-taking is often a utility-maximizing strategy of a self-seeking bureaucrat. But the downside of one's willingness to take bribes is that such actors disqualify for professions where their commitment would be vital.

A similar thought arises for heads of government, as explored in Chapter 4. They might transfer public funds into their private pockets. But they are not trusted by investors if they disrespect law. The advantage from bribery turns against its actors. This is at the core of understanding the social costs of grand corruption, the type of corruption that takes place higher up in hierarchy.

Chapters 3 and 4 at the same time provide readers with an up-to-date assessment of research, both empirical and theoretical. Such an assessment is also provided in the various boxes of this book, which allow readers to obtain a quick grasp of empirical research. I hope such details do not distract readers from the core message of the book. There is a multitude of social costs invoked by corruption. This ascertains that we cannot avoid the negative consequences of corruption but must fight corruption itself. We are given no alternative but to devote our efforts to reducing corruption.

Chapter 5 asks whether we should facilitate or impede corruption. The answer appears straightforward in favor of the latter option.

But we must note that the traditional rent-seeking theory argued differently. It opted in favor of facilitated corruption because otherwise competition for preferential treatment would waste resources for lobbyism, engaging lawyers for lawsuits, or harassing politicians with public campaigns. I show that this conclusion is misguided – our effort must be directed toward increasing the transaction costs of corruption.

Chapter 6 shows how in practice corrupt actors attempt to secure reciprocity. This chapter might be misunderstood as a how-to-bribe guide for criminal actors. But learning how to arrange bribes is a fruitful starting point for reform. We must understand our enemies if we want to defeat them. We must understand corrupt actors' temptation to betray each other in order to encourage precisely this behavior.

Chapter 7 brings our thought to the international arena. The invisible hand of competition brings about good markets. But does it destroy good governance? This proposition, fortunately, would take things too far. The reason for ethics to survive market pressures relates to the skills required in corrupt transactions. I address this topic by raising an empirical question: do differences in skills affect trade? Are some exporters advantaged in entering corrupt markets? The answer is a clear yes. The skill of bribery is at the core of understanding some remarkable differences in trade patterns of large exporting nations. Ethical behavior can survive market pressure. Whereas some actors may refrain from corruption owing to moral concerns, others are simply untalented. One application of this finding relates to corrupt intermediaries. These offer expertise on corrupt transactions to the untalented. Certification should be offered to those intermediaries who are willing to commit to anticorruption.

Chapter 8 picks up the international perspective of Chapter 7 and confronts it with a challenging position. While I claim that transaction costs of corruption should be increased we hear investors complain about the unpredictability of corruption. Should we prefer corruption to be predictable? Is reliability and reciprocity always a good thing? This is not an academic debate. Politics is often involved in guaranteeing international reciprocity even when corruption was involved. I argue that this practice must be stopped. The unpredictability of corruption is precisely what may put an end to it. We must make sure that corruption remains a risky and capricious activity.

Chapter 9 brings us back to the question of how corrupt actors reciprocate. It shows that corrupt transactions are often embedded in regular, legal business transactions. These transactions can provide the breeding ground by establishing the trust and the reciprocity necessary to engage in illegal deals. This chapter is crucial for understanding that there is no "corrupt marketplace." There is hardly ever a given demand for corrupt services and supply of such, with a going rate for bribery being determined in equilibrium. Corruption is restricted to insiders with established links. Corruption is open only to those who exploit long-standing relationships for a criminal career.

Chapter 10 summarizes. Other guiding principles for anticorruption such as repression, prevention, or transparency may run out of steam. The principle of the invisible foot should be at the core of anticorruption and provide future inspiration. A plethora of building blocks can emanate from this principle; this book does not try to be exhaustive in this regard. One focus that deserves recognition is the design of the legal system. Penalties may mark the starting point of a corrupt career. An asymmetric design of penalties may avoid this problem and inhibit corrupt reciprocity. This is only an example for the overarching principle of the invisible foot. To state it again: corrupt actors can neither commit to honestly serving the public nor credibly promise reciprocity to their corrupt counterparts. Reform is about exploiting this handicap.

1 Introduction

There are several good protections against temptations,
but the surest is cowardice.

Mark Twain,
Following the Equator, 1897

1.1. Why this book?

Corruption, the misuse of public power for private benefit, turns out to be a relatively new challenge for social sciences. It has been an issue for politics and society for many centuries, but its systematic scientific treatment is rather novel. However, most researchers consider corruption to be just another application of preexisting theories without sufficiently considering their adequacy. This, I believe, is like putting new wine into old wineskins. Just as wine causes the skins to burst corruption ruptures preexisting theories. Just as we lose wine in old skins we may fail to understand corruption without considering its intrinsic dynamics and logic. Applying old theories then falls short of an adequate understanding of the phenomenon.

A lecture that I run on the economics of corruption starts with a game: students are supposed to derive a strategy of how to win a public tender when they have insufficient funding to take the official route.[1] I find myself time and again appalled by the variety of unusual, innovative, and totally criminal proposals. This is what corruption is about: someone violates the rules of the game in a way that was not anticipated by others. To apply models of perfect foresight, rational expectations, competition with a level playing field, and similar models are, hence, no longer enlightening. In this spirit, a variety of

[1] I owe this idea to Krassen Stanchev, Institute for Market Economics, Sofia, Bulgaria.

orthodox approaches to corruption appear less useful. Some examples are provided here.

There were some economists who started with the indisputable notion that corruption in the form of bribery represents a mutually beneficial exchange. Microeconomists consider such an exchange to be desirable and inevitable; functionalists assume that its mere existence indicates its useful function. Given that briber and bribee are better off after striking a corrupt deal, on what grounds can we claim that the deal is detrimental to economic well-being? But this notion disregards how corruption constrains decision-making. When officials cannot credibly promise to reject side-payments from clients, they are not trustworthy at the outset and may not be employed in the first place. Corruption turns out to be harmful even to those who have the chance of striking illegal deals.

For example, it may well be worthwhile to construct good-quality roads. But the government may choose to cancel the project if bad quality is expected to result from bribes being paid to inspectors. Or imagine that a fair and efficient tax system should be established, but tax collectors cannot be kept from taking bribes in exchange for turning a blind eye to underreporting. A country may have to continue living with the old system. If a state auditor cannot guarantee that she will not fake reports in exchange for a bribe, her contribution loses value. She may not be hired in the first place – even though an honest exchange would have been favorable to all.

Other researchers argued that instead of fighting corruption itself one should combat its causes, of which they claimed excessive government intervention, market restrictions, and a burdening bureaucracy to be most prominent. These arguments have been pointed out by early writers (Bayley 1966; Nye 1967; Huntington 1968; Leff 1964; Morgan 1964) and still make their way into modern economic textbooks such as Mankiw (2000: 123). Corruption is then nothing else but a symptom of inadequate state intervention (Ades and Di Tella 1999). This transforms the problem into something which is more akin to economic theories. State intervention is widely dealt with in economics. The standard recipe for containing corruption would be to get rid of government intervention. Take the case of Philadelphia's Department of Licenses and Inspections where officials accepted money from plumbing contractors in exchange for a quick approval of job-site work.

A standard 'tip' was $20, a source said, and it could grow if a plumber was in a bind of some kind. "A lot of it would occur when a plumber would need to close an excavation hole where they'd buried pipe, and it couldn't be closed until an inspector approved it, "the source said." So you could stand around with your crew waiting, or you could page an inspector and get him out there real quick, and thank him for it."... the payments to inspectors have been suspected for years but that they were hard to crack since those paying the bribes were happy for the speedy service. (*Philadelphia Daily News*, March 14, 2001: "Plumbers Allegedly Bribed Inspectors")

The case reveals how regulation to obtain an inspector's approval induced corruption. But the case shows at the same time that simple recipes for cracking down on government regulation are not feasible. Inspections are necessary so as to guarantee the delivery of proper quality, and their abandonment is likely to do more rather than less harm, maybe even increase corruption further.

One of the biggest cases of systematic corruption also related to market distortions: in the Iraqi Oil-for-Food program between 1995 and 2003, oil was allowed to be sold only in exchange for humanitarian goods. The extreme public desire for much-needed goods not only provided ample opportunities to mark up prices but it also led to high-ranking UN officials turning a blind eye to massive corruption.[2] According to an estimate, Saddam Hussein's regime was able to collect as much as US$1.8 billion. Of the 4,500 private firms involved in the program, close to half were involved in the payment of bribes. One paradigmatic case relates to a truck being sold by Daimler Chrysler. While the regular price would have been US$130,000, the company charged US$143,000 and passed on US$13,000 to a Swiss bank account of an Iraqi official. Likewise, oil left the country too cheaply and kickbacks were paid in exchange. This case well fits standard economic modeling on the distortionary effects imposed by market restrictions. Such restrictions create opportunities for systematic corruption. But at the same time, the common economic advice to abolish market restrictions is far from obvious. The standard economic recipe would be to prevent the UN Security Council from imposing trade restrictions as a way of sanctioning countries; this is not at all a suggestion that will gain undisputed approval.

[2] The full report by the Volcker Commission is available at www.iic-offp.org. Accessed November 2006.

The experience from the Iraqi Oil-for-Food program will rather lead to considerations of how better to monitor the purchases and control malfeasance.

These two cases are representative of many other incidences of corruption. Regulation is often an integral and much-needed part of government. Suggestions to avoid regulation are more revealing of a writer's negative attitude toward government, in general, rather than a useful contribution to reform.

For the last decade, most economists have been much less lenient on corruption than their predecessors and have clearly emphasized its adverse welfare consequences. But the remedies suggested have been embedded into economic orthodoxy. The thrust of some approaches has been to be critical of government *in toto*. If corruption involves a self-seeking government whose members attempt to enrich themselves, one needs to crack down on the government itself; see Becker (1994), and for a critical review see Orchard and Stretton (1997).

Boyko *et al.* (1996) suggest that privatization is a means of reducing corruption and increasing efficiency at the same time. A downsized "grabbing hand regime" would have less opportunities for milking the citizenry (Shleifer and Vishny 1998). This argument is well embedded into economists' belief in the market and distrust toward politicians, suggesting that corruption can be contained by minimizing the public sector. However, the findings reported in Box 1 are not supportive of this approach.

Box 1 Corruption and the size of the public sector

It has been suggested that the overall size of the government budget relative to GDP may be positively correlated with levels of corruption. This is shown by LaPalombara (1994: 338), who uses a sample of countries in which Scandinavian countries are disregarded by assuming them to be an exception. The reverse finding is reported by others. Elliott (1997: 182–3) reports for a sample of eighty-three countries that the size of the government budget relative to GDP decreases with levels of corruption. This is supported by Adsera *et al.* (2000). Gerring and Thacker (2005: 245–6) report insignificant results. Graeff and Mehlkop (2003) observe that corruption significantly decreases with government size in the high-income countries.

These considerations suggest that a more promising focus would be on particular types of government expenditures in their potential to cause corruption. In this respect it is suggested that redistributive activities as opposed to other government activities are more likely to cause corruption. La Porta *et al.* (1999: 242) show a positive correlation of the total government transfers and subsidies relative to GDP with corruption. However, the variable correlates too closely with total government expenses, bringing about the aforementioned problems. In sum, there is no convincing evidence on the size of government expenses as a cause of corruption.

Elliott (1997) concludes that types of government activities may be more important than the size of their budgets. Regressing corruption on the government's budget (relative to GDP) might also be affected by reverse causality: corrupt governments have difficulties in obtaining funding, be it through taxation or loans. See Box 21 for respective evidence. This lack of resources then forces them to operate on a rather small budget. Another criticism of the hypothesis put forth by LaPalombara is provided by Husted (1999: 342, 350, 354). He argues that governments are larger in societies characterized by a greater acceptance of authority. Such acceptance would be a cultural determinant of both corruption and the size of the government budget.

Overall, there is little correlation between the overall size of the public sector and corruption, as shown in Box 1. Privatization may have its clear economic advantages, but its effect on containing corruption appears ambiguous. This might be owing to privatized firms experiencing a "privatized" form of corruption. The bribes formerly taken from public servants would then be requested from the private firms' staff. Privatization also does not provide a guarantee that the newly founded units are no longer serving politically motivated interests. Similarly, whether a downsized government is less capable of milking the citizenry is equally questionable: privatized firms can be equally exposed to public interference and demands for bribes. What was formerly taken from state-owned enterprises is then extorted from private firms. More often than not, private firms pay more in bribes than their well-connected state-owned counterparts (Lambsdorff and Cornelius 2000: 76–7). Finally, many transition economies experienced massive corruption in the course of privatization programs. This may be another reason why downsizing the public sector does not help in reducing corruption, at least not in the transition period. Long-term positive effects from privatization may certainly be possible, where competitive pressures are superior in avoiding inefficiencies and corruption, as opposed to bureaucratic control. But such advantages are likely to require best practice in the process of privatization.

On a similar note, some authors assume that decentralization could be a means for reducing corruption by ripping the state off its extortionate capacities and bringing government closer to the people. But the alternative to a large centralized public sector is sometimes a weak local government that is captured by strong local players. It requires little imagination that such a regime may be equally unattractive to investors, and similar adverse effects on welfare are quite likely to arise. As shown in Box 2 a simple economic "recipe" like decentralization does not unequivocally ameliorate the problems of corruption. The pros and cons of decentralization are an important issue. But they are the wrong battleground if one aims at containing corruption.

One issue highlighted by Box 2 is that arguments pertaining to decentralization seem to be dependent on how decentralization is precisely quantified. Apart from this, one cannot exclude that certain cultural determinants drive both decentralization and the absence of corruption. Countries characterized by civic cooperation and trust among people as well as those with well-developed subnational units may be in a position to decentralize and lower corruption at the same time.

Box 2 Corruption and decentralization

Some authors observe a positive correlation between corruption and a country's size, measured by total population (Fisman and Gatti 2002; Root 1999; Treisman 1999). These correlations are robust to the inclusion of further variables. This might be taken as an indicator in favor of decentralization. Smaller countries might be in a better position to establish a decent administration and to monitor their politicians. Using the results from a cross section of countries might be taken as an indicator that decentralizing government power could be a means to curb corruption.

But Knack and Azfar (2003) provide a clear warning against these findings. They show that the correlation between corruption and population size results from sample selection problems. Ratings on corruption are only provided for those countries in which multinational investors have sufficient interest. These tend to be large nations and, among the small nations, only those that are well governed. Knack and Azfar (2003) conduct regressions for larger samples of countries and observe that the relation between corruption and population disappears. Damania *et al.* (2004) show that population density decreases corruption in a sample of sixty-nine countries; it remains to be seen whether this finding survives the test for sample selection, as proposed by Knack and Azfar.

Another variable for measuring the extent of decentralization is presented by Huther and Shah (1998) and Fisman and Gatti (2002). The authors interpret the share of subnational expenditures in total public spending as a measure of decentralization. In a sample of eighty countries, this index correlates positively with various measures of good governance. Huther and Shah report a correlation with lack of corruption larger than 0.5. However, the authors do not include further explanatory variables. One cannot exclude that more developed countries are less corrupt and more decentralized at the same time. Biased coefficients are therefore possible. The approach by Fisman and Gatti (2002) makes use of the same variable on decentralization yet tests whether the outcome is robust to the inclusion of further variables. For a wide range of specifications, they find that fiscal decentralization in government spending is significantly associated with lower corruption. The authors also suggest that corruption may be larger when spending is decentralized, while revenue collection remains in control of the central government. They base their empirical findings on levels of corruption in local states of the United States. Arikan (2004) employs various measures on decentralization and observes mostly an insignificant relationship to corruption. A high ratio of non-central government employment to total government employment, however, seems to go along with lower levels of corruption.

Treisman (1999) takes a more direct approach to investigating the effect of decentralization. Rather then regressing corruption on total population, he distinguishes between federal and centralized

Box 2 (*Cont.*)

states. He reports significant evidence that federal states are more corrupt than centralized ones. But Treisman (1999) argues that this relationship falls to insignificance when other variables are included. Adsera *et al.* (2000) and Panizza (2001) also fail to obtain a significant impact. Damania *et al.* (2004) even report a significant impact of federalism in reducing corruption. On the contrary, Goldsmith (1999: 878), Kunicova (2002), and Kunicova and Rose-Ackerman (2005) claim federalism to increase corruption, even when controlling for GDP per head. In a more recent publication, Gerring and Thacker (2004) are also supportive of a significant adverse impact of federalism on corruption. They distinguish between nonfederal, semifederal, and federal states and mix these characteristics with the extent of bicameralism where no or only a weak upper house exists, where the upper house is not dominated by a lower house, and where nondominance goes along with a different partisan distribution between the houses. The authors find evidence against federal states and in favor of unitary governments throughout a variety of regressions.

Testa (2003) investigates differences between unicameral systems and bicameral systems. She shows for a cross section of forty-three democracies that bicameralism lowers corruption in rather ethnolinguistically homogenous states. But bicameralism increases corruption in countries with a high level of ethnolinguistic fractionalization. The suggested reason for this finding relates to bicameralism hindering lobbyism (and corruption) by doubling the legislators that a lobby must buy. But where two chambers differ in politics, which is likely to arise in countries with high levels of fractionalization, legislators are used to seeking compromises and lobbyism may require few resources. The extent of fractionalization is also investigated by Alesina *et al.* (2003). They show that countries characterized by ethnic, linguistic, or religious fractionalization are rated worse by PRS/ICRG with respect to the political instability related to corruption.

Many economists point to one major cause of corruption: bad regulation. Ill-designed institutions are considered to be at the frontline of assigning adverse incentives to policy-makers, bureaucrats, and the public in general. Box 3 reviews studies that are supportive of a close association between bad regulation and corruption. Such a viewpoint would accept that government serves useful functions and that, thus, downsizing government is not the vision for reform. Reform should rather avoid complicated rules or those that are difficult to administer and align with individual decision making. From this perspective, some "good" regulation may even be helpful in containing corruption. For example, privatization in Eastern Europe involved bribery because there was too little "good regulation," that is, too few legal requirements that restricted corrupt deals.

As a result, detecting bad regulation and misdirected state intervention can be helpful in becoming aware of areas where corruption is likely to occur. However, bad regulation and corruption are quite often two sides of the same coin. When local firms are given preferential treatment in public tenders, this may induce corruption, but it may also be the outright result of strong private interests that capture public funds. In other cases, corruption causes bad regulations, and not the other way round.

Quite striking is an example from Pakistan. The gold trade was formerly unregulated and smuggling was common. Shortly after Benazir Bhutto returned as Prime Minister in 1993, a Pakistani bullion trader in Dubai proposed a deal: in return for the exclusive right to import gold, he would help the government regularize trade – and make some further private payments. In 1994, the payment of US$10 million on behalf of Ms. Bhutto's husband was arranged. In November 1994, Pakistan's Commerce Ministry wrote to the bullion trader, informing him that he had been granted a license to be the country's sole authorized gold importer – a profitable monopoly position (*The Straits Times*, Singapore, February 1, 1998, "Paper Trails Points to Illicit Bhutto Hoard," and June 2, 1998, "The Scandals").

When monopoly rights are given in exchange for bribes, it is rather corruption that drives market distortions. Claims that the monopoly right should be abandoned so as to get rid of corruption appear misplaced, because at the core of the problem would be criminally innovative politicians and businesspeople, and their capacity of inventing bad regulations. A final concern: the difference between "bad" and "good" regulation is far from obvious. One criterion could be whether regulation creates opportunities for corruption. But in this case the argument becomes circular and we are not provided with a causal theory of corruption. Overall, looking for "bad" regulation provides some hints for detecting corruption but it falls short of an overarching approach to reform.

Box 3 Corruption and regulatory quality

Broadman and Recanatini (1999) show for a sample of transition economies in Europe and Central Asia that higher barriers to market entry lead to higher corruption. Djankov *et al.* (2002) are equally concerned with the nature of entry regulation. They determine the number of procedures required for starting a new business for a cross section of seventy-one countries, along with the necessary time and official costs. The authors find a strong correlation of these variables with a country's level of corruption for a variety of specifications and control variables. Svensson (2005: 29) finds a positive correlation between corruption and the number of business days needed to obtain legal status. These findings support the argument that entry regulation often does not serve to correct for market failure but brings about problems of its own.

Treisman (2000) finds that "state intervention" tends to increase corruption. The former variable is measured by a subjective index compiled by IMD. But as other explanatory variables enter into the regression, the relationship breaks down. Another correlation between corruption and a measure of policy distortion for thirty-nine countries is presented by the World Bank (1997: 104, 168). Unfortunately, the study lacks a precise definition of policy distortions. Also, the robustness of the results is not tested by including further explanatory variables.

Gerring and Thacker (2005) report a positive correlation between regulatory quality and absence of corruption. Ades and Di Tella (1997; 1999) provide a more detailed analysis of policy distortions. The authors use an index that measures "the extent to which public procurement is open to foreign bidders" and another index that measures "the extent to which there is equal fiscal treatment to all enterprises." Both variables, and also a corruption variable, are taken from the survey by IMD. Both variables significantly explain the level of corruption, even controlling for other explanatory variables. This leads the authors to conclude that policy intervention causes corruption. Goel and Nelson (2005) observe a positive association between corruption and government regulation of and involvement in the financial sector, the latter index being from the Heritage Foundation. The finding for a sample of sixty-three countries is robust to various tests.

Many authors acknowledge that corruption may cause policy distortions and not vice versa, bringing about problems of simultaneity bias. Ades and Di Tella (1997) claim that their instruments for policy distortions ascertain the direction of causality. Certainly, policy distortions and corruption are quite often just two sides of the same coin. In this case, instruments have to carry a heavy burden.

A simple correlation for a sample of twenty-six African countries is provided in Lambsdorff and Cornelius (2000). They show that corruption is positively associated with the degree to which "government regulations are vague and lax." These results are interesting in shifting the focus away from the total burden of regulation to their application. Vagueness and lax application of regulation supplies public servants with the bureaucratic discretion necessary for requesting bribes. Clear rules might present a burden to business but would not necessarily trigger corruption. However, the regressions are not yet controlled by further variables, neither are they extended to a broader sample of countries.

In a similar vein, Gatti (1999) argues that a highly diversified trade tariff menu fuels bribe-taking behavior, whereas uniform trade tariff rates limit public officials' ability to extract bribes from importers. She reports a positive association between the standard deviation of trade tariffs and the level of corruption for a small sample of thirty-four countries. Causality may be difficult to ascertain, because corrupt public servants may impose diversified tariffs so as to be in a better position to ask for bribes.

Some researchers claim that corruption simply mirrors the absence of economic competition; see Box 4 for a review of evidence. Competition among suppliers drives down prices. In public procurement, for example, the resulting rents for private firms decrease. Consequently, public servants and politicians have less to "sell" in exchange for bribes, reducing their motivation to start with a corrupt career. On the contrary, where competition is restricted, profits increase and politicians can grasp the opportunity to assign these profits, in exchange for a share. Again, we would be favorable to this general association. However, the argument adds little to the overall economic dispute as to whether restrictions on competition can in rare instances be beneficial and sheds no light on the process of dealing with natural monopolies. Above that, the argument can easily suffer from reverse causality: the prospects of corrupt income may motivate private firms to pay bribes and politicians to offer market restrictions. The case on p. 9 is illustrative of this. We would end up in a vicious circle. Instead of being provided with ideas for reform, we would observe rather that encouraging competition and reducing corruption can be two sides of the same coin.

On the other hand, competition may sometimes increase rather than decrease corruption. Where companies compete with quality rather than with prices, competition may force firms to myopic behavior. Instead of cultivating a high-quality reputation they would rather bribe inspectors, inducing them to turn a blind eye to the delivery of substandard quality.

Box 4 Corruption and competition among private firms

Government restrictions on economic freedom are likely to reduce competition and thus encourage corruption. Henderson (1999) argues that corruption is negatively correlated with different indicators of economic freedom. This result is largely supported by Goldsmith (1999: 878) for a sample of sixty-six countries, where the regression is controlled for GDP per head, and by Paldam (2002) who includes further explanatory variables in a sample of seventy-seven countries. Goel and Nelson (2005) report similar findings. Such arguments, however, might be tautological. The Heritage Foundation's Economic Freedom measure, for example, includes an assessment of corruption. This implies that a measure of the dependent variable is placed on the independent variable side of the equation (Sandholtz and Gray 2003).

Graeff and Mehlkop (2003) relate corruption to the subcomponents of the index of Economic Freedom by Gwartney and Lawson (2000) for a sample of up to sixty-four countries. Controlling for a variety of further influential variables they find that a variety of these subcomponents is insignificant. An assessment of the legal security of private ownership rights, the viability of contracts, and the rule of law is found to lower corruption, particularly in rich countries. Another aspect of economic freedom that is associated with less corruption is the freedom of exchange in capital and financial markets. The argument on this latter subcomponent, however, may be disputed. This variable includes the percentage of deposits held in private banks and the percentage of credit given to the private sector. Instead of being a cause of corruption such indicators may rather result from a low-corruption environment. Interestingly, the freedom of citizens to own foreign currency bank accounts domestically and abroad is found to increase corruption, at least in the poorer countries of the investigated sample. The authors conclude that not all aspects of economic freedom deter corruption because some regulation may increase the transaction costs of corrupt deals. In a related investigation, Neeman *et al.* (2003) argue that financial openness is detrimental to development because the income from corruption is allowed to be allocated abroad rather than being re-invested in a country; see also Box 16 for details.

Ades and Di Tella (1995) test the influence of two other indicators of competition. These are taken from the survey by IMD. A subjective index of "market dominance" measures the extent to which dominance by a limited number of firms is detrimental to new business development. Another index of "anti-trust laws" measures the effectiveness of these laws in checking non-competitive practices. The authors conclude that the less competitive a market environment, the higher will be the extent of corruption. However, the authors note the problems of causality and acknowledge that corruption may provide incentives for politicians to support monopolies.

One measure of competitive pressures is the integration of a country into the global economy. If competition reduces corruption, then increased openness to international trade and investment should go along with less corruption. A report in Foreign Policy (2001) indeed found that increased globalization is associated with less corruption. However, the study neither controls for further variables nor provides insights into a possible causality. Sandholtz and Gray (2003) report that the more international

Box 4 (*Cont.*)

organizations a country belongs to, and the longer it has been a part of the major international institutions such as the United Nations, GATT/WTO and the IMF, the lower its level of corruption. Furthermore, they report that corruption decreases with other factors of openness such as international telephone minutes per capita and air freight per capita. Responding to the criticism by Knack and Azfar (2003), as described on p. 7, Sandholtz and Gray (2003) show that their results are not affected by sample selection criteria.

Ades and Di Tella (1995; 1997; 1999) demonstrate that openness, defined as the ratio of imports to GDP, is negatively associated with corruption. They apply corruption data from BI (in a cross section of fifty-five countries) and IMD (in a cross section of thirty-two countries). With both approaches the results are robust to the inclusion of further explanatory variables. The authors conclude that international economic competition reduces corruption. A similar finding is reported by Sung and Chu (2003) and Gerring and Thacker (2005). However, Treisman (2000) did not find significant evidence for such an impact using the TI-index.

Another possible measure of the extent of competition in a country can be derived from the number of years it has been open to trade, as assessed by Sachs and Warner (1995). Treisman (2000) and Leite and Weidemann (1999) provide evidence that this variable negatively and significantly impacts on the level of corruption. In line with this thought, one may conjecture that liberalization does not immediately reduce corruption. In fact, Tavares (2005) claims that the immediate effect of liberalization is to increase rather than decrease corruption. Once tariffs are reduced below 40 percent, nontariff barriers relate to less than 40 percent of imports, a socialist economic system is abandoned, no major black market premium is paid for the exchange rate, or major exports are no longer a state monopoly, the level of corruption as measured by Political Risk Services/International Country Risk Guide (PRS/ICRG) increases. Given that our knowledge on trends in levels of corruption is still limited, certainly, the results may require further validation.

Other researchers were engaged in trying to find "shortcuts" in the fight against corruption. One of these shortcuts is to assume that some forms of corruption are more tolerable than others. Krueger (1974: 302), for example, prefers favouritism in government over competitive forms of rent-seeking. Tullock (1980b: 109–11) considers nepotism to be less problematic as compared with competitive lobbying (I will deal with this issue in more detail in Chapter 5). Unusual as these arguments may appear, they tend to provide excuses for some types of corruption instead of providing us with an approach for reform. Along similar lines, Murphy *et al.* (1993: 413) argue that the problems with corruption are mitigated when corrupt rulers can collect bribes efficiently. Perfecting corruption rather than fighting it is the avenue suggested for reform.

But such conclusions are misleading when the underlying model is too limited for an adequate discussion of a multifaceted problem. In a similar spirit it is sometimes assumed that the adverse effects of corruption relate largely to the accompanying uncertainty. Bribers have no legal recourse after making the payment and face threats of demands for further bribes. Some authors assume that it is this type of uncertainty that deters investors, less so corruption itself. But the more predictable form of corruption is likely to bring about other disadvantages. A predictable type of corruption less forces investors to seek legal alternatives, facilitating the further spread of this type of corruption (this issue will be examined in Chapter 7). Corruption has a large variety of disastrous effects that make it difficult to prefer one type to another. Clearly, corruption is a complex phenomenon and its diverse variants are likely to bring about quite different effects. But whether this allows us to rationally prefer one type to another is likely to remain open to dispute.

1.2. Defining corruption

Definitions of corruption can be discussed at length without necessarily providing an actual value added to the reader. Still some researchers display their endeavors in this area. They are willing to go into time-consuming debate and are fierce in preferring one approach to another. Such debate, however, tends to absorb much of the energy that is desperately needed elsewhere. Recognizing this, some colleagues have started to avoid definitions of corruption, claiming that most cases of corruption are unambiguously perceived by most observers. This is somewhat along the lines of Weber's (1920: 30) definition of the spirit of capitalism. He rejects a definition and claims that this term is composed by the various fragments and conceptions provided in his subsequent writing. This is similar to the problems faced by United States Supreme Court Justice Potter Stewart in 1964 when he argued "I can't define pornography, but I know it when I see it."

In such a perspective, a definition of corruption would be rendered at the end of the reading, rather than being provided upfront. I tend to share this notion and propose the reader might simply skip the following paragraphs. For the sake of completeness, I nonetheless provide a rather uncontroversial, rough sketch and description of what should be understood by the term corruption. Some readers may profit more from this reading after having completed the book.

Corruption is commonly defined as the **misuse of public power for private benefit**. The term "private benefit" relates to receiving money or valuable assets, but it may also encompass increases in power or status. Receiving promises for *future* favors or benefits for relatives and friends may also be considered a private benefit. With regard to favors for relatives and friends, the terms nepotism and favoritism are also common.

"Public power" is exercised by bureaucrats, appointed to their office, and by politicians, who are elected to their position. Such public power is exercised in a variety of sectors, such as the judiciary, public procurement, business regulations and granting of permits, privatization, foreign exchange (including customs, trade permits, and international financial transactions), taxes (including the granting of tax exemptions), police, subsidies, public utility (water, electricity, telephone, garbage collection, health care), and government services (health, education).

The term "misuse" can either relate to a behavior that deviates from the formal duties of a public role (elective or appointive), that is in contrast to informal rules (established by public expectations or somewhat standardized as codes of conduct), or, more generally, where narrow interests are followed at the expense of the broader interests of the public at large. In a functioning government system these definitions fall into one: public interests are supposed to feed into the public's expectations vis-à-vis office holders. These, in turn,

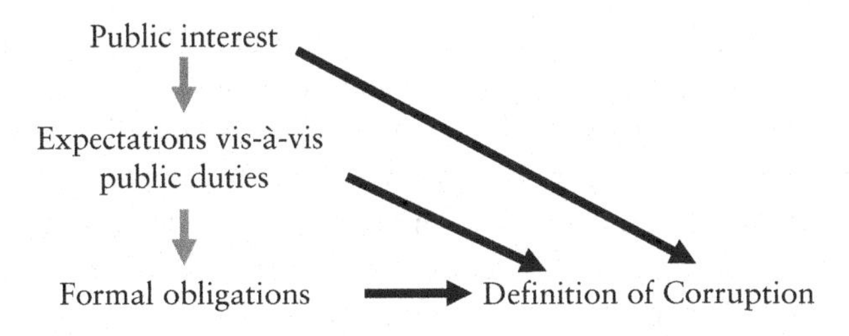

Figure 1.1. Defining corruption

are supposed to define formal obligations in line with the public's interest; see Figure 1.1. However, corruption is about government failures, which provides some problems to our definitions. Corruption as a real-world phenomenon thus destroys the foundation on which the just given formal definition rests.

When those who dictate formal obligations operate without regard to public expectations, a definition of corruption can no longer relate to formal obligations. This problem is sometimes observed for parliamentarians. They are reluctant to follow a rigid rule for themselves and rather oppose the related legislation. This renders the parliamentarians' own bribe-taking as permissible. Hence, the taking of bribes would not violate the law, but clearly it is in contradiction to public expectations. A definition that sticks narrowly to formal obligations would therefore be of little use. Instead, a definition would have to refer directly to public expectations. This, certainly, comes at the cost of reduced precision of the term. In some rare instances such as civil war or ethnic or social cleavages, the public may even no longer develop consistent and generally shared expectations vis-à-vis the operation of public office holders. Corruption must then refer to an even more abstract term: the public interest. It goes without saying that such a definition tends to become vague. But under such rare conditions, public interest would be the only adequate reference for establishing a meaningful understanding of corruption.

A world free of corruption is associated with public servants who intend to serve the public, be it through intrinsic motivations, incentives, threats of penalties, or peer pressure. Concerning the institutions that help establish such a behavior, at least four aspects are commonly emphasized: first, the arms-length principle, stating that pertinent arguments in public decision-making should not be overshadowed by personal relationships and that equality of treatment for all economic agents should be achieved; second, citizen participation and involvement, giving people a say in public decision-making; third, transparent procedures with regard to public decision-making, limiting the discretion among office holders; and fourth, competition among office holders, giving voters and clients the chance to exchange nonperforming individuals with others.

Corruption, certainly, is defined differently in different regions of the world. Across countries the public forms different expectations about public roles. How officials should serve the public can be up to purely local taste. The four aspects mentioned above may obtain different weightage in different countries. Equality of treatment may be less relevant in societies characterized by strong personal relations, where relatives and friends expect office holders to provide favorable treatment. Transparency and participation may be given less significance in societies that are convinced that only pertinent arguments are relevant for bureaucrats. What seems to be universal, though, is that the public commonly considers self-seeking behavior by politicians and bureaucrats as corrupt when this goes along with a blunt neglect of their expectations and interests.

Corruption is an exchange of favors between two actors, an agent and a client; see (Andrig and Fjeldstadt 2000). The agent is entrusted with power by her superior, the principal.[3] The principal delegates a task to the subordinate, his agent, and sets up the rules as to how this task is to be fulfilled. The agent is supposed to serve the client in accordance to these rules. Bribery, extortion, embezzlement, and fraud in the public sector are variants of corrupt behavior, amounting to the agent "defecting" from her rule-bound behavior. In the case of **bribery** the client acts as a briber and makes a payment (also called kickback, baksheesh, sweetener, payoff, speed- or grease-money) to the agent, who then is called a bribee. In return the client obtains an advantage such as a service or license he is not entitled to obtain, for example, a tax rebate or a public contract. In the case of **extortion** the agent uses her power to extract money or other benefits from the client. The client may have to pay for a service, although he is legally entitled to obtain it without such payment. The agent uses coercion,

[3] Throughout the book, I use the female pronoun for agents, supervisors, and middlemen, and the male pronoun for principals and clients.

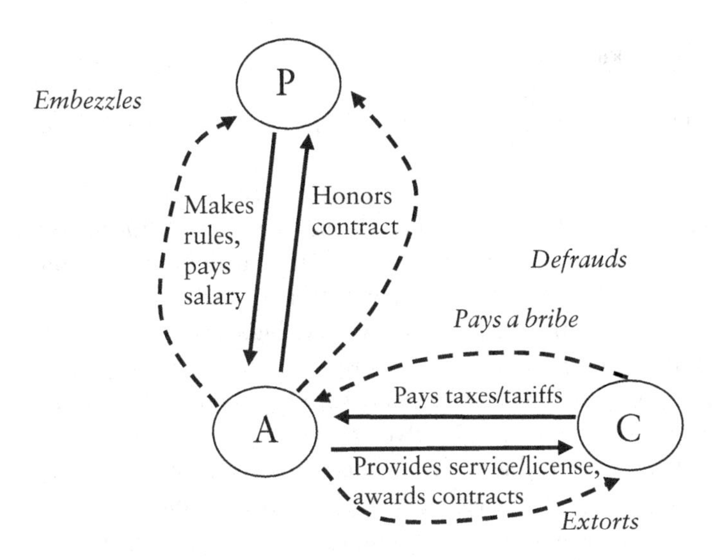

Figure 1.2. Corruption in a principal–agent–client model

violence, or threats in order to obtain this payment. **Embezzlement**, in contrast, is simply theft of public resources by the agent. Without an involvement by the client a disloyal agent steals from the principal. Bribery, extortion, and embezzlement imply that the principal's rules are trespassed and his interests are hurt. The agent is commonly better informed about details of her daily tasks and her efforts devoted to their fulfillment. This implies that she can benefit from informational advantages. The agent can also actively conceal information from the principal with the help of trickery, swindle, deceit, manipulation or distortion of information, facts, and expertise. In this case the term **fraud** is used. See Figure 1.2 for an overview.

Corruption must be distinguished from certain other forms of criminal conduct that involve only private parties. Tax evasion, contraband, black markets, insider dealings at the stock exchange, production of counterfeit money, and subsidy fraud can be carried out without misusing public power. Actors involved in such activities are private businesspeople, for example, taxpayers, who are not entrusted with public power.[4] A wider definition of corruption would also include this type of behavior. When a private firm's sales

[4] These activities may also go along with corruption when public office holders are paid to refrain from prosecution, to grant impunity, or to provide inside information on criminal opportunities.

manager takes kickbacks in exchange for contracts, he misuses "entrusted" power. But clearly, the position of power was not provided by the public, suggesting differences to the common definition of corruption.

One may distinguish between various forms of corruption based on other criteria, as well. One criterion is whether the briber or the bribee obtains the larger benefit from a corrupt deal, depending largely on which side has the stronger bargaining power. "Clientilist" corruption takes place if the briber obtains the higher benefit, while "patrimonial" corruption occurs where the bribee obtains the bigger share. One may equally distinguish between petty and grand corruption, where the former involves frequent, small payments to public servants lower in hierarchy, while the latter relates to large, one-shot payments to higher ranks. The terms "political" and "administrative" corruption are defined according to the key actors, being either politicians or bureaucrats.

Some behavior would be termed corrupt equivocally by all observers. But "gray areas" exist where viewpoints differ. Lobbying is one such gray area. While its presence may suggest that decisions in the public sector are for sale, it is often legal, carried out in a transparent and competitive manner, and involves not the narrow interests of individuals but those of larger business sectors. This distinguishes it from ordinary types of corruption. Gift-giving to public servants is another such gray area. While it involves the danger of dependency and reciprocity by the receiver, it may not require obfuscation, which is a characteristic of corruption. Gifts, in contrast to bribes, can always be given in an open, transparent manner.

1.3. Measuring corruption

Given the recent interest in corruption, attempts to quantify the extent of corruption have become vital. Most prominent among these is the Transparency International Corruption Perceptions Index (CPI), which provides assessments of perceived levels of corruption for a cross section of countries. The CPI is a composite index, using the assessments by risk agencies and surveys carried out among elite businesspeople. While perceptions should never be confused with reality, the given consensus provides some confidence that the perceptions gathered are informative on actual levels of corruption.

The CPI is an annual index, compiled since 1995. I started the operational work behind the index many years ago at the University of Goettingen; this work is carried out now at the University of Passau under my supervision. The index has assumed a central place in research on the causes and consequences of corruption, based on regressions for a cross section of countries. An appendix to this chapter on pp. 236–255 provides technical detail to the methodology behind the index. All the data between 1996 and 2005 as well as historical data can be obtained at www.ICGG.org.

The goal of the CPI is to provide data on extensive perceptions of corruption within countries. This is a means of enhancing the understanding of real levels of corruption and how these differ from one country to another. In an area as complex and controversial as corruption, no single source or polling method has yet been developed that combines a perfect sampling frame, a satisfactory country coverage, and a fully convincing methodology to produce comparative assessments. This is why the CPI has adopted the approach of a composite index. Box 5 lists the various sources that enter the index.

Box 5 Sources of the 2005 CPI

- State Capacity Survey by Columbia University (CU), 2003; ninety-five countries are assessed by a panel of largely academic experts from the United States.
- The Economist Intelligence Unit (EIU), Country Risk Service and Country Forecast 2005, (www.eiu.com); 156 countries are assessed by staff.
- Freedom House Nations in Transit (FH), 2005 (www.freedomhouse.org/research/nattransit.htm); twenty-seven transition countries are assessed by a panel of experts.
- The Institute for Management Development, Lausanne (IMD), World Competitiveness Yearbook. I use data for 2003–2005 (www.imd.ch); fifty-one countries are assessed, based on more than 4000 annual responses by local executives in top and middle management of domestic and international companies.
- Information International (II), 2003, (www.informationinternational.com); thirty-one countries are assessed, based on 382 assessments from 165 expatriate business executives.

Box 5 (*Cont.*)

- Merchant International Group (MIG), Grey Area Dynamics Rating, 2005 (www.merchantinternational.com); 155 countries are rated by expert staff and a network of local correspondents.
- The Political and Economic Risk Consultancy, Hong Kong (PERC), Asian Intelligence Newsletter. I use data for 2003–2005, (www.asiarisk.com/); fourteen Asian countries are assessed, based on roughly 1000 annual responses by expatriate business executives.
- United Nations Economic Commission for Africa (UNECA), African Governance Report 2005 (www.uneca.org/agr/), twenty-eight African countries are assessed by a panel of roughly 100 resident experts per country.
- The World Markets Research Centre (WMRC), 2002, (www.wmrc.com); 186 countries are assessed by staff.
- The World Economic Forum (WEF), Global Competitiveness Report. I use data for 2003–2005 (www.weforum.org); 117 countries were assessed in 2005, based on more than 10,900 responses of local senior business leaders of domestic and international companies.

As the data collected relates to perceptions rather than to real phenomena, it has to be considered whether such perceptions improve our understanding of real levels of corruption. Since actual levels of corruption cannot be determined directly, perceptions may be all we have to guide us. However, this approach is undermined at least to some extent, if the perceptions gathered are biased. Such a potential bias might originate from the particular cultural background of respondents. For example, Bayley (1966: 721) argues:

> The western observer is faced with an uncomfortable choice. He can adhere to the Western definition, in which case he lays himself open to the charge of being censorious and he finds that he is condemning not aberrant behavior but normal, acceptable operating procedure. . . . On the other hand, he may face up to the fact that corruption, if it requires moral censure, is culturally conditioned . . . [and] it may be necessary then to assert in the same breath that an official accepts gratuities but is not corrupt.

Taking up this perspective, it becomes essential to investigate how the underlying sample of respondents may define and quantify corruption. While the sources all aim at measuring the extent of corruption, the sample design differs considerably. Basically, three different types of samples are used. A first group of sources, namely, CU, EIU, FH, MIG, and WMRC, assemble the perceptions of nonresidents, turning in their expert opinion with regard to foreign countries. These assessments are largely carried out by respondents from developed countries of the western hemisphere such as North America and Western Europe. These would be the respondents that are faced with Bayley's "uncomfortable choice."

A second group of sources, namely, represented only by II, also assembles the perceptions of nonresidents, but these respondents are largely from less-developed countries. There is an advantage to perceptions vis-à-vis foreign countries because they are not vulnerable to a "home-country bias." Such a type of bias would be relevant if respondents assess their home country purely according to local standards. Such a standard would be problematic because it can differ from one country to another, impairing the validity of cross-country comparisons.

A third group of sources, namely, IMD, PERC, and WEF, gather assessments made by residents with respect to the performance of their home country. These respondents are partly nationals but also expatriates from multinational firms. While such data might be susceptible to the aforementioned "home-country bias," they are not susceptible to introducing an undue dominance of "western business people's" viewpoint. Such a viewpoint would be inadequate if foreigners lack a proper understanding of a country's culture.

The data correlate well with each other, irrespective of these different samples. The high correlations mitigate fears that any of the aforementioned biases are important to the results. Residents may therefore have a rather universal ethical standard and adequately position their country as compared with foreign countries. Likewise, those respondents who assess foreign countries seem to have a good grasp of a country's culture and provide appropriate assessments in the light of this. In sum, the perceptions are a helpful contribution to the understanding of real levels of corruption.

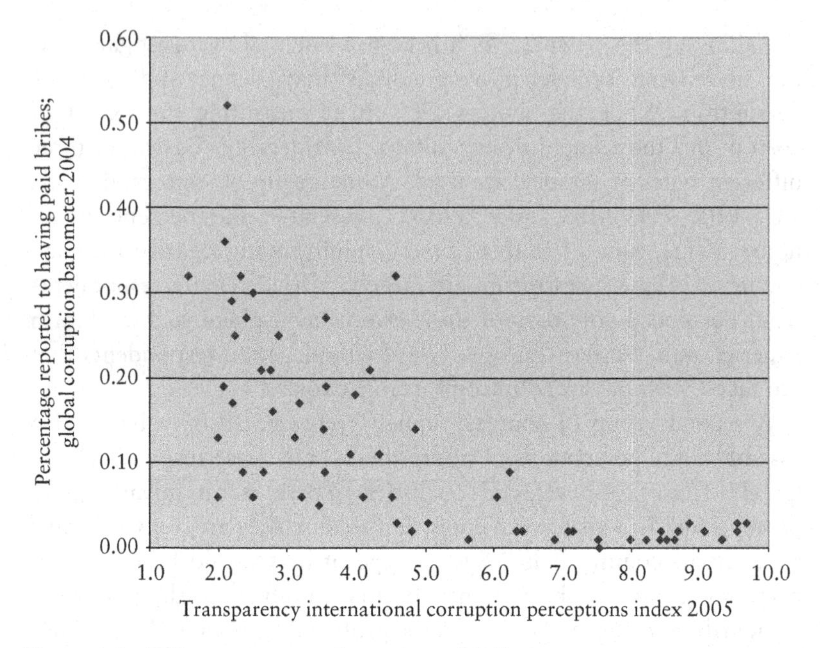

Figure 1.3. CPI versus reported payment of bribes

Interestingly enough, the data also correlate well with actual experience. Experience-based data has been produced by the International Crime Victim Survey (ICVS). They poll the general public in more than forty countries. In 1996 they asked "in some areas there is a problem of corruption among government or public officials. During 1995, has any government official, for instance a customs officer, police officer or inspector in your own country, asked you or expected you to pay a bribe for his service?" While less than 1 percent agreed in most developed countries, figures went as high as one-third in less-developed countries. These data clearly relate to personal experience. Still, for a sample of forty-three countries the data correlates well with the sources entering the CPI, commonly with a coefficient higher than 0.8. This supports the validity of the CPI.

More recently, Gallup International incorporated questions on corruption commissioned by Transparency International in its 2004 survey "Voice of the People," an annual poll of the general public in fifty-four countries. Question 5 reads: "In the past 12 months, have you or anyone living in your household paid a bribe in any form?" Figure 1.3 depicts a scatterplot where the results are portrayed against

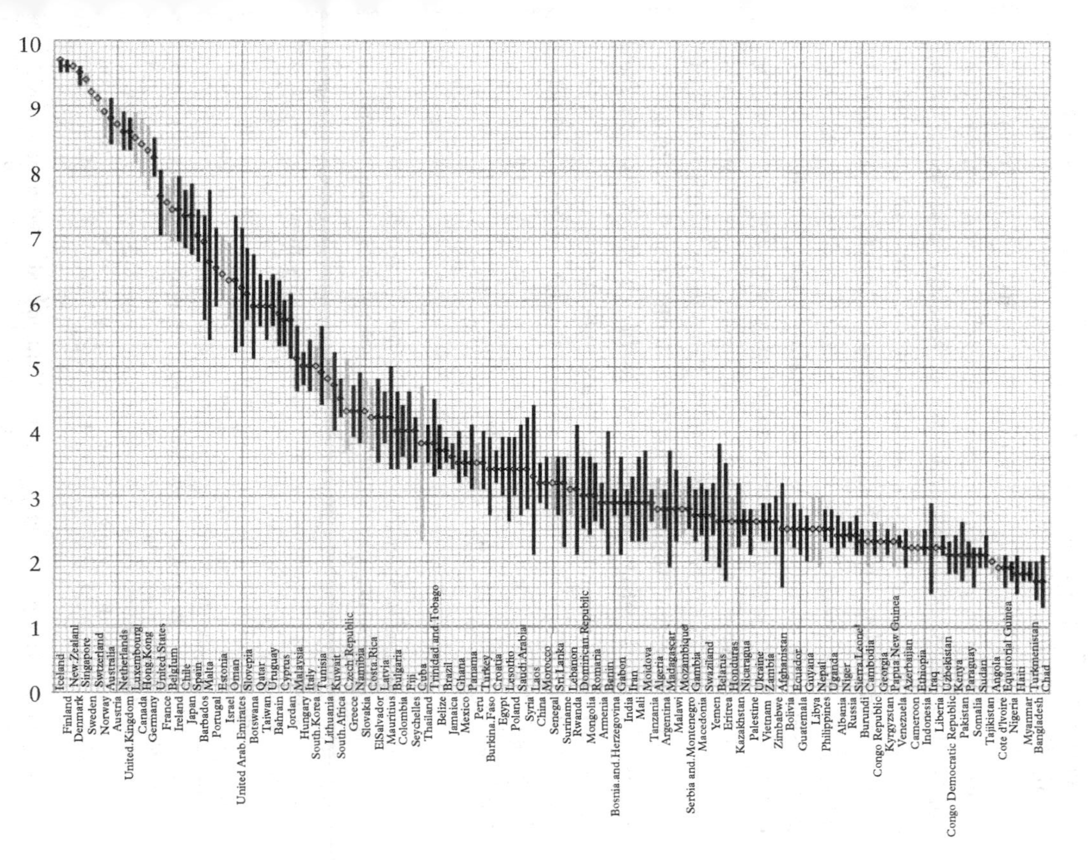

Figure 1.4. 2005 Corruption Perceptions Index and approximate confidence intervals. The coverage probability is 65–75% (gray lines) or 80–90% (black lines)

the CPI 2004. This reveals a 0.70 correlation coefficient for the data, again supporting the overall validity of perceptions.[5]

These results also imply that the perceptions are not distorted by media reports. Respondents might rely on media coverage and reports obtained from others. Certainly this influence cannot be excluded and necessarily contributes to perceptions. Yet, in its extreme form such an influence may suggest that respondents rely only on hearsay. The potential problem with this influence is that the assessment of a country might then reflect the quality of the press in uncovering scandals and particularly its freedom to do so. Countries that suppress a free press may escape a bad reputation for corruption among their population. Such an influence would certainly undermine the validity of the CPI and its usefulness as an aid to understanding real levels of corruption. However, the CPI tends to correlate positively with press freedom; see p. 46 for respective results. Perceptions of high levels of corruption are rather found in countries with little press freedom. Media reports therefore do not seem to bias perceptions. On the contrary, perceptions appear to be robust indicators.

Figure 1.4 shows the 2005 CPI, along with the confidence ranges. These depict the precision of the respective scores. The appendix to this chapter on pp. 235–255 provides technical details to the CPI.

[5] A similar correlation is reported by Mocan (2004) relating to data on experienced corruption by the United Nations Interregional Crime and Justice Research Institute (www.unicri.it/icvs). But she claims that this relationship breaks down once regressions are controlled for the quality of institutions in a country. She concludes that perceived corruption relates more to such indicators than "real" levels of corruption. This conclusion, however, is easily overemphasized. First, the data on experienced corruption are distributed differently than the CPI. This can easily result in residuals not being normally distributed. In my own regressions, I chose a more adequate functional form for the relationship. This produced normally distributed residuals and the CPI was strongly significant, even when controlling for other variables on institutional quality. Second, data on reported corruption are not necessarily "real." Standards of definition may vary from one country to another. Minor gifts may already be termed a bribe in Norway, while in Nicaragua facilitation payments may be considered legitimate. In Norway a payment to the public servant's distant relatives may be considered illegitimate, while in Nicaragua only favors going directly to an official may qualify as a bribe. Third, individual confrontation with corruption is likely to relate more to the street-level, petty type of corruption as observed by households; Svensson (2005: 23–4). The Corruption Perceptions Index (CPI) includes also the extent of grand corruption and focuses on the impact of corruption on the costs of doing business.

2 *Enemies of corruption*

Corruption has emerged high on the agenda of multinational development agencies, private firms, and policy-makers. This increased interest in the phenomenon of corruption has produced a multitude of policy prescriptions, reform initiatives, and conferences. The world is not short of ideas on how to tackle corruption. While good intentions abound, we currently know little about their likely success.

Being short of empirical evidence and profound experience, there is clearly no theory available that allows us to put the various approaches for reform into comparative perspective. How should bureaucrats be punished? How should administrative procedures be reformed? How far should parliamentarians be held accountable to the public? What piece of information should be made publicly available? Is transparency always helpful? Is it possible to reward honesty? Can corruption be effectively fought by focusing on technical and organizational issues? What role should be assigned to civil society? How far can we expect bureaucrats to follow their narrow self-interest as opposed to ethical considerations? How much of our resources should we spend for improving the judiciary? How should we deal with whistle-blowers?

A recent cohort of anticorruption activists requests high levels of integrity as part of a moral crusade against corruption. Standard policy recommendations embrace the "strengthening" of diverse legal foundations and procedural guidelines. They include the "promotion" of integrity in various sectors, or they relate to "capacity building" in the public administration. These and similar buzzwords repeatedly enter topical guidebooks by various donor agencies, consultancies, and multilateral institutions. But they leave the reader with the uncanny impression that the approach is circular. Integrity, strength, and capacity are exactly what are in short supply, and the reader obtains little inspiration on how to escape the vicious circle.

Moreover, the moral rigor of some recommendations sounds rather like a doctor suggesting a tight fitness program as a treatment after a heart attack. If we had an army of benevolent and well-trained public servants, we may be successful in fighting corruption in a top–down manner. If we have alert and well-educated citizens who unite in their opposition against corruption, we can contain corruption in a grassroots movement. But corruption exists precisely because we are short of one or the other. In order for reform to be successful, we must start with the recognition that only imperfect tools are available.

While there are numerous questions that are crucial to anticorruption, a holistic approach to reform is mostly suggested (Pope 2000). This viewpoint is reasonable because corruption in one sector breeds malfeasance in another. Anticorruption, therefore, is similar to destroying the Gordian knot; piecemeal approaches appear futile. However convincing such a holistic approach may appear, it does not clearly provide direction to reform. It alerts the public that much has to be done, without exactly proposing what measures have to be taken and where to set priorities. We need more theoretical inspiration that is able to direct our energies better in the fight against corruption. A consistent economic theory may provide valuable insights, but the task at hand is too complex to rely on a single theoretical tradition. If we want to generate sound policy advice, then only an interdisciplinary approach is likely to be successful. This is what this book is about.

In order to provide a first cut through this maze, the results from empirical research are instructive. There exist unavoidable levels of corruption that cannot be addressed by reform, at least not in the short or medium term, but must be regarded as given. These natural causes of corruption are manifold. At first, there are cultural causes of corruption.

2.1. Unavoidable corruption

In contrast to economists, sociologists are often quick in pointing to cultural causes. Among these, generalized trust, religion, and acceptance of hierarchy play a crucial role. These studies tend to provide important contributions. Box 6 reviews the relevant studies.

The link between culture and corruption is strong. Given the invariance of cultural variables over time, we have reason to assume that the causality runs from culture to corruption and not the other way round. Countries with high levels of generalized trust, a large share of Protestants, and little acceptance of hierarchy are perceived to be less affected by corruption. At the same time, the findings provide little inspiration to reform. At best, they suggest that superficial reform might be futile because societies may return to the culturally determined level of corruption. It appears that cultural issues must be addressed in a long-term reform strategy. However, culture explains only a fraction of the variance of levels of corruption, leaving sufficient prospects for countries to change for the better even if their cultural preconditions are less favorable.

Another conclusion originating from the link between culture and corruption suggests that reform should consider cultural preconditions. Husted (1999) argues that effective measures to fight corruption are dependent on culture. Countries where power is distributed unequally, and where hierarchy is accepted, will require different treatment than others. In such countries, a top–down approach to anticorruption may have better prospects as compared with a grassroots movement. On the other side, where a strong desire for material wealth is given, ethical training may not fall on fertile ground.

Box 6 Corruption and trust

Some societies are characterized by a high level of trust among its people, while in others people tend to have misgivings about each other. Investigating the consequences of such forms of "social capital" has been made possible with data from the World Values Survey, which surveys 1,000 randomly selected people since the 1980s in an increasing number of countries. One question is, "Generally speaking, would you say that most people can be trusted or that you can't be too careful in dealing with people?" La Porta *et al.* (1997: 336) argue that trust can be helpful in fighting corruption, since it helps bureaucrats to cooperate better with each other and with private citizens. In a sample of thirty-three countries, the authors show that trust has a significant negative impact on corruption, while controlling for GDP per head. This finding is corroborated by Adsera *et al.* (2000). Uslaner (2004) supports the negative association between trust and corruption. Concerned with the causality, he claims that trust lowers corruption while the opposite causality is less robust. Björnskov and Paldam (2004)

Box 6 (*Cont.*)

undertake a first attempt to construct time series with the TI data on corruption. Seeking explanatory variables, they find that trust is about the only one with significant impact.[1]

Also the role of religion in contributing to the level of corruption is examined by La Porta *et al.* (1997: 337). The authors consider the Catholic, the Eastern Orthodox, and the Muslim religions to be particularly hierarchical and believe that such hierarchical forms of religion are detrimental to civic engagement, a factor that should help reduce corruption. For the same sample of thirty-three countries mentioned above, the authors report a positive association between the percentage of population belonging to a hierarchical religion and corruption, controlling for other influences. For a larger section of 114 countries this relationship is reproduced by La Porta *et al.* (1999: 251–2). But here the relationship becomes rather weak as soon as GDP per head is included. A strong association between religion and corruption is obtained by Treisman (2000). He relates corruption to the percentage of Protestants in the total population in a sample of up to sixty-four countries and obtains a highly significant negative impact on corruption, controlling for other variables such as GDP per head. This is corroborated by Lipset and Lenz (2000) and Gerring and Thacker (2005: 244–6). In contrast to these studies, however, Sandholtz and Gray (2003) claim that Protestantism loses significance both in larger samples and when one controls for a variety of indicators on openness. A more in-depth analysis of the impact of various religions is provided by Paldam (2001). He identifies eleven different groups of religions and tests their impact on corruption, controlling for other variables. While in countries with a large fraction of Reform Christianity and tribal religions corruption is lower, higher levels of corruption can be found in countries with a large influence of Pre-Reform Christianity, Islam, Buddhism, and Hinduism. However, the impact is only significant for Reform Christians (Protestants and Anglicans).

[1] As pointed out repeatedly, the time-series value of the TI data is distorted because of annual changes in the composition of sources. Björnskov and Paldam (2004) refer only to ordinal changes in the data over time, that is, whether a country improves in rank relative to others. Because of this approach, it might be possible that one-shot changes that are of purely methodological nature play a minor role as compared with actual trend information.

In line with the argument by La Porta *et al.*, the idea that hierarchies contribute to corruption is supported by Husted (1999), who uses a totally different dataset. Based on surveys by Hofstede (1997), he employs the resulting data on cultural values. One variable defined there is called "power distance" which measures "the extent to which the less powerful members of institutions and organizations within a country expect and accept that power is distributed unequally" (Husted 1999: 343). This variable is shown to have a positive impact on the level of corruption in a sample of forty-four countries in various regressions, while controlling for other explanatory variables. Concomitant with this indicator, two further cultural variables positively and significantly impact on the level of corruption: first, the extent to which the quest for material success dominates over a concern for the quality of life[2] and, second, the extent to which members of a culture feel threatened by uncertainty or unknown situations. The latter variable must clearly be distinguished from risk avoidance, which might be expected to lower corruption. The idea is that corruption may give its beneficiaries the hope of reducing the level of uncertainty they face. Robertson and Watson (2004) largely reproduce these findings.[3]

Anderson and Tverdova (2003) investigate the impact of corruption on the trust in civil servants and the evaluation of the political system. For this purpose they employ survey data from the 1996 International Social Survey Program. They find that corruption significantly reduces trust in civil servants, as reported by respondents. Another finding relates to respondents' evaluation of the political system: "all in all, how well or badly do you think the system of democracy in your country works these days?" The authors find that this assessment is significantly worse in countries with high levels of corruption. Interestingly, they report that both these impacts are significantly attenuated among supporters of the incumbent political authorities.

[2] This variable is called masculinity–femininity. I avoid this misleading term.

[3] Robertson and Watson also claim that changing levels of FDI impact on corruption, because they produce an unexpected surplus to local businesspeople, who resort to corruption as a means of grasping profitable opportunities. While the theoretical reasoning may require further consideration, FDI tend to vary considerably over time and the changes from 1998 to 1999 employed by the authors may not be a solid measurement.

Other cultural variables that are tested relate to "traditionalism." Societies that cultivate secular-rational attitudes toward authority (i.e., where impersonal values are more important as opposed to particularistic or familistic values) are perceived to be less corrupt, unlike those where traditional religious values dominate. Also a high respect for one's family increases levels of corruption. The reason might be that family interests might be in conflict with official duties. Where respect for one's kin is high, a nepotistic type of corruption might emerge. A review of relevant studies is given in Box 7. Suggestions for reform, however, would be difficult to derive from such a finding.

Box 7 Corruption, values, and colonialism

Sandholtz and Taagepera (2005) determine two cultural dimensions from the World Values Survey conducted between 1995 and 2001. A first dimension measures traditional versus secular-rational attitudes toward authority. A second dimension relates to survival versus self-expression. This dimension measures the extent to which people are focused on personal and economic security, or on personal self-expression and quality of life. African and Muslim countries have traditional attitudes and a high extent of "survival" due to their low income. Protestant countries are oriented toward self-expression and have secular attitudes. Former communist countries have a secular tradition, but again a high level of "survival" due to their low income. They give up on God while still feeling insecure and unhappy. Respondents from Latin America, the United States, Ireland, Canada, and Australia are committed to self-expression but have some traditional attitudes toward authority. These countries combine belief in God with the feelings of security and happiness. The authors show that a strong "survival" orientation contributes twice as much as a strong "traditional" orientation to higher levels of corruption. The authors, unfortunately, are not very concise in explaining how these dimensions are determined. They also do not control their regression for some standard variables, such as GDP per head. In light of this, the significant result for tradition appears more interesting than the one for survival, which is likely to be less significant when controlling for income per head.

A higher level of corruption in post-communist countries is also reported by Gerring and Thacker (2005: 245–6), who show that a socialist legal tradition increases corruption.

Lipset and Lenz (2000: 120) create a scale to measure "familism" and then test the relationship between familism and corruption. Their data on familism is the percentage of respondents from the World Values Survey agreeing that, regardless of the qualities and faults of one's parents, a person must always love and respect them. A second item measures the percentage of people who think that divorce is unjustifiable. In regression analysis, the measures of familism are positively related to corruption, even when controlling for per capita income.

Fisman and Miguel (2006) observe a correlation between corruption and the behavior of UN diplomats in New York City. Diplomatic immunity means that there is essentially zero legal enforcement of diplomatic parking violations. Conformity with parking rules would thus be driven by intrinsic motivation alone, and the latter aspect might be well depicted by the level of corruption of the diplomat's country of origin. Indeed, the study finds that diplomats from high corruption countries have significantly more parking violations.

There are still no full-fledged studies about the impact of colonialism on the level of corruption. But variables of colonial heritage sometimes enter as control variables in studies investigating the causes of corruption. This is the case in Swamy *et al.* (2001) and Treisman (2000). According to Treisman, former British colonies exhibit lower levels of corruption than other countries, controlling for the level of income per head and various other variables such as the existence of a common law system. This result is reproduced by Swamy *et al.* (2001).[4] Both studies found that colonies of other countries do not exhibit the same reduction in the level of corruption.

It is surprising that colonialism does not increase the level of corruption, as suggested by anecdotal evidence. But as outlined above, these studies did not primarily intend to investigate the

[4] Lederman *et al.* (2001), however, disagree. In their regressions the British legal tradition did not lower corruption. This may relate to their use of the PRS data on corruption.

Box 7 (*Cont.*)

impact of colonialism on corruption. To arrive at sound conclusions, further analysis is required, which should go beyond the use of dummy variables and take into consideration more detailed characteristics of colonial rule.

The role of social structure in advancing corruption has been of interest lately. One concern relates to gender. Male-dominated networks could go along with corruption. They might be set up to advance particularistic interests at the expense of those of society at large. Improved women's rights may emanate as a method for lowering corruption. Once parliamentary debates embrace both sexes and bureaucratic decisions are communicated across sexual boundaries, the resulting increased transparency may decrease corruption. Box 8 lists the relevant studies. Whether individual women are intrinsically less corrupt, as has been hypothesized by some authors, appears to be beyond the scope of cross-country analysis. Testing such a hypothesis requires an analysis of female-dominated societies, of which we hardly have any in our sample. All we observe is that a better mix of sexes as opposed to male dominance appears to lower corruption.

Yet, there are reasons for the presence of reverse causality. Low levels of corruption may impose restrictions on male-dominated networks and provide women with legal recourse and improved access to higher positions. Women's rights would be difficult to establish in corrupt countries, and they would contribute little by themselves to lower corruption.

Box 8 Corruption and gender

The impact of gender on corruption is investigated by Swamy *et al.* (2001) and Dollar *et al.* (2001). The authors determine the percentage of women in the labor force and in parliament. Both indicators negatively impact on the level of corruption in a cross section of up to sixty-six countries. The influence is large in magnitude, highly significant and robust throughout a large variety of regressions, controlling for various variables. These findings are in line with some microevidence reported by Swamy *et al.* and suggest that policies designed to increase the role of women may help lower the level of corruption. Similar results are reported by Sung and Chu (2003).

However, both female participation and corruption might be driven by other factors. This is the argument advanced by Sung (2003). He shows that the impact of gender on corruption decreases considerably once controlling for further variables such as rule of law, press freedom, and democracy. His results are robust to the inclusion of standard control variables. He concludes that female participation barely lowers corruption. The data are more suggestive of institutional preconditions advancing both women's rights and integrity.

Besides cultural preconditions, some geographic variables can foster corruption. Abundant natural resources, high levels of corruption among one's neighboring states, and a large distance to the world's major trading centers are observed to significantly increase corruption. Box 9 provides a review. Such findings, again, do not inspire reform. At best, they might provide societies with a benchmark for a feasible level of corruption.

Box 9 Corruption and geographic preconditions

Ades and Di Tella (1999) and Leite and Weidemann (1999) argue that an abundance of natural resources creates opportunities for rent-seeking behavior and gives rise to corruption. Both studies measure the first variable in terms of a country's exports of fuels and minerals as a share of GNP. Throughout various specifications this variable is found to significantly increase the level of corruption. These results are robust to the inclusion of various explanatory variables, different samples of countries, and the use of different indicators of corruption. A similar finding is reported by Kunicová (2002). Montinola and Jackman (2002) argue similarly, but employ a dummy variable for OPEC member states instead, which relates to abundance of oil. This variable also significantly increases a country's level of corruption. Another study by Gylfason (2001) argues that the abundance of natural resources can be measured by the proportion of the labor force employed in primary production. He reports a positive association of this proxy with corruption, controlling for income per head.

Box 9 (*Cont.*)

Sandholtz and Gray (2003) show that countries surrounded by corrupt neighbors exhibit higher levels of corruption. Neighbors may share similar cultural affinities and norms; attitudes toward corruption may spill over from one country to another owing to strong regional exchange. Gerring and Thacker (2005) observe that corruption decreases with a country's distance from the equator. Ades and Di Tella (1999) and Wei (2000a) provide evidence that corruption increases with a country's distance to the world's major trading centers. The likely reason for this impact relates to the higher transportation costs and the resulting limitations of competitive pressure. These limitations may make it easier for local monopolies to evolve and to protect their position with the help of bribes.

Geographic conditions can be responsible for increased international competition in a country, measured by a higher level of openness. As evidenced in Box 4, this can be a cause of reduced corruption. Wei (2000a) investigates whether such geographic conditions or open trade policies are crucial to reducing corruption. He determines a measure of "natural openness" as the extent of openness that is caused by a country's total population and its remoteness from world trading centers. Both these measures tend to lower a country's openness, the former because large countries tend to trade less with the outside world and the latter because transport costs make foreign trade less attractive. These indicators are independent of a country's trade regime, and thus exogenous to a regression. He finds that natural openness significantly lowers a country's level of corruption, pointing to the helpful role of competition in reducing corruption.[5] The residual openness (i.e. the part which is not explained by country size and geography) is a measure of a country's trade regime and its policy decisions in favor of global competition. Yet Wei does not find a significant impact of this variable, suggesting that geographic conditions rather than open trade policies are crucial for the level of corruption.

[5] The finding by Knack and Azfar (2003), cited on p. 7, casts doubt on Wei's conclusion. They argue that the correlation between population size and corruption is merely an artifact of sample selection. The "natural openness" by Wei would be affected by this criticism, because it depends on population size.

2.2. Candidates for reform

In theoretical studies a large array of reform measures has been discussed. Only a few of them were subject to empirical research. Although penalties are assumed to deter corrupt behavior and play a major role in theory, related empirical studies are still missing. The difficulty of finding cross-country comparable data on penalties might be a reason for the absence of such studies.

Research on legal standards is also rare. Stratmann (2003) constructs an index on the strictness of campaign financing rules in fourteen countries and observes, surprisingly, that strictness goes along with higher levels of corruption. This surprising finding may relate to endogeneity and the lack of control variables. High levels of corruption may lead to the adoption of contribution limits so as to operate as a remedy. The finding should thus not discourage the implementation of campaign financing rules.

Another strand of research lately focused on the role of increased official salaries. The reason for this impact relates to fears of being fired when caught taking bribes. High salaries provide office holders with prospects of a future income premium, which would be lost in case of being fired. Also the intrinsic motivation of public servants may increase with salary. However, as shown in Box 10, the related empirical evidence is poor.

Box 10 Corruption and official wages

Evans and Rauch (2000) investigate the impact of merit-based recruitment on corruption in thirty-five developing countries. Higher values in the merit-based recruitment index are associated with a greater proportion of higher-level officials in the core economic agencies who are either in possession of a university degree or who enter the civil service through a formal examination system. Controlling for income, this index is negatively associated with corruption.

Van Rijckeghem and Weder (2001) examine the extent to which the level of public sector salaries is linked to the amount of corruption. They argue that low salaries force public servants to supplement their incomes illicitly. At the same time, high salaries are a premium that is lost if a public servant is caught and fired.

Box 10 (*Cont.*)

In a small sample of thirty-one developing countries, they find a significant negative correlation between higher civil service wages (relative to manufacturing wages) and corruption levels. Doubling the civil service wage will improve the corruption index on the order of one point of the TI index.[6] The authors also point out that the association may be driven by reverse causality: corrupt countries tend to have a poor budgetary performance or may subscribe to the view that civil servants earn sufficient income from corruption, prompting them to reduce civil service pay. Such endogeneity problems diminish the prospects of fighting against corruption by increasing wages. Even disregarding these issues, pay increases are a costly approach to fighting corruption.

Other studies provide equally poor results for the impact of wages on corruption. Manow (2005), Swamy *et al.* (2001), and Treisman (2000) investigate the ratio of average government wages to per capita GDP, controlling for a variety of other influences. The results are ambiguous, and mostly insignificant, depending on the indicator for corruption employed and the inclusion of control variables.

While the effect of wages in aggregate, cross-country investigations tends to be poor, Di Tella and Schargrodsky (2003) find that wages of procurement officers at hospitals had a negative effect on the prices they paid for standardized health products. Price markups, on the other hand, would have been indicative of corruption. This effect, they argue, was particularly relevant at a time where a moderate level of auditing was carried out. There thus seems to be scattered evidence that higher wages accompanied by basic auditing can make a difference.

Another reform proposal has been to invigorate democracy. Its favorable effect on containing corruption has been largely related to increased competition for political mandates. At first, competition for the political positions should enable societies to get rid of those performing particularly poorly. Leaders who care only about their personal income could be voted out of office. Candidates from the

[6] The authors refer to a 0.5-point improvement in a corruption index by the PRS. This index has about half the standard deviation of the relevant subsample of countries in the TI index.

opposition could easily seize power when promising minor improvements (Rose-Ackerman 1978: 28). With competition, incumbents can be held accountable for their actions more easily, and voters can better identify and sanction self-seeking behavior (Rose-Ackerman 2005: 4). Competition may thus operate like an invisible hand, substituting a possible lack of benevolence among politicians with a mechanism that makes sure that public welfare is pursued. This is a standard argument in political economy at least since Schumpeter (1942).

The assumption of benevolence is sometimes overemphasized in economic modeling. Politicians may not be primarily motivated by productive efficiency, or the public interest, and they are not even seeking an optimally balanced set of hierarchical controls and monitoring mechanisms (Moe 1984: 761–2). Governments may even be purely self-serving. If an intrinsic motivation to serve the public is rare, competition may be all that societies have to generate some basic level of stewardship among their leadership.

For an empirical assessment of the effect of democracy on corruption, see Box 11. As evidenced by these studies, improvements in democracy reduce corruption, but not immediately, not the lukewarm type of democracy, and not the type with little electoral participation. Before transforming authoritarian systems into half-hearted democracies it is worthwhile considering whether such systems have established their peculiar methods of honoring integrity and how these might be endangered during transition.

Box 11 Corruption and democracy

The impact of the Gastil index (Freedom House; see Gastil (1986)) for political rights, that is, democracy, on corruption is tested by Paldam (2002). While the correlation between these variables is large, in multivariate regressions this relationship breaks down as soon as GDP per head enters into the equation. Similar results are reported by many others (Goldsmith 1999; Persson *et al.*, 2003; Sandholtz and Koetzle 2000). But Treisman (2000) finds a significant impact for a selection of sixty-four countries when he tests his sample for the impact of established democracies, those with a tradition for democracy going back to 1950. He argues that while the current degree of democracy is not significant, a long period of exposure to

Box 11 (*Cont.*)

democracy lowers corruption. Gerring and Thacker (2004; 2005) provide significant results using the cumulative number of years a country has been democratic since 1900.

Montinola and Jackman (2002) employ a broader measure of democracy, where the Gastil index enters besides an assessment of (1) freedom of group opposition and (2) the effectiveness of the legislative body. They find a nonlinear impact on corruption. As compared with autocratic regimes, moderate levels of democracy do not decrease corruption. Only after a certain threshold is passed do democratic practices inhibit corruption. Manow (2005) supports this finding with the help of more topical data. Manow concludes that corruption in medium-democratic regimes is even (slightly) higher than in totally authoritarian countries. Once this threshold is passed, he provides evidence for democracy reducing corruption. Sung (2004) tests different functional forms for the relationship between corruption and democracy and finds that a cubic form best fits the data. This form reveals an ambiguous impact for countries scoring between seven and two in the Freedom House index. Only the good score of one brings about decreased corruption. However, he fails to control for income per head, making it difficult to judge on the robustness of the findings. Adsera *et al.* (2000) obtain significant results for electoral participation. Controlling for various variables they find that countries with higher participation elicit lower levels of corruption. This also provides a more intricate picture of democracy.

One important constraint imposed on rulers, a president or prime minister, is often the power exerted by parliament. Parliament may sometimes follow its own self-seeking goals, but even in this case, by power of its independence, it can effectively limit the ruler's self-seeking behavior. As reviewed in Box 12, parliamentarism tends to go along with lower levels of corruption, while systems with powerful presidents are perceived to be more corrupt.

But, again the results are controversially discussed among political scientists, owing to an omitted variable bias. One missing variable is the quality of political parties (Shugart 1999). Presidentialism might be a second best alternative in countries where political parties are not devoted to broad national interests. In this case, presidentialism might be a response, rather than a cause, of high levels of corruption.

Box 12 Corruption and parliamentarism

Gerring and Thacker (2004) investigate the capacity of parliamentary systems to contain corruption, as opposed to presidential systems where policy-making power is divided between the legislature and the president. They find evidence that parliamentary systems are associated with less corruption. A similar result is reported by Lederman *et al.* (2001) and Panizza (2001). Kunicová (2005) reports the same finding for a sample of more than one hundred countries controlling for a battery of further variables. She extends her analysis by introducing a dummy variable for presidents with term limits. She reports that presidentialism increases corruption significantly when it goes along with term limits. She argues that this is likely to result when incumbents have little to lose at the end of their term. In addition, she shows that corruption increases where presidents are more powerful, that is, where their range of power expands across both legislative and nonlegislative functions. For a sample of forty-three presidential countries she shows that corruption increases with this indicator of power. Kunicová and Rose-Ackerman (2005) investigate parliamentarism versus presidentialism and plurality voting versus proportional representation. The systems most prone to corruption are presidential systems with closed-list proportional representation.

Adsera *et al.* (2000) obtain an unexpected positive impact for presidentialism on the control of corruption. This might result from their different quantification of presidentialism. This variable is no longer determined as a dummy variable, but takes on the values of 0 if the president is elected directly, 1 if the president is elected by the assembly, but has substantial powers, and 2 if the system is purely parliamentarian. The different finding might also result from their inclusion of a variable on political instability, which increases corruption and could be associated with constitutional structure.

Competition among politicians is another issue considered to contain corruption. Competition may not only limit self-seeking among the government, but also force political leaders to tightly control subordinates. A contested ruler may be effectively pressurized to secure bureaucrats or party members to serve the public (Breton and Wintrobe 1975). A contested government may not only be held responsible for its own self-seeking but also for the bureaucratic corruption among its various agents. Those politicians who are least able or willing to contain corruption at lower ranks may fear being ousted. The government will therefore be induced to monitor how well its members and the administration contribute to public welfare, hence disallowing shirking, laziness, and corruption.

Yet, the power of competition should not be overestimated. Moe (1984: 762) argues that competition does not guarantee that inefficient programs are eradicated and that dishonest politicians are disposed of. One reason for this arises when corruption is used to subvert the selection process. Politicians with control over corrupt income may spend these resources in return for staying in power. Corruption and the power to allocate rents to supporters can be helpful instruments for guaranteeing political survival. Honest politicians have fewer such resources at their disposal and may perish as a result of competition for political positions (Buchanan 1993: 69). Those who can bargain best for political assistance are in a prime position for survival. Even benevolent rulers may trade in some of their generous motivation for political support. Competition alone may be insufficient to ensure that benevolence among the leadership prevails. Also Rose-Ackerman (2005: 4) points to the risk of electoral defeat having the potential to increase corruption. The risk of losing office makes it harder for party leaders to secure loyalty. This may induce them to compensate their supporters by other favors. This type of partisan favoritism may open the door to outright corruption, because partisan politicians may dislike the restrictions imposed on their favoritism by regulations on transparency and accountability. In this respect, recent empirical evidence on the impact of electoral systems on corruption is illustrative; see Box 13. As argued there, electoral systems can enhance competition among candidates, but the resulting effect on corruption might be ambiguous.

Box 13 Corruption and voting systems

Persson *et al.* (2003) test the impact of electoral rules on corruption in a cross section of more than eighty democracies. They argue that smaller voting districts, characterized by few representatives from each district, increase corruption because they impede the entry of new candidates. Small voting districts require increased efforts for a candidate or a political party to adapt to local requirements and needs, lowering competition among candidates and their accountability toward their constituency. In contrast, larger districts imply lower barriers to entry for new parties or new candidates, and this increased competition helps reduce corruption. They report a negative impact of the size of voting districts on corruption. However, this impact is significant only at a 10 percent significance level and is not robust throughout different specifications. Also Damania *et al.* (2004) and Panizza (2001) report less significant findings. Another, more significant finding by Persson *et al.* relates to party lists. The authors find that corruption is higher in countries whose parliamentarians are elected from party lists, rather than as individual candidates. The likely reason is that such election systems go along with less individual accountability. The authors suggest that Chile's strong score might be largely attributable to its electoral rules, which avoid small districts and limit party lists.

Chang and Golden (2004) criticize the simplified variable on party list voting in the approach by Persson *et al.* They argue that closed-list voting, where voters only cast votes for parties, should be distinguished from open-list voting, where voters both select a party and rank candidates given the party's selection of candidates. They argue that the two types fare differently, depending on the size of the voting district. They find that, in the case of large voting districts, closed-lists help in containing corruption, while in small voting districts open lists limit corruption. They point out that politicians need to amass (possibly illegal) resources to triumph over their opponents in open-list voting. This effect becomes stronger in large voting districts, suggesting why closed lists turn out to be superior.

Box 13 (*Cont.*)

Persson *et al.* (2003) observe a positive correlation between the size of the voting district and the prevalence of voting from party lists. A voting system tends to be characterized either by plurality rule, where seats are awarded to the individual candidates receiving the highest vote shares in small voting districts, or by proportional representation systems, where political parties compete in larger voting districts. These large voting districts are preferable with respect to lowering corruption, but the prevalence of candidates coming from party lists increases corruption. They find that the latter effect is stronger, indicating that proportional election, even in large districts, increases corruption. This unfavorable finding on proportional representation is supported by Kunicova and Rose-Ackerman (2005). They find that electoral systems with proportional representation are associated with higher corruption than plurality rule. Westminster democracy is most capable of reducing corruption.[7]

All these findings are challenged by Manow (2005) who claims that political parties' influence in elections reduces corruption. He argues that a political party's time horizon is typically longer than that of individual candidates, suggesting that the malfeasance of a single party member brings about severe damage to the reputation of the political party. This explains parties' willingness to discipline their members. The favorable role often played by established political parties and their capacity in containing corruption, he argues, deserve to be reconsidered. Manow shows that the negative impact of party lists by Persson *et al.* breaks down when restricting the sample to more mature democracies or countries with a high level of political freedom (those that score between three and one on the Freedom House index).

An explanation to these contradictory findings might be found in Panizza (2001: 326, 336, 338). He employs an index on "particularism" in regressions for 101 countries. This variable depicts the extent to which party control is subverted by individual candidates. It embraces party (lack of) influence as to which

[7] This result survives the inclusion of dummy variables for British colonialism and British legal origin. However, they point out that the effects of electoral rules are rather small as compared with that of other variables.

candidates use the party's label, whether votes relate to candidates or pools of candidates, and whether voters can voice preferences for parties or candidates. Panizza finds no linear impact of this variable on the extent of corruption. However, he obtains a nonlinear impact: countries with moderate party influence and some limited power among individual candidates fare best, (Panizza 2001: 336, 338). In the light of this nonlinearity, the selected sample of countries can seriously affect the results. For example, disregarding African, Latin American, and Eastern European countries, where elections are rather party-centered and corruption is rife, would provide results that are rather favorable to political parties, in line with Manow's findings. There is no simple right or wrong with respect to choosing the sample – and no iron-clad advice to be obtained from the existing studies on particularism.

Overall, competition for political positions can be helpful in avoiding a self-seeking leadership. But it requires more than just general elections to effectively reduce levels of corruption. Also the precise technicalities of the voting system appear to have a rather mixed impact on levels of corruption. Guaranteeing fairness and honesty during an election process is one crucial prerequisite for electoral competition to bring about the desired fruit, but this is precisely what may be in short supply. Political competition may certainly be desirable on its own right, helping to bring power closer to ordinary citizens. But the technicalities of the voting system provide little avenues for reform.

Another more promising candidate for reform relates to the freedom of the press. More than the fear of being prosecuted and sentenced, politicians may be deterred by the danger of losing their reputation. While the process of public scandalization may not necessarily be fair and impartial, it nonetheless induces public office holders to refrain from corruption. One basic precondition for a press to contain corruption is its freedom and independence. Indeed, as revealed in Box 14, substantial evidence supports a negative correlation between corruption and press freedom. Thus, reform aimed at improving the quality, freedom, and independence of the media is influential in reducing corruption.

Box 14 Corruption and press freedom

By regressing various indices of corruption on indicators of press freedom, Brunetti and Weder (2003) show that a free press effectively deters corruption. The latter variables consist of "laws and regulations that influence media content," "political influence over media content," "economic influence over media content," and "repressive actions" as compiled by Freedom House. These four separate indices and an aggregate index of press freedom all impact negatively on the level of corruption in various specifications. This negative association between freedom of the press and corruption is also confirmed by Lederman *et al.* (2001). Besley and Prat (2006) observe a correlation between corruption and state ownership of newspapers as well as with a high concentration in ownership of newspapers. However, they fail to control their regressions for standard explanatory variables. Another weakness of these studies is the choice of the corruption index, which is that by PRS. Still, Brunetti and Weder (2003) corroborate their findings also by using alternative indicators, providing us with some more confidence with respect to their findings. Sung (2002) confirms a strong negative association between press freedom and corruption using the TI CPI, albeit missing to control for income per head. Corrupt authoritarian regimes may restrict press freedom, suggesting that part of the causality may run the other way. Nevertheless, Brunetti and Weder (2003) show that their findings survive the use of instruments, claiming that a good share of the causality runs from a free press to less corruption. Adsera *et al.* (2000) employ data on daily average newspapers per person. These figures vary from 0.7 daily copies per person in Hong Kong to 0 in Mauritania. They show that the amount of newspapers per person is negatively associated with corruption, particularly in democracies. This equally suggests that a successful media is a strong impediment to corrupt politics by making it difficult for elites to get away with corrupt behavior.

Lindstedt and Naurin (2005) also show that freedom of the press reduces corruption, but that this impact is largely limited to democracies and countries with higher levels of education. Focusing anticorruption alone on press freedom, one may conclude, would be insufficient.

Another area for reform relates to the judicial system. A high quality of the judiciary acts as a deterrent to corruption. But even in the dismal case where verdicts can be bought and judges be bribed a judiciary might still reduce corruption. As long as the judiciary is independent, courts endanger the corrupt transactions of a country's elite. To the contrary, in some countries politics has a strong influence on the judiciary, making it possible for the big fish to escape prosecution. In some cases the judiciary might even operate in favor of corrupt elites by enforcing their corrupt deals. As revealed in Box 15, empirical evidence is supportive of judicial independence lowering corruption. This should also embrace the independence of prosecutors. But it requires more than just changing laws. It is rather the de facto independence that seems to be at play. Such reform proposals should certainly not overlook the fact that freeing the judiciary from corruption is also an important contribution to reform.

Box 15 Corruption and the judiciary

An approach by the World Bank (1997: 104, 168) focuses on the quality of the judiciary. While controlling for other explanatory variables, an index of the predictability of the judiciary from WB/UB significantly influences the level of corruption in fifty-nine countries. Herzfeld and Weiss (2003) exhibit a strong negative correlation between law and order and corruption. The former variable by ICRG measures the soundness of political institutions, the strength of the court system, and whether provisions are in place for an orderly succession of power.

A correlation between corruption and the independence of the judicial system is proposed in Ades and Di Tella (1996). Also Sung (2002) reports this result, albeit missing to control for income per head. Damania *et al.* (2004) show that corruption diminishes with a composite index embracing as diverse issues as people's tendency to abide by the rules of society, perceptions of violent and non-violent crimes, predictability and efficiency of the judiciary, and the enforceability of legal contracts. Given the broad definition of

Box 15 (*Cont.*)

this variable and its potential endogeneity, however, the coefficient could easily be biased upward.

Voigt *et al.* (2004) investigate the impact of prosecutorial independence on corruption. They provide data on independence with a help of a questionnaire sent to Supreme Court judges, law professors, lawyers, and anticorruption activists. The authors distinguish between de jure independence (e.g. life tenure, appointment and promotion by persons other than politicians, lack of executive power to substitute prosecutors working on a specific case) and de facto independence (dependence would be assumed, for example, in case of forced retirement, frequent changes in legal foundations, and decreasing income and budget of prosecutors). They find that de facto independence decreases corruption, and relate this to the disciplining effect on the executive and on influential politicians. Interestingly, de jure independence increases corruption. This finding is surprising. De jure reform might be futile in some cases, but inducing an increase of corruption is counterintuitive. One explanation to this finding relates to endogeneity. Rather than de jure independence impacting on corruption, it is rather corruption that brings about de jure independence. The higher corruption is among the executive, the higher the willingness to pay lip service to prosecutorial independence.

Apart from these results, our knowledge of reform is rather limited. Above that, we are lacking a sound theoretical framework that can serve as an inspiration.

2.3. A novel inspiration to reform

Theoretical modeling has often hindered rather than inspired reform. One early approach to the connection between corruption and welfare was provided by the rent-seeking theory. Chapter 5 deals extensively with this approach. The viewpoint taken by rent-seeking theory is that corruption is an alternative to lobbyism. Privileges can be provided by public decision-makers, and these are for sale due to the presence of corruption or lobbying. Comparing these two evils, it becomes evident that corruption provides benefits to politicians, while lobbying may rather molest them, because it goes along with time-consuming responses to public campaigns, efforts to avoid lawsuits, and defending one's public reputation. The private firms' expenses for rent-seeking are simply wasted in the case of lobbying, while they bring about benefits to public servants in the case of corruption. Thus, corruption entails smaller transaction costs. The problem with rent-seeking theory is its odd policy prescription: because of these transaction costs it claims that corruption should be preferred to lobbying. This line of thought has hindered comprehensive anticorruption efforts for some decades. The policy prescription by rent-seeking theory was quite unusual: corruption should be condoned; efforts should rather be directed to lowering the waste that goes along with the sale of privileges. Nepotism should be preferred to competitive lobbying. Arbitrary decision-making in politics fares better than transparent political contests. The transfer of benefits to politicians should not be hindered because this would increase the transaction costs.

The approach to reform suggested in this book is plainly the opposite: transfers to politicians should be made as difficult and costly as possible. In order to justify this approach, Chapter 5 is devoted to disproving the early rent-seeking theory. Its conclusions rest on one-sided assumptions regarding the causes of corruption. The results change dramatically, once taking into account that the prospects of receiving bribes induce politicians to offer privileges. If bribes are unavailable, there is a chance that the pertinent arguments in public decision-making are not overshadowed by other considerations and that privileges and rents are not created in the first place.

Given the crucial role of transaction costs in affecting the behavior of politicians and bureaucrats, we must understand their roots. We must investigate the link between norms, trust, and the precise mechanisms by which corrupt relationships are established. A theoretical approach that links the corrupt exchange of goods and services with the underlying social patterns, moral sentiments, and the necessity to find trusted partners is provided in Chapters 6–9. We have to identify those institutions that are employed or that evolve in order to meet the coordination needs of corrupt exchange.

While high levels of corruption are generally deplored, academics commonly wonder why they are not even higher. With self-seeking being the presumed nature of human beings, opportunities for self-enrichment should always be seized. Distrusting public decision-makers should be the natural consequence; trusting them appears to be a naïve attitude. Given that we sometimes have reason to wonder about astonishingly high levels of integrity, social scientists must confess that they are lacking a theoretical explanation. Also in recent experiments, researchers found that integrity was higher (and corruption lower) than predicted (Schulze and Frank 2003).

One approach to explain this paradox is to focus on the (mostly informal) institutions needed for arranging and securing a corrupt deal. Partners in a corrupt exchange face a challenging task in negotiating the terms of their agreement and in making sure that each side adheres to its promises. At the same time they are constantly tempted to betray each other. Such betrayal can be a good thing from the point of view of the society at large, because it assures that corruption is a troublesome business and convinces potential participants to refrain from becoming involved in corrupt deals. When public officials are paid with counterfeit money, as it recently happened in India, or with fake antiques, as it took place in China, the resulting insecurity for public servants may effectively deter them from asking for bribes in the future.[8] Similarly, when public servants, who take bribes, decline to deliver on their promises, businesspeople may become less likely to continue with their illegal strategy.

One of the salient functions of institutions is to safeguard economic exchange from opportunistic behavior. Yet, these safeguarding mechanisms can be used in two different ways: some can protect legal transactions and help to economize on transaction costs, while others are used to enable transactions that run counter to the formalized canon of legal activities – corrupt transactions being one of them.

Corrupt transactions usually do not take place in an anonymous marketplace. Consequently, corrupt actors have scope in designing the institutions of their exchange. Informal institutions such as reciprocity, loyalty and honesty in corrupt transactions can be increased by a variety of institutional settings. In a recent publication,

[8] See *International Herald Tribune* (March 8, 2002: "One Corrupt City Shows the Plague that Afflicts All of China"); *The New Zealand Herald* (March 28, 2002: It's Hard Graft When Bribes are Crooked); *Asia Times* (April 4, 2002: "Rampant Corruption Threatened by Corruption").

Figure 2.1. Cartoon by J. Shapiro, Daily Mail and Guardian, South Africa, July 11, 1999

different authors have contributed valuable insights on this topic (Lambsdorff *et al.* 2004). The contributions provided in this book lay out the foundations of this newly developed research area. Exploring how far corruption is vulnerable to opportunism, the focus is on transaction costs. These are costs that occur as a consequence of exchanging services or goods for a return. They typically include costs associated with searching for partners, determining contract conditions, and enforcing the agreement thereafter.

A close investigation of the transaction costs in corrupt agreements reveals remarkable differences to those of legal transactions. First, corruption does not allow for legal recourse;[9] second, corruption must be hidden from the public; and, third, because of the ever-present threat of mutual denunciation, partners of a corrupt agreement are "locked-in" to each other even after an exchange has been finalized. As a consequence, opportunism is particularly difficult

[9] Uslaner (2004) provides the only counterexample I have encountered up to now. An Italian court ruled that the nondeliverance of a promised (corrupt) favor would have been penalized. Clearly, this example is an exception rather than the rule.

A man of principle. He accepted the bribe but he wouldn't give me the licence because that would be against the rules.

Figure 2.2. Cartoon by Laxman, Times of India

to avoid in case of corrupt contracts. Transaction costs are higher than in the case of legal contracts.

Courts would reject the enforcement of corrupt agreements, forcing the actors to explore alternative mechanisms. They must employ methods to make their agreement self-enforcing. Various forms of institutional solutions come into play and provide direction to reform. Corrupt parties who lack trust in each other often employ intermediaries. Practical insights into the dealings of intermediaries have been reported recently (Aburish 1986; Andvig 1995; Moody-Stuart

1997). Their function is to build bridges from one side to another by being trustworthy to both. Such middlemen can help in identifying corrupt partners, where searching in the open is too risky. They may even provide a legal appearance to a corrupt deal, camouflaging a bribe as a commission. Middlemen can monitor how well public servants stick to their promises, providing reasons for public servants to invest in their reputation as "honest bribees." But employing middlemen is not without its own risks. Intermediaries might be costly, cheat their clients, sign unenforceable contracts, and render their clients vulnerable to blackmail (Bray 1999; 2004). Middlemen are at best an imperfect solution to the problems faced by corrupt actors. Corrupt opportunities may be missed when enforcement problems remain unresolved.

A functioning type of corruption is commonly regarded as the lesser of two evils. Although costly to businesspeople, it allows at least for some predictability and confidence. This sometimes misleads observers to conclude that the adverse effects of corruption might be avoided by divesting it of its unpredictability. But these arguments are misguided because a lack of confidence in those supposed to deliver corrupt services also acts as a deterrent to corruption. This is investigated in Chapter 7, which focuses on the interaction of reciprocity, social embeddedness, and corruption. The chapter argues that unpredictable corruption might be the lesser of two evils, because unpredictability acts as a deterrent to a further spread of corruption.

In a similar spirit, Herrera and Rodriguez (2003) investigate the link between the size of bribes, the impediments to doing business, and the predictability of corruption. Using firm-level data on the reported payment of bribes by the 2000 World Bank Business Environment Survey, they report that the frequency of bribe payments is higher where corruption is predictable, that is, where the size of the payment is known in advance and where public servants deliver as promised. Thus, predictability can induce the further spread of corruption. A similar result is provided by Tonoyan (2004), using data from the 1995–1996 World Values Survey. She observes that individual perceptions of high levels of corruption ("How widespread do you think bribe-taking and corruption is in this country?") are positively correlated to the importance of friends. She argues that high-trust societies are often associated with lower levels of corruption. But this holds true only for generalized trust, that is, trust in anonymous others and institutions. The opposite is true for particularized trust, that is trust in specific persons (friends). A lack of generalized trust is substituted by particularized trust. The latter type of trust, for example, is fostered within close business networks. This, in turn, can be a breeding ground for corruption (Lambert-Mogiliansky 2002).

Preexisting social relationships can lay the foundation for economic exchange by providing the required safeguards against opportunism. Social structures facilitate economic exchange by embedding individuals in long-term relationships (Granovetter 1992). For members of a social structure, the advantages to be gained from benefiting another member may outweigh the motivation to behave opportunistically or to denounce another member. Such social structures can facilitate the sealing of a corrupt contract (Rose-Ackerman 1999: 98). Social structures may also be helpful in spreading information on corrupt opportunities. Group members can be entrusted with delicate pieces of information that must not leak to third parties. Consequently, networks are preferred to markets, where anonymous recipients of information may deliberately cooperate with law-enforcement authorities. The extent and type of social embeddedness may offer favorable prerequisites for securing corrupt deals.

Another approach to enforce corrupt agreements is at the disposal of business partners who have an already established ongoing exchange with each other. Once a relationship of mutual trust, repeated legal exchange, or hierarchical control has been established, this can be misused for striking a corrupt agreement. A corrupt transaction would be embedded into a broader context of exchange. A legal transaction may thus act as a "guarantor" for the corrupt deal. For example, a repeated legal market exchange between business partners can serve as a basis for a corrupt deal, because the threat to end the legal relationship effectively prevents opportunism with respect to the corrupt deal. Also, a hierarchical relationship within a firm may help in arranging a corrupt exchange, because it provides control mechanisms for sanctioning opportunism and harassing an offender. This issue is further explored in Chapter 9, which has been written jointly with Utku Teksoz. This chapter shows that various types of market or hierarchical interactions can be exploited for striking a corrupt deal. Once trusted relationships have developed and legal threats been established, these can be misused for guaranteeing an additional corrupt contract. This stresses that corruption usually does not take the form of market exchange but is often restricted to well-acquainted business partners. Corruption is embedded into a regular exchange that deteriorates so as to comprise illegal elements.

That opportunism represents a substantial threat to informal contracting has recently been corroborated by laboratory experiments. In some recent studies participants play bribery games or face problems similar to those explained above. For a comprehensive review, see Dušek *et al.* (2005). The results emanating from this research are that reciprocity takes place even when this is in contrast to immediate self-seeking. There is a tendency to "do good to those that did us good." This is sometimes termed "positive reciprocity." Returning a favor is thus done even if it does not promise future gains to the giver. But while some players tend to reciprocate, others are opportunistic. They would not return favors; they may not feel thankful to those who did them well or at least would not translate their thanks into favors. From the viewpoint of fighting corruption, this opportunism is a good thing, because it also impedes illegitimate deals between corrupt actors.

Drawing on the gift-exchange literature, Abbink *et al.* (2000) let two participants hope for reciprocity when handing over gifts. In case of defection one of them could spend resources on punishment. Game theory would predict that such punishment would not be carried out because it does not increase the punisher's income. Expecting the absence of sanctions, the counterpart would have no incentive to return a gift. This suggests that none of the participants hands out gifts in the first place. However, contrary to game theoretic predictions retribution was found to be quite common. Dušek *et al.* (2005) summarize that "hostile actions are consistently punished while the friendly ones are less consistently rewarded." There emerges a second type of reciprocity: doing bad to those who did us bad. This type of "negative reciprocity" is also chosen, even where it is costly to the punisher. The risk of retribution and how it impacts on the stability of a corrupt exchange will be dealt with more explicitly in Chapter 6.

To root out corruption, it may be necessary to risk destroying some of the confidence that goes along with it – the trust that expects corrupt favors to be reciprocated. Fjeldstad and Tungodden (2001) argue that the way the customs services was downsized in Tanzania was a failure, because those officials who were fired at a later stage became middlemen and created trusted corrupt relationships. After a first crackdown on corruption, the corruption networks were revitalized and strengthened, and corruption returned to its original level. Apparently, strategies in fighting corruption can fail if they do not adequately take notice of the network ties and the mechanisms that facilitate corruption.

For example, rotating staff can be helpful in destroying confidence in a bureaucrat's potential to return a favor. In a recent experimental study, this effect has been corroborated (Abbink 2004). A trust game was designed by letting fixed pairs play repeated games where they can jointly profit only from cooperation but defection would be individually optimal. In a second treatment, participants were rematched in each round. The effect of this rematching is similar to that of rotating personnel. The number of bribery attempts and their volume was cut by about half in the second treatment.

Regulating middlemen can impede them in creating networks of trusted relationships. But only scant ideas can currently be observed concerning the attempt to regulate the behavior of corrupt middlemen. For example, in India the payments of commissions in public arms contracts are prohibited. This can effectively discourage corrupt middlemen. Equally, in Algeria laws prohibiting the engagement of middlemen in public procurement were enacted in 1978 and improved further in 1988. In Singapore, subcontracting in public procurement is illegal – intervening purchasers may otherwise engage as corrupt intermediaries. All these are diverse ideas of how to make life more difficult for corrupt middlemen. Many practical approaches in this spirit deserve recognition.

Another effective means to destroy the confidence among corrupt partners is to encourage whistle-blowing. This includes advising citizens on how to make a complaint and establishing institutions that will handle the resulting cases (Pope 2000). An effective system of whistle-blowing lowers the confidence among corrupt partners, cuts through secrecy and thus increases the transaction costs of corrupt agreements. Making sure that courts stay firm in rejecting the enforcement of corrupt agreements is another necessary contribution to anticorruption. Finally, politics can also contribute to the destruction of confidence among corrupt partners. Politics must stop the honoring of potentially corrupt agreements.

Before devoting our efforts to reform, we need to see Chapters 3 and 4, which are dedicated to the welfare consequences of corruption. These chapters show that corrupt actors are unlikely to be chosen for public duties where abstinence from corruption would be vital. Bribes impede actors from performing official duties. This feature turns against those who encounter opportunities for corruption and those who cannot ascertain that they will not give in to this temptation. This failure is at the core of the welfare losses of corruption. By recognizing this, we notice that even those who might engage in corruption sometimes want to partner in anticorruption campaigns.

3 *What is bad about bureaucratic corruption? An institutional economic approach*

THAT corruption adversely affects economic development has become a commonplace assertion in academia and public discussion. Identifying the precise reasons for this impact is not straightforward, however. I show here that at the core of understanding the social consequences of corruption is the bureaucrats' failure to commit to honesty once they are ready to take bribes. The downside of public servants' willingness to take bribes is that these officials disqualify for professions where their commitment to honesty would be vital. This downside effect may certainly also hurt the reputation of honest colleagues in the public service without compensating them by income from bribery.

Corruption involves the malfunctioning of some (or all) areas of the public sector. Crucial to this malfunctioning is that individuals or whole units within these sectors serve themselves and not the public. Those who study the effects of corruption on welfare are confronted with a multitude of models. Since each has its specific benefits and deficiencies, the choice of an adequate model is complicated and crucial at the same time.

Crucial to an understanding of the effects of bureaucratic corruption is its relationship to bureaucratic discretion and distorting regulation. I claim that a sound assessment of the effects of corruption on public welfare remains inconclusive when regulations are considered exogenous to the analysis. This results because corruption and bad regulation are often two sides of the same coin. A principal–agent model is taken as a framework of analysis for the subsequent sections. For a recent formal treatment, see Aidt (2003). I assume a self-serving bureaucrat (agent) and the government taking the role of a benevolent principal. The crucial reason for welfare losses to arise relates to informational asymmetries. Corruption constrains the contractual space available to agents and principals, and disallows agents from committing themselves to honest dealings.

That governments are not necessarily benevolent should be plausible to readers of a book on corruption. Yet we delegate the consideration of nonbenevolence among the government to Chapter 4.

3.1. Corruption and market distortions

Corruption often entails the provision of a service by a public servant or politician in exchange for a bribe. As long as this takes place voluntarily, both actors will be better off, making it arduous to argue that total public welfare suffers. Negative externalities may be imposed on others, for example on unsuccessful competitors that are better qualified than a bribe-paying firm. Taking this into account, a common conclusion is that the total welfare effect of corruption cannot be determined *a priori* but depends on the size of these externalities. Given circumstances of cumbersome regulation, excessive bureaucracy, or market restrictions, some economists tended to emphasize the positive effects of corruption (Bayley 1966; Huntington 1968; Leff 1964; Morgan 1964; Nye 1967). Crucial to these effects is the existence of market distortions caused by government intervention, preventing markets from equating supply and demand, and allocating resources efficiently. In such an environment corruption is a symptom of inadequate state intervention (Ades and Di Tella 1999).

These interventions are harmful to market participants. They generate the above-mentioned externalities. In contrast, corruption is seen to ameliorate these problems. Corruption helps to open up new contractual possibilities and to reestablish market efficiency. Corruption has even gained recognition in economic textbooks. Mankiw (2000: 123) argues that with regard to state-imposed price ceilings on rental fees "bribes bring the total price … (including the bribe) closer to the equilibrium price."

For example, the United States imposed quotas of $1.7 billion a year on thirty-eight textile and garment categories shipped from Vietnam in order to curb imports. Le Van Thang, 50, deputy director of the Ministry of Trade's Import and Export Department, and staff member Bui Hong Minh, 33, were arrested in Hanoi in September 2004 for taking bribes. Thang was responsible for selecting the local textile and garment companies to meet the quotas. This equipped him with ample opportunity to take something in exchange for providing preferential treatment. The case was exposed, however, when some companies came forward to the police (*Wall Street Journal*, September, 15 2004: "Two Vietnam Officials Arrested for Alleged Bribery").

As this case indicates, market restrictions such as import quotas create opportunities for corruption. In many other cases of quantity restrictions corruption can be a consequence of state intervention. But one wonders about Mankiw's argument that the price that results with corruption should be close to the initial equilibrium price in an undisturbed market. Bribes act as a wedge between the price that suppliers are requesting and the price that customers are willing to pay. Owing to the artificial scarcity imposed by state intervention, the price (including the bribe) that customers must pay is larger than the initial equilibrium price. In our case, US customers of Vietnamese garments paid higher prices because of import restrictions, and Vietnamese officials seized part of this markup by demanding bribes. It is not at all apparent that bribes eased the burden.

Even where corruption is caused by superfluous regulation and bothersome government intervention it does little to overcome these restrictions. In an attempt to crack down on corruption, the Vietnamese government could sell the right to export garment with the help of a public tender. But in reality, once corruption becomes embedded such initiatives are quickly abandoned because the huge rents achievable by corruption allow for buying off politicians in exchange for turning a blind eye to bureaucratic corruption. In light of these considerations, the causality is often found to run from corruption to profitable market distortions. Corruption becomes a cause of distortionary regulation (Lambsdorff 2002b; Chapter 5 of this book; Rose-Ackerman 1999: 9–17). For example, the investigation of excessive bureaucratic regulation in De Soto (1989) leads the author to conclude that they were largely motivated by the desire to generate corrupt revenues. A vicious circle can exist whereby inefficient regulation leads to corruption, which in turn cultivates the further spread of troublesome regulation so as to enhance administrative power and the opportunity to exact further payoffs. As expressed by Myrdal (1956: 283),

> In many underdeveloped countries . . . the damaging effects [of quantitative controls] have been serious. The system tends easily to create cancerous tumors of partiality and corruption in the very center of the administration,

where the sickness is continuously nurtured by the favors distributed and the grafts realized. Industrialists and businessmen are tempted to go in for shady deals instead of steady regular business. Individuals who might have performed useful tasks in the economic development of their country become idle hangers-on, watching for loopholes in the decrees and dishonesty in their implementation.

Bureaucrats, once bribed, may turn a blind eye to market-distorting rules imposed by the government. But at the same time they have an interest in keeping precisely these distorting rules in place. Public servants can take bribes for disregarding rules – but without these rules they would have nothing to profitably disregard. This is well illustrated by the cartoon, in Figure 3.1. Considering this vicious circle a welfare analysis of corruption must incorporate the investigation of institutions and regulation and must not consider them exogenous to the analysis.

There exists by now plenty of evidence that countries riddled by corruption exhibit poor government institutions. For example, corruption leads managers to waste more time negotiating with bureaucrats (Kaufmann and Wei 1999). There is therefore consensus nowadays that corruption does not "grease the wheels," as suggested in some older pieces of literature. For a recent empirical assessment, see Méon and Sekkat (2005). Corruption does not help to overcome cumbersome regulation but acts as an inducement to public servants to create artificial bureaucratic bottlenecks. Corruption acts, therefore, as sand in the wheels. See also Box 3 for further empirical evidence.

In line with this, countries with high levels of corruption are characterized by vague and lax regulation and hidden import barriers – because vagueness allows bureaucrats to request something in exchange for easing the burden. Entry regulation is equally distorted by corruption. These distortions include a high number of procedures required to start a new business, alongside with more time and official costs necessary to work through official and unofficial requirements. Politicians and bureaucrats who impose excessive and cumbersome regulation cause the aforementioned distortions. Once such bottlenecks have been created, private firms face the alternative of either staying out of business or paying a bribe to work around these impediments. A vicious circle emerges because excessive regulation, once in place, provides opportunities for future corrupt transactions. Once corruption becomes the rule, self-seeking

Look, I want to announce some rigid rules and regulations – so that I may liberalise them to give relief to the people!

Figure 3.1. Cartoon by Laxman, Times of India

bureaucrats attempt to increase their income by imposing further troublesome impediments on the private sector.

3.2. The principal–agent approach

An alternative approach to the creation of rules is provided by the principal–agent theory. While this model was initially developed for analyzing the relation between private contractual parties such as owners and managers of a firm, it has also been utilized to model bureaucracy and public institutions. Its application to the investigation of corruption goes back to Rose-Ackerman (1978: 6) and has, in the meantime, become standard to many economists' work (Jain 1998; Klitgaard 1988: 73).

From a principal–agent approach the design of rules becomes the actual object of analysis. A principal (i.e. the government)[1] is assumed to create rules directed at assigning tasks to the agent (e.g. the tax authorities). These rules are intended to regulate exchange with a client (e.g. the taxpayer). Such exchange relates, for example, to the payment of taxes and customs tariffs, the provision of services and licenses, or the awarding of contracts. By nature of individual goals tending to differ, a conflict of interest arises between the principal and the agent. This conflict is unavoidable because both actors depend on each other. The principal is insufficiently skilled or faces time constraints that favor delegation of tasks to the agent. But the agent will, in turn, have an informational advantage over the principal, which provides her with discretionary power. Either her effort level is not observable by the principal (she can hide her true effort level from the principal after the contract is negotiated) or she can obfuscate her qualifications before the contract is sealed. An example of the latter case is that agents may have a certain propensity to behave honestly that is hidden to the principal (Besley and McLaren 1993).

Given this informational advantage, it may not be possible to write contracts contingent on the agent's quality. Likewise, a contract that specifies the agent's effort level may not be enforceable because information on effort is not available to the principal or to courts and arbitrators (Furubotn and Richter 1998: 179–80). The principal thus faces problems of moral hazard and adverse selection. One solution suggested for the relationship between private parties is to make the agent partly the residual claimant of the operation. This incentive induces compliance to the terms of the contract. But in reality the role of such economic incentives is lower than that predicted by theory

[1] This study uses the terms principal and government as synonyms. Another approach would be to assign a government the role of the agent, facing the constituency as the principal. Yet, since the power of the constituency is highly limited, this approach does not fit into our analysis.

(Furubotn and Richter 1998: 202). Not only does the common assumption of the agent's risk-aversion restrict the attempt by principals to make agents residual claimants of the operation but such incentives also play a minor role particularly for bureaucracies because there is no measurable economic surplus accruing to an administrator of a bureaucratic unit serving as a yardstick for remuneration (Moe 1984: 763).

Owing to this failure, governments, instead of rewarding honesty, rather tend to levy a "tax on honesty." For example, Hart (1970: 875–87) argues that taxpayers have tremendous scope for concealing their true income and may even bribe the revenue agent, such that honesty becomes expensive. Instead of providing monetary inducements, principals may try to substitute costly incentives with an appeal to an agent's intrinsic honesty. Or else they may attempt to impose psychological barriers against agents' self-serving behavior, for example by encouraging moral conformity through the help of ethical training. Easier to describe in economic terms are attempts by agents to make credible commitments where the resulting signals of honesty are informative to the principal. While the term "informational asymmetry" is an "amoral" term that does not involve normative assessments, these mechanisms may explain why, in reality, principal–agent relationships are often supported by social norms like customs or professional standards.

Whether the self-serving behavior of agents can readily be termed corruption or not is food for debate. There is an unavoidable normative element in the judgment on whether an agent is regarded as being entitled to maximize her self-interest or, alternatively, whether this is a misuse of public funds and a breach of the trust she was given. Particularly when the size of funds involved is small and the agent is simply lazy, the term corruption seems inappropriate. But in the case of large-scale cost padding and embezzlement, some observers may consider this term adequate.[2]

[2] Whether embezzlement represents a type of corruption can be up to dispute because it does not require an exchange between two parties at the cost of others – that is, the existence of a client. But in order to conceal the true costs of a project and to overinvoice, agents often require the cooperation of outsiders. They employ clients who provide fake documents, falsely certify the provision of services, and pay kickbacks for obtaining inflated prices in procurement.

Another crucial characteristic of corruption can be seen in the agents' relationship to third parties. A client adds another dimension to the principal–agent approach, because he provides further opportunities for the agent to cheat. Corruption is deemed to take place when an agent trespasses on the rules set up by the principal by colluding with the client and promoting her own benefit. She obtains a bribe that is hidden to the principal. The aim of a bribe is to loosen loyalty between the agent and the principal, and to induce the agent to bend the rules in favor of the client. It is particularly this type of collusion between a client and the agent that distinguishes corruption from simple self-serving behavior among agents.

Another variant of the principal–agent model emerges when a supervisor/auditor is introduced, who is supposed to monitor the agent and report truthfully to the principal, so as to alleviate the informational asymmetries faced by the principal. But if a supervisor can collude with the agent, she can be induced to falsify her reports. In exchange for a bribe, she might turn a blind eye to the agent's noncompliance. For a review of the relevant literature, see Khalil and Lawarree (1995).

3.3. Welfare implications

Being concerned about the overall damage posed by corruption, one may refer to the total size of bribes collected by public servants. This clearly is not a good measure of welfare losses because bribes are foremost a reallocation of resources – someone gains and another person gives. Harm is resulting because corrupt agents are disloyal to their principals and consequently distort their decisions. This type of distortion is not easy to pin down.

A first apparent effect is that corruption will lower the agent's effort. If she colludes with supervisors who falsely certify a high effort level, the agent slacks off and devotes more of her time to leisure. The payment of speed money ironically even aggravates this problem. Hoping for the payment of speed money public servants are induced to create further artificial bottlenecks and to increase the queue in front of their office. The longer the queue, the dearer the price for cutting it. Speed money increases the velocity of services only for the briber. But the incentives given to public servants operate in the opposite direction, suggesting that the slowest service obtains the highest rewards.[3]

There is also an important impact on the quality of goods. An agent may have to choose between various clients. In case of corruption, her decision would be biased in favor of those clients who pay the largest bribe, instead of those who provide high quality. This can be best illustrated in the case of an auction, where corruption may be a means for inefficient firms to win a public tender. In perfectly competitive markets, those who produce most efficiently can also afford the largest bribes, suggesting that the best firm is chosen even if this selection is influenced by bribes (Beck and Maher 1986; Lien 1986).[4]

But markets are typically imperfect and competitors will differ in their inclination to offer bribes. For the case of exporting countries this is dealt with more explicitly in Chapter 7. Apart from moral concerns, such differences result from the large transaction costs associated with the making of corrupt deals. Owing to the associated risks and the private institutional arrangements required to enforce corrupt deals, the circle of those in a position to make corrupt deals is limited to some insiders. We deal with this in detail in Chapter 6. Clearly, those who are most inclined to bribe and best connected for arranging a corrupt transaction are not necessarily the most efficient. Welfare losses would be unavoidable.

In public procurement corrupt officials tend to prefer those who are better connected and more skilled in arranging hidden payments as opposed to those who provide quality at reasonable prices. The

[3] Lui (1985) argues in favor of allowing speed money because he considers it capable of inducing agents to exert higher levels of effort and to process cases according to urgency. Opposing arguments have already been circulated earlier (Myrdal 1968: 952–923; Rose-Ackerman 1978: 90). Lui assumes a total failure of bureaucratic "carrots and sticks" as an inducement to efficiency. This extreme assumption appears overemphasized. Also an intrinsic motivation among bureaucrats can contribute to efficiency. Thus, there appears little necessity to allow speed money to bureaucrats. But there can be reasons for abstaining from imposing harsh penalties on agents who take speed money. Threatening penalties for a minor offence can badly backfire if a first misbehavior occurred out of ignorance. Suddenly, bureaucrats have something to conceal something. They might view themselves as belonging to the criminal side of the watershed. This may mark the starting point of a corrupt career. See Box 28 for details to this argument.

[4] As shown in these studies, this conclusion is even valid when information about competitor's actions is incomplete.

Figure 3.2. Al Capone as a child; *source*: www.cartoonstock.com

cartoon in Figure 3.2 provides a good grasp of this logic. Certainly, sandcastles are rarely procured in reality, but the true effects of corruption in public procurement are similar to those shown in the cartoon. A similar effect will be obtained in job provision, where applicants are preferred when they are inclined to bribe and are trustworthy in promising corrupt reciprocity.

Furthermore, the very act of creating market distortions can be the explicit goal of collusion between agents and clients. When clients pay agents for restricting competition by harassing their competitors, distortions are a straightforward consequence of the corrupt dealings (Bardhan 1997: 1322). The police might be bribed to arrest a competing businessperson; regulators might be induced to fake evidence and close down a rival firm; lawmakers can be paid in exchange for restricting market entry. Perfect competition in this case does not ameliorate problems. It does not help if all competitors do the same. Even if the most efficient firm wins the dirty battle, welfare suffers owing to a lower level of competition.

Another apparent example of adverse welfare consequences arises when clients pay agents (or supervisors) for turning a blind eye to the use of substandard material (Frisch 1999: 92–94; Klitgaard 1988: 36–48; Svensson 2005: 20). This is illustrated by a Christmas disco fire in central China that killed 309 people. Corruption is the key to understanding the sequence of mistakes. One of the public servants on trial was a fire department inspection officer who visited the building on many occasions and wrote false reports. Other defendants on trial include two police officers, three city industry and commerce department officials, and a cultural department official, who turned a blind eye to the fact that the disco operated illegally. Two construction officials faced charges for allowing the building manager to rent out the fire escape route outside the building to a man who built a shop, blocking the rear exit and also all the first-floor windows.[5] The creation of a distortionary decision, here the writing of false reports, becomes the actual intention of the corrupt inducement.

Not only will the wrong competitors be chosen but the wrong projects will also be favored by bribe-taking bureaucrats. Customized goods present better opportunities to arrange for hidden payments than off-the-shelf products. Shleifer and Vishny (1993) report on a bottle-making factory in Mozambique that needed a new machine for fixing paper labels onto the bottles. A simple machine could have been bought for US$10,000, but the manager wanted a more sophisticated version for ten times that price. Since there was only one supplier of this machine, this provided sufficient room for overinvoicing and paying a kickback to the manager. Winston (1979: 840–841) argues that the risk associated with corruption increases with the number of transactions, the number of people involved, the duration of the transaction, and the simplicity and standardization of the procedure. Because the risk does not clearly increase with the value of a transaction, large, one-shot purchases create a more efficient base for a kickback. This causes the decisions made by corrupt public servants to be biased in favor of capital-intensive, technologically sophisticated, and custom-built products and technologies. The most

[5] See Agence France-Presse, August 15, 2001: "Inferno Trials Expose Web of Corruption."

visible sign of the adverse impact of corruption are "white-elephant projects," that is, projects that totally disregard public demand or that are wrecked shortly after completion (Mauro 1997a).

3.4. Corruption as the principal's choice

Given the harm generated by corrupt agents, their principal will adjust. He may seek ways to counter self-serving behavior by the agent. He may try to induce the agent to truthfully reveal her actions. In case this inducement is unsatisfactory, the principal may surrender and consider corruption among his agents to be unavoidable. In this case he would anticipate the agent's income from corruption and profit by lowering the official salary.

As a result of such consideration, the level of corruption is partly the principal's choice. The principal sets incentives with the aim of increasing honesty; he determines sanctions for those who are detected, and he hires supervisors and auditors. Such actions aimed at reducing corruption are costly to implement. Costs may arise from detection and punishment (Klitgaard 1988: 26), from inducing agents to behave honestly (Kofman and Lawarree 1996; Laffont and Tirole 1993; Olsen and Torsvik 1998; Strausz 1995), or from attracting more honest agents for government positions (Besley and McLaren 1993), or it may arise because reducing corruption may require downsizing government and permitting the persistence of market failure (Acemoglu and Verdier 2000). The optimum choice of the principal then includes a level of corruption that balances the advantages from increased honesty among agents against these costs in the best manner possible.

Lower levels of corruption may not be entirely beneficial if they can be achieved only through excessive expenses for detection, enforcement, and incentives, or if they go hand in hand with a cut down public sector that insufficiently corrects for market failures. Insofar as the principal can effectively influence the level of corruption, he will be assumed to choose an optimum level. Living in an optimum should naturally lower our concern for the adverse effects of corruption. So, should we be worried about bureaucratic corruption? Should we adhere to the perspective that a benevolent and rational principal contains our worries about corruption? I believe not for two reasons.

First, there can be limits to the principal's influence. Whether agents take bribes or not may be little influenced by the principal's rules. It may relate instead to ethnic or religious fractionalization that is supportive of nepotism or simply to powerful multinationals bribing their way through the administration of poor countries. The resulting exogenous increase in corruption would not be due to the principal's choice. Welfare losses would be apparent.

Second, even where the principal chooses the "optimum" level of corruption, losses still arise for all concerned parties. This loss is due to the fact that potentially beneficial contracts to both sides are no longer tenable. Those contracts that require honesty and the absence of corruption will not be sealed when the principal faces an agent who will take advantage of the arising opportunities. Hence, the benefits such a contract would provide to both parties cannot be achieved. An illustrative example on this is provided by Bates (1981). He argues that in sub-Saharan Africa peasant farmers avoided corruption by taking refuge in subsistence production. The welfare-enhancing profits from a division of labor could not be achieved because farmers had no guarantee that they would not be cheated (Svensson 2005: 37).

Some of the approaches presented in Section 3.2 suggest that welfare-enhancing economic actions are restricted by legislation and regulation, that these restrictions should be assumed to be exogenous to the analysis, and that corruption can enlarge the set of possible actions to be taken by the parties involved. Yet, as seen from an agency perspective, the possibility to behave in a corrupt manner does not enlarge the contractual possibilities. On the contrary, contractual possibilities are constrained further when agents do not adhere to the prohibition of accepting side-payments. When agents cannot credibly promise to reject side-payments from clients, they are not trustworthy when writing contracts that require the absence of such payments. Principals will be reluctant to offer such contracts in the first place.

The public may be willing to pay taxes in exchange for good-quality roads. But they would urge their principals to cancel such projects if bad quality is expected to result from unavoidable collusive behavior. A similar decision would result if tax collectors cannot be kept from taking bribes in exchange for turning a blind eye to underreporting. A related situation arises for the principal's relation to a supervisor. If the supervisor cannot guarantee that she will not fake reports in exchange for a bribe, her contribution loses its value for the principal. She may not be hired in the first place – even though an honest exchange would have been favorable to all.

The public will be unwilling to pay taxes if government projects provide them with little benefit as a result of bribery. Additional resources would be willingly handed out to public servants with a binding commitment to honesty. But such public servants are in short supply. This results in an unwillingness to pay taxes – and politicians would not gain support when attempting to increase taxes because they have little to promise in return. This provides reason for taxes to deteriorate with corruption, as evidenced in Box 21, and the little correlation with the size of the public spending, as evidenced in Box 1.

That corruption reduces contractual possibilities had already been mentioned by Marshall (1897: 130), one of the most famous economists of the last century:

> Everyone is aware of the tendency to an increase in the size of individual businesses, with the consequent transference of authority and responsibility from the owners of each business to its salaried managers and officials. This would have been impossible had there not been a great improvement in the morality and uprightness of the average man: for even as late as the seventeenth and eighteenth centuries we find the great trading companies breaking down largely in consequence of the corruption and selfishness of their officials.

3.5. Evidence

To ascertain the overall adverse effect of corruption, attempts have been undertaken to link corruption to lower income per head. The relevant studies are summarized in Box 16. There is no doubt about a strong correlation between GDP per head and corruption. But there is equal agreement that no unambiguous causality can be derived from this. Researchers attempt to solve the problem of endogeneity by detecting instruments that affect only corruption but not directly the income per head. Given that income and corruption are so highly intertwined, these instruments have to carry a heavy burden. Not all readers can easily be convinced that a chosen instrument satisfies these requirements. Owing to this, other researchers preferred to relate corruption to variables other than income per head, variables where endogeneity issues appear less pressing.

Box 16 Corruption and income per head

While corruption is likely to lower GDP per head, poorer countries lack the resources to effectively fight corruption (Husted 1999: 341–2; Paldam 2002). A simple regression would not provide a causal link between corruption and GDP but report some correlation of unknown origin. Besides, cultural determinants are likely to drive both income and absence of corruption. The same problem emerges when correlating corruption with human capital. Svensson (2005: 27–30) shows a positive association between corruption and the number of years in school. But he alerts that causality is likely to run both ways.

One attempt to disentangle this simultaneous relationship is provided by Hall and Jones (1999). The authors regress output per worker on an indicator of social infrastructure, which includes a measure of corruption among other variables. There exist a variety of potential simultaneity problems that are addressed by the authors. One of them is related to the fact that the indicator of corruption is based on perceptions. If countries at equal stages of development differ in the extent of corruption, perceptions are undisturbed and may be particularly informative. But in case countries widely differ in their development, perceptions may be overshadowed by these differences and be less reliable. The idea advanced by the authors is that these problems of simultaneity can be solved by instrumental variables technique. The approach by Hall and Jones (1999) is applied by Kaufmann *et al.* (1999b: 15) and Wyatt (2002) to the relationship between corruption and GDP per head. Results indicate a significant adverse impact running from corruption to GDP per head. However, the results must be taken with a grain of skepticism because the instruments carry a heavy burden. It is crucial to their validity that they impact on corruption and not directly on GDP per head. Given that corruption and GDP per head are highly intertwined, such a requirement is difficult to obtain.

Neeman *et al.* (2003) observe that the correlation between corruption and GNP per head is strong in economies that are financially open. In contrast, in closed economies there is no relationship at all. The authors argue that in economies with lower barriers to capital movement, it is easier to transfer income from corruption abroad. In financially closed economies, illegally obtained income is more likely to stay within the country and contribute to economic development. A related argument is provided by Graeff and Mehlkop (2003), who argue that levels of corruption, and not the impact of corruption on income, increase with financial openness; see Box 4.

Efforts have been made to ascertain the influence of corruption on the *growth* of GDP. Overall, the findings are ambiguous with various researchers reporting insignificant findings. See Box 17 for a review.

Already theoretically the link between corruption and growth of GDP is tricky. When we regard the absence of corruption, similar to other aspects of social and human capital, as a factor for production, corruption would impact on income per head. This suggests that growth of GDP would not be explained by absolute levels of corruption but by a change in these levels. In an unpublished study, I use responses to a 1998 WEF survey question on whether corruption has decreased in the past five years. This variable is shown to better explain growth of GDP as opposed to absolute levels of corruption. But since issues of endogeneity are difficult to assess these are not iron-clad results, but should rather be interpreted as suggestive to the issue at hand.

Box 17 Corruption and growth of GDP

Knack and Keefer (1995) report a variable of institutional quality by PRS, which incorporates corruption among other factors, to exert a significant negative impact on growth of GDP. Tanzi and Davoodi (2001) provide evidence for corruption (measured by the CPI) lowering growth for a cross section of ninety-seven countries. Brunetti *et al.* (1998: 369), Li *et al.* (2000), and Svensson (2005) produce insignificant results. Abed and Davoodi (2002: 507) obtain insignificant results for a cross section of twenty-five transition countries

Box 17 (*Cont.*)

once including an index of the success with respect to structural reforms. Mauro (1995) found a slightly significant impact in a bivariate regression. But as soon as the ratio of investment to GDP is included as an explanatory variable, this impact disappeared.[6] Ali and Isse (2003) find corruption to lower growth but base their regressions on the data by PRS/ICRG. They carry out tests for Granger-causality to ascertain the direction of causation. But their findings suffer from the fact that most data on corruption are not valid for time series analysis.

Anoruo and Braha (2005) employ panel data analysis to investigate the impact of corruption on growth for eighteen African countries. They observe corruption to significantly reduce growth, even when controlling for the ratio of investment to GDP. However, given that the data on corruption is valid for cross sections but less for time series analysis, the finding must be taken with a grain of skepticism. Another approach is provided by Wedeman (1997). Based on simple cross-tabulation of growth and corruption he observes many corrupt countries exhibiting high growth rates. He concludes that certain kinds of corruption might have more significance for growth rates than the overall level of corruption as such. Rock and Bonnett (2004) provide supportive evidence. They show that corruption has an overall adverse impact on growth. However, it is found to increase growth in the large East Asian newly industrializing economies. The authors speculate that the rather stable exchange of government promotional privileges for bribes may explain this East Asian paradox. In sum, earlier investigations provide mixed evidence on the relationship between corruption and growth of GDP.

Some more recent investigations are more favorable to corruption lowering growth. Making use of data on corruption provided by PRS, Mauro (1997a) produces significant results at a 95 percent confidence level. Leite and Weidemann (1999: 24) and Poirson (1998: 16) also report a significant positive impact. An adverse impact of corruption on growth in African countries is reported by Gymiah-Brempong (2002).

[6] Mauro thus argues that the impact of corruption on growth is largely via its impact on the ratio of investment to GDP.

Mo (2001) finds a significant adverse impact of corruption on growth between 1970 and 1985 for a cross section of forty-five countries. As in the above studies, standard control variables are included such as initial GDP per head, population growth, and political rights. He modifies the regression by successively including further explanatory variables in the regression. In particular, these are the ratio of investment to GDP, the level of political stability (measured by the number of assassinations per million population per year and the number of revolutions), and human capital formation (measured by average schooling years). By adding these variables the impact of corruption on growth becomes insignificant. Mo traces this to the multicollinearity of corruption with these variables and argues that the results help in identifying the channels by which corruption impacts on growth. He finds that more than half of corruption's impact runs via its effect on political stability, more than 20 percent via its impact on the ratio of investment to GDP, another 15 percent via its adverse impact on human capital formation, and the rest is of a direct nature.

In a similar spirit, Pellegrini and Gerlagh (2004) trace the impact of corruption on the growth of GDP to the ratio of investment to GDP and to a country's openness. Méon and Sekkat (2005), equally detect an adverse impact of corruption on growth. This impact survives the inclusion of a variable on the ratio of investment to GDP. The impact becomes even stronger in countries with a low quality of governance. For the latter issue, indicators of "rule of law," "government effectiveness," and "lack of violence" are used. The results by Méon and Sekkat contradict the "grease the wheels" view of corruption, which postulates that corruption may help compensate for bad governance.

Overall, the evidence on the link between corruption and GDP or the growth of GDP has its empirical and theoretical weaknesses. Given this, researchers have sought alternative variables that might be responsive to levels of corruption but are less likely to be by themselves a cause of corruption. For a review of such investigations, see Box 18. These investigations embrace regressions on the quality of roads, the economic rate of return of aid projects, the value of stocks, the quality of health care, and the effectiveness of environmental protection.

Of interest is also the distortion corruption imposes on human capital. Corruption is a form of rent-seeking behavior where human capital is allocated to redistributive tricks rather than productive activities. Seeking loopholes in public laws or searching for windfall profits due to preferential treatment by public decision-makers would distract students from studying engineering – alternative disciplines such as law might equip them better for future challenges.

Box 18 Corruption, productivity, and quality

Tanzi and Davoodi (1997) examine the impact of corruption on the quality of investments. Referring to panel data on corruption for 1980–1995, the authors suggest that corruption lowers the quality of the infrastructure as measured by the condition of paved roads and power outages. They support their hypothesis by reporting a high significance in their statistical results.[7] Isham and Kaufmann (1999) and the World Bank (1997: 39) present an alternative approach. They correlate the economic rate of return on World Bank-financed projects with indicators of institutional quality and present a positive association of these variables. Successful economies tend to adjust more rapidly from primary-sector-intensive to manufactures-intensive exports. In this respect, the size of manufactured exports relative to GDP signals a prosperous economic development. Méon and Sekkat (2004) obtain a significant negative impact of corruption on this variable. Their use of the TI-data as panel data, however, is debatable.

Lee and Ng (2004) show that firms from countries scoring badly in the CPI are valued lower by international investors. This valuation is measured either by the ratio of firm's price to book value or by the price to earnings ratio. The authors control their regressions for a variety of variables, business sectors being one

[7] Based on own regressions for a cross section of countries and using the TI CPI 2001 it was not possible to reproduce significant results. This sheds some doubt on the robustness of the findings to different methodologies. Also, the corruption index used by Tanzi and Davoodi (1997) is the one from PRS/ICRG. See page 238–9 for a criticism of this indicator.

of them. They relate their findings to the risks associated with corruption and the higher rate of return requested by investors from firms operating in more corrupt countries. A decrease of corruption by one point of the CPI increases the valuation of stocks of the respective firms by roughly 10 percent.

Gupta *et al.* (2001) show that countries with high levels of corruption are associated with inefficient government services and a low quality of public health care provision, as subjectively assessed by respondents. Such subjective associations may certainly relate to respondent's impressions rather than reality. The authors therefore expand their investigation with more objective proxies for the quality of government services: child and infant mortality as well as the percent of low-birthweight babies in total births as a proxy for the quality of public health care provision and student dropout rates as a proxy for the quality of public education. All these variables react significantly to levels of corruption. Child mortality rates in countries with high levels of corruption are about one-third higher than in countries with low corruption; infant mortality rates and the share of low-birthweight babies are almost twice as high, and dropout rates are five times as high.

The poor quality of environmental regulation as a result of corruption is investigated by Welsch (2004) for a cross section of more than one hundred countries. The author argues that corruption increases pollution. This is attributed to both a direct impact of corruption, reducing the effectiveness of environmental regulation, and an indirect impact, through which corruption lowers income. An adverse impact on emissions cannot be found. The author suggests that this may relate to corruption adversely impacting on the truthful reporting of this data. But, significant results can be found for ambient pollution of air (the urban sulfur dioxide and suspended particulate concentration) and water (dissolved oxygen demand and suspended solids). These results hold controlling for income (which is assumed to have a nonlinear, U-shaped impact on pollution). Only the direct effect is depicted in this case. Pellegrini and Vujic (2003) employ survey data on environmental policy stringency for the agriculture sector. In regressions for up to forty-one countries the authors observe that

Box 18 (*Cont.*)

corruption reduces stringency directly, as well as via its impact on income per head. Damania *et al.* (2004) show that in countries with high levels of corruption respondents to a survey by the WEF agree to the following claim: "compliance with international environmental agreements is a high priority." For a sample of sixty-one countries these findings survive the inclusion of a variety of variables.

In line with these findings, Esty and Porter (2002) also provide evidence that highly corrupt countries tend to have lower levels of environmental quality. Smith *et al.* (2003) investigate the impact of corruption on biodiversity, arguing that corruption limits the success of conservation projects. They show that countries with high levels of corruption tend to experience decreases in the population of elephants and black rhinoceroses, a lower variety of species, and a reduced total coverage of forest.

Tanzi and Davoodi (2001) determine the ratio of college enrollment in law relative to college enrollment in engineering in 1980 and report a significant impact of the level of corruption. Corrupt societies, they argue, distract students from jobs aimed at increasing production toward those jobs where legal opportunities and loopholes are sought. Faccio and Parsley (2006) investigate the value of political connections by observing whether the stock valuation of firms decreases if politicians from related geographic regions die. They find that this decrease is more pronouned in corrupt countries. Political connections are thus more valuable in corrupt countries – making it likely that resources are spent for rent-seeking rather than for production.

The evidence on corruption reducing the quality of public services and the productivity of firms and projects is convincing. In Lambsdorff (2003a) I provide a macroeconomic approach to determining the adverse effects of corruption. This study uses the ratio of GDP to capital stock as a macroeconomic proxy for a country's average capital productivity. The capital stock is determined by a perpetual inventory method, that is, the sum of all past investments net of depreciation. A significant negative impact of corruption on this ratio is found in a cross section of sixty-nine

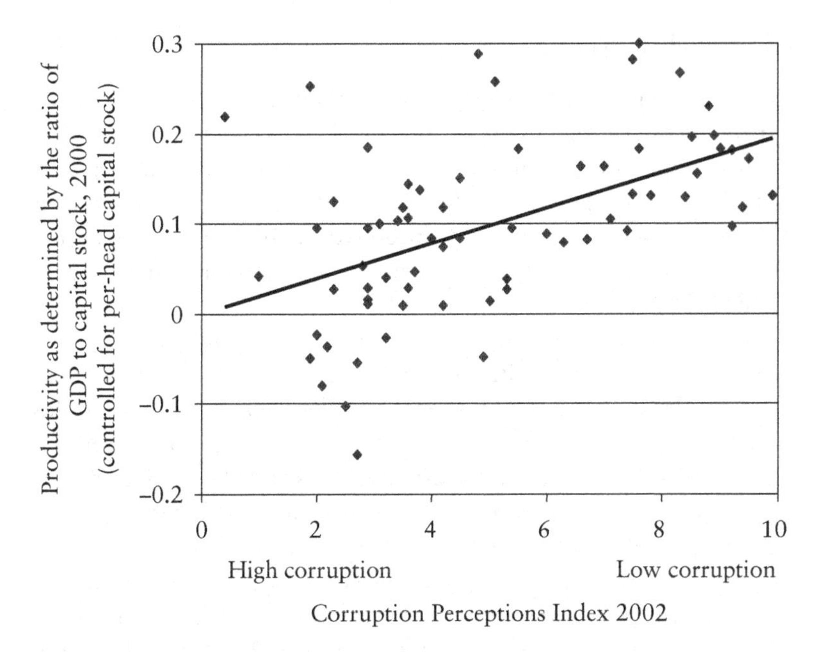

Figure 3.3. Corruption and productivity

countries, controlling for the total capital stock and testing for various other variables. These results are robust to the use of different indicators of corruption, the inclusion of further governance indicators, sample selection, and endogeneity issues.

It is concluded that a six-point improvement in integrity on the TI index – for example an increase in Tanzania's level of integrity to that of the United Kingdom – would increase GDP by 20 percent.[8] The income of an average person would increase by this amount and the income of the honest, noncorrupt citizens is likely to increase even more than that of the dishonest. This impact is shown in Figure 3.3. The finding is well related to our theoretical considerations. For example, bureaucratic corruption is likely to advance projects that provide a good base for kickbacks as opposed to those that increase production.

[8] Interestingly, this coefficient falls when controlling for an index depicting countries' bureaucratic quality. This suggests that productivity is reduced because corruption goes along with bureaucratic inefficiency.

3.6. Conclusions

Corrupt bureaucrats are likely to base their decisions on expected corrupt income rather than on the potential benefit to the public. Wrong competitors are chosen, wrong projects promoted, and quality control is up for sale. But a truly benevolent government may react. It may design monitoring systems, incentives, and threats of penalties. But such attempts will be imperfect because of informational asymmetries.

The government therefore faces an uncomfortable choice – to continue public service with existing levels of corruption or to close down whole branches of administration. The second reaction unfolds the unavoidable welfare loss of bureaucratic corruption: given the informational advantage, the bureaucracy is unable to ascertain its honest delivery of public services. But this in turn threatens it own endurance. Bureaucracy itself might be better off if being unable to take bribes – because it would be delegated further authority by the public and the government. The scope of obtaining extra-legal income reduces the value of bureaucrats, just as a car seller's potential to sell us lemons reduces the value of second-hand cars.

Corrupt opportunities, rather than broadening the choice for bureaucrats and their clients, constrain the contractual space available to public servants and the government. Those contracts, which require the absence of corruption, cannot be sealed. The welfare effects by and large relate to governments omitting economic transactions, because agents cannot credibly commit themselves to honesty. The public may become unwilling to pay taxes where the outcome of public projects is so. They will evade taxes or vote for politicians who lower official tax duties. This explains why in empirical research taxes deteriorate with corruption; see Box 21. With reduced taxes public expenditure will also shrink. These arguments may explain why in empirical research government size tends to decrease with levels of corruption; see Box 1.

4 The dilemma of the kleptocrat
What is bad about political corruption?

WHAT is bad about grand, political corruption? Similar to the problem of a corrupt bureaucrat, a government's head fails to credibly commit to honesty if being guided by corrupt goals. He thus disqualifies for attracting investors. The advantage from bribery turns against its actor because investors are stripped of guarantees that their property will be honored. Even those politicians who are primarily career-oriented may try to avoid this downside effect and prefer to commit to anticorruption instead.

Corruption has been defined as the misuse of public power for private benefit. But the term "misuse" is open to different interpretations. In Chapter 2, it involved the rules set up by a benevolent principal, which were trespassed by a self-serving agent. While this approach was appropriate for bureaucratic corruption, it appears misguided for political corruption. A self-serving principal, a government that disregards its duty of serving the public, might create an environment where laws do not prohibit its own self-enrichment or that of a ruling class. Corruption can even accompany and underlie the writing and enforcing of rules designed with the intention of furthering the principal's narrow interests.

In case the principal is not benevolent, a definition of corruption as a violation of rules would be misleading. This can be illustrated with a case study from Thailand. It is reported that strict rules prohibit ordinary citizens from taking away anything from the tropical forest in Thailand, even leaves and pebbles. But the Forestry Department was largely in power to make regulations so as to benefit its own interests. What should have been protected was officially converted into tourist attractions, or destroyed for gas pipelines, for the benefit of the department.[1]

[1] See *Bangkok Post*, September 17, 1998, "Killing what is its to protect".

The term corruption may be misplaced when applied to a disobedient agent who is disloyal to rules that are themselves the result of self-serving. Instead, it may be more accurate then to locate corruption at the level of the principal's own self-serving behavior. In this case "misuse" is not clearly related to the trespassing of rules (in the legal sense). Instead, it relates to acts that the general public regards as illegitimate or that contradict the *public interest.*[2] Political corruption may be regarded as the behavior of public decision-makers where preferential treatment is provided to individuals and where narrow interests are advanced at the expense of the interests of broader segments of society.

When dealing with bureaucratic corruption we are primarily concerned with the distortion that results from the principal's limited capacity to control the agent. This can be adequately addressed in an agency approach, as it was presented in Chapter 2. With respect to political corruption, it is not limited control that concerns us. Distortions and welfare losses are likely to arise as a result of limited benevolence on the part of the principal. The resulting welfare losses therefore differ. If control is not carried out to benefit the public, it becomes ambiguous whether the limitations faced by the principal are a bad thing. A prerequisite to the agency approach would be that honesty among agents allows for a deal with the principal that also benefits the public. But if the loyal agent serves the corrupt goals of the principal, unusual circumstances must be imagined in which this loyalty also increases public welfare. Other approaches are needed to model corruption and to relate corruption to losses of public welfare. A more promising way to assess the effects on welfare is by a straightforward reference to the goals pursued by the principal and less to the principal's limitations.[3]

[2] See Heidenheimer *et al.* (1989: 3–14) for a review of various approaches to defining corruption. Pages 15–20 of this book deal more explicitly with issues of defining corruption.

[3] One may defend the applicability of agency theory by arguing that government should be regarded as an agent and the general public as the principal. But there is no consistent treatment of this scenario in the literature. The principal is commonly assumed to be benevolent and to have the power to design contracts that best serve his purposes. If these two characteristics, benevolence and sovereignty in designing contracts, do not fall hand in hand, one may assign the principal's role either to the benevolent party or to the one with the actual power. I pursue the second approach here.

4.1. Inefficiency by design

One such approach whereby the principal seeks to strike deals, which are unfavorable to the general public, is provided by representatives of the Chicago School (Posner 1974; Stigler 1971). In their view, lobbying groups and politicians design regulations so as to create rents and promote the narrow interests of individuals or private parties. The welfare losses, it is argued, are different from those arising in an agency model. Posner (1974: 337–9) suggests that governments operate with reasonable efficiency. In contrast to the slackness among agents within agency theory, public servants are considered here to be well motivated, in a way similar to private businesspersons. They are subject to similar supervision as well as competition from colleagues and other agencies. But inefficiency results from the kind of goal pursued by governments. This comes about as politicians supply protection against troublesome competition by means of subsidies, import quotas, tariffs, tax exemptions, and preferential treatment to interest groups paying for this service (Stigler 1971). Governments operate with reasonable efficiency to purposefully attain deliberately inefficient goals (Posner 1974: 337–9).

While the term "corruption" is not mentioned in this context, the approach by the Chicago School emphasizes that the inefficiency of government operation does not result from its limitations or lack of motivation. As seen by representatives of the Chicago School, it is not even the principal's self-serving behavior that is responsible for the inefficiency of laws and regulations but rather the strong leverage that interest groups have over government operations. The government is not intentionally self-serving but falls victim to the interests of private actors. This argument suggests the existence of two types of self-serving regimes. A first type is called a "predatory government," a "grabbing hand" regime (Djankov *et al.* 2002), characterized by rules and regulations that are designed so as to profit the government. A second type is described by the Chicago School as a regime where lobbying groups are in a strong position and regulations are created to generate rents for their benefit. In both cases, the problem rests with a government's goals and not its limitations. Contrary to the agency approach, limitations faced by the principal may actually be beneficial to the public instead of being a source of inefficiency, since representatives of the Chicago School consider government to strive for inefficient goals.

The contributions by Tullock (1980a: 27) and Shleifer and Vishny (1993) can be regarded as a contribution to the analysis of the "grabbing hand" regime. They argue that self-seeking governments that are monopolized are superior to disorganized, predatory governments. In the latter case a businessperson must bribe several departments simultaneously for the operation of his business, for example, the local legislature, the central ministry, the fire authorities, the police, and the water authorities. Each of these institutions acts independently and extorts the businessperson. The arising problem is that a businessperson needs permission from all of these units. As a result of their independent revenue maximization, the departments "overgraze" the market and suffer from the "tragedy of the commons." Each public servant ignores the fact that the bribe she charges reduces business operations and, consequently, the bribes all the other departments can pocket. The departments therefore suffer from lack of cooperation. This case is pretty much similar to that of groups of road bandits along a single road. Taking into account that extortion lowers road traffic, each group will determine the optimal "fee" it charges for using the road. But it does not take into consideration that the fee it charges also reduces the revenues of other road bandits. As a consequence of poor cooperation, the bandits will rob travelers excessively, who may stop using the road altogether.

Minimizing government size may be a straightforward means of reducing its distorting impact. We argued in Chapter 2 that a downsized public sector would be the consequence of bureaucratic corruption because the public finds little benefit in public programs where bureaucrats cannot commit themselves to honesty. The argument with respect to political corruption is parallel; see, for example, Becker (1994) and, for a critical review, Orchard and Stretton (1997). The public may prefer a small government if predation is all that the government aims at. However, at the same time, this regime is exactly the one where our public requests will remain unheard. The argument to downsize government may be well heard in public debate but only rarely accepted by a self-serving ruler. This self-serving ruler prefers to downsize government where government serves the public but resists such temptations where it benefits himself.

One clear difference emerges between containing bureaucratic corruption and avoiding political corruption: the level of control exercised by the principal would be helpful in avoiding bureaucratic corruption by providing government with the necessary instruments. A top–down approach to anticorruption emanates from an agency perspective where the principal is guided by benevolence. On the contrary, with respect to political corruption, it is precisely the control exercised by government that is the root of our concern. The approach to reform would entail the strengthening of grassroots movements. Anticorruption would be the task of civil society in broadening the freedom of its decisions, of the private sector in strengthening market forces as opposed to government force, and of the media in limiting the government's scope of self-seeking.

4.2. The constrained principal

In reality, the control exercised by government is already limited in various dimensions. The government faces restrictions by other independent actors, such as a strong bureaucracy that is better informed about technical details of administrative procedures. Constitutional constraints often regulate the scope of government actions. An independent judiciary may obtain act as a veto player, keeping a tight rein on rulers. The media often provide another limitation to government actions. Finally, strong private interests may be able to lobby the government into decisions and be successful in defending their turf. Various such constraints have been investigated and their impact on welfare discussed. Let me mention some examples.

Agents can constrain their principal. They can obtain a powerful position vis-à-vis the principal. Niskanen (1975), for example, has been prominent in arguing that the bureaucracy has a strong position vis-à-vis the Congress. Politicians face restrictions from countervailing powers and they may have to seek the support of their agents to secure their own survival. Also, because of a division of power there might be multiple principals in place who all want to control the agent. The agents, in turn, may be in a position to favor one principal over another and obtain a stronger bargaining position. One further reason for the agent's power arises with principals who are contested and must fear being ousted from their position, be it through election, coup, revolution, or by powerful rival factions within the government. Agents become more powerful when their principals are contested.

For example, they can inform (or misinform) the public about a corrupt act of the principal or they can provide political support to the principal's opponent. Support by the agent may therefore be helpful to the principal in securing his power and the agent can effectively demand some leeway in return.[4]

Principals can also be constrained by powerful lobbies. Such lobby groups may provide campaign funding or be instrumental in pursuing the principal's political goals. In return, the government may offer distortionary laws and regulations that are of interest to lobbies. They create bottlenecks and market distortions and offer the resulting artificial rents to their beneficiaries. The government then becomes dependent on its supporting private interests. Tullock (1993: 26) posits that politicians are not in a powerful position to pursue their own interests. Rather, they are merely acting on behalf of other's interests. The principal is merely a "passive broker among competing private rent seekers" (McChesney 1987: 102).

As derived in Chapter 5 of this book, apart from economic distortions there are also expenses for rent-seeking that are detrimental to public welfare. These expenses embrace the lobbies' costs such as those for organizing public campaigns or hiring lawyers so as to increase one's chances of obtaining the artificial rent. Expenses for lobbying, while wasteful to the public, may prove helpful to principals, for example when they include donations to finance election campaigns or to harass rivals. These resources are not used to serve consumers and the public by increasing the size of the cake, but rather to battle for a larger slice of the given cake for oneself. These expenses represent a form of waste because they go along with effort but not with increasing overall public welfare.[5]

As a result of the restrictions faced by the principal, his self-serving behavior is likely to cause allocative distortions. He may be able to favor a private interest in one sector only. Organization of a corrupt

[4] A suitable approach to model the resulting welfare effects has been offered by the theory of x-inefficiency. While this approach was modeled for different purposes, it has also been utilized for describing the adverse impact of corruption and government operations on public welfare (Button and Weyman-Jones 1994: 91–2; Isham and Kaufmann 1999).

[5] While the existence of this form of waste appears plausible, it is not clear how it can be avoided. North (1984: 39) argued that the form of waste identified by traditional rent-seeking theory may simply be a form of unavoidable transaction cost in political decision-making.

system may be feasible only in one branch of government operations. This would imply that other sectors and branches would have to suffer by paying the higher prices demanded by the favored sector (Klitgaard 1988: 39; Rose-Ackerman 1999: 28–9).[6] Valuable resources would be misallocated. Public servants would prefer to start their career in the protected government departments rather than where their human resources are most needed. As a result, in some countries instead of working in the private sector the customs department is the place to make a career. As expressed by a CEO in Thailand, "I hope to be reborn as a custom official" (Svensson 2005: 19). Likewise, students become lawyers as opposed to engineers in order to seek legal loopholes rather than increase production; see Box 18 for empirical evidence. Creating these misallocations would already result in a case of bureaucratic corruption. But governments can impose restrictions in a more forceful way by making them part of law.

A further limitation faced by governments relates to the media. If rulers fear public dismay or the strengthening of rival factions resulting from allegations of corruption, their self-enrichment must be kept confidential. Even at the end of a political career the need for secrecy may endure if keeping one's ill-gotten gains requires a political ally as a successor. As a result of the necessity for concealing payments, some sectors are preferred to others. As argued on p. 68 with respect to bureaucratic corruption, customized goods present better opportunities for arranging for hidden payments than off-the-shelf products. One reason for this impact relates to the secrecy that surrounds negotiations related to custom-built products. This secrecy would make custom-built products also attractive to corrupt politicians.

A corrupt politician would have to misallocate resources to favor sectors where lobbies are in a position to return the ill-gotten favors, where agents do not impede but be helpful in organizing the corrupt transactions and where the public is unlikely to be informed and rebel. As a result, politicians are likely to distort budget allocation. Box 19 provides supportive evidence.

[6] There are also examples of corruption lowering prices, particularly when it accompanies fraud. Customs officials may collect only the bribe rather than a more costly official duty. Tax collectors may lower the amount owed in exchange for a cut (Shleifer and Vishny 1993). At the legislative level tariffs can be lowered for favored sectors or tax privileges may be given to industries in exchange for bribes. In this case, the tax burden of other sectors would increase.

Box 19 Corruption and distorted budget allocation

Those who allocate resources may have better opportunities to extract illegal income from large investment projects than from small labor contracts. Public investments are particularly susceptible to this kind of misallocation. In extreme cases, public investments fail to meet public demand, resulting in "white-elephant projects." Mauro (1997a) thus suggests that corruption may increase public investment. But the subsequent regressions provide no significant evidence. This is in contrast to Esty and Porter (2002) and Tanzi and Davoodi (1997), who claim significant evidence for overinvestment in public infrastructure. The latter investigation refers to panel data on corruption provided by PRS for 1980–1995. Given the nature of this data on corruption and the mixed results, the evidence for this link appears to be rather poor.

However, there is convincing evidence that corruption lowers government spending on education. This result is analyzed in detail in Mauro (1998), the argument being that other expenditures offer public servants better opportunities to collect bribes. Mauro's results hold for various specifications, yet suffer a little from the low explanatory power of the regressions. Gupta *et al.* (2002) and Esty and Porter (2002) confirm the finding, providing us with some more comfort. Similar considerations suggest that expenditure on maintenance is too low, particularly when a corrupt government can better extract bribes from new investments (Tanzi and Davoodi 1997).

Corruption may also lead to higher spending on the military. Mauro (1998) provides rather insignificant evidence on this link, contrary to anecdotal evidence. Gupta *et al.* (2001a) investigate this relationship more intensively, basing the regressions on four different sources for corruption and up to 120 countries during 1985–1998. They claim that corruption is significantly associated with higher military spending or higher arms procurement (as a share of either GDP or total government spending). The evidence for cross-section regressions is significant and robust.

4.3. The kleptocrat's dilemma

While a constrained self-serving principal imposes the aforementioned welfare losses on society, ironically, he is unhappy about these losses. A principal, self-serving or benevolent, always dislikes welfare losses because they absorb what he regards his own. A self-serving principal will therefore be opposed to welfare losses. For example, corruption resulting in price increases is particularly distorting when it bears on some goods while the prices of others are unaffected. But such a distortion will not arise if prices for all goods and services increase evenly. When the impact of corruption is equal on all economic sectors, resource allocation will not be distorted to favor one sector over another. Instead of placing this additional burden on society, a self-serving government will prefer a corrupt system that operates as smoothly as a tax. The logic is not one of benevolence but rather that a well-functioning bribe-system allows extracting even more.

Still, bribes will be worse with regard to public welfare than taxes, because they must be concealed (Rose-Ackerman 1978: 8; Shleifer and Vishny 1993). Self-serving governments may have to obfuscate their self-enrichment and employ costly mechanisms for gathering bribes. As a result, Rose-Ackerman (1999: 117) notes "efficient regulatory reforms will be opposed by the kleptocrat if the reforms would convert illegal into legal pricing systems." On the other hand, secrecy is not an issue when the media and the judiciary can be forced to play along with political leaders who demand their cut.[7] If a self-serving government also controls the revenues that result from the legal pricing system, it does not have to distort allocation to favor illegal pricing systems.

The option of price discrimination would also avoid a distortional allocation. Self-serving governments may want to charge their customers according to their willingness to pay, discriminating with their prices between the needy and the less interested. There seems to be empirical support for this hypothesis. Svensson (2003) shows for Ugandan firms that bribes increase with the firm's ability to pay. While this discriminatory power may cause the public to feel uncomfortable and deprived of its consumer's rent, the classic welfare

[7] Githongo (1997) provides evidence that the Kenyan press was largely free to report on corruption but that its impact was so minor that the government was basically indifferent to widespread revelations of high-level corruption.

loss does not come about. Instead, a corrupt government can seize the full rent, and all deals that are mutually profitable are carried out.

A strong government will even seek to contain low-level corruption among the bureaucracy. This behavior is already known with regard to laziness. Superiors, even those who are self-serving, will discourage slack behavior among subordinates, because this absorbs "slack resources," which are otherwise available to them (Moe 1984: 763; Posner 1974: 337–9). Similarly, a self-serving principal will avoid corruption among agents simply because any self-enrichment by the bureaucracy takes away from the resources the principal considers to be his own. Furthermore, a self-serving principal cannot gain from allowing substandard quality in public procurement. He either prefers to embezzle the required funding right away, or hopes for future economic (corrupt) gains resulting from an improved public infrastructure – which then has to be of good quality.

It appears unlikely that favoritism toward unqualified contractors in tendering procedures will be helpful to a corrupt regime. A strong government would disallow the waste identified by rent-seeking theorists. If the principal is sufficiently strong, he would disallow lobbyists wasting their time and resources with public campaigns. Strong leadership would contain welfare losses because lobbies would have little impact on the principal's decisions. In contrast to the argument by the Chicago School, distortionary regulation may also not be an issue for self-serving governments. McChesney (1997: 153–5) argues that such regimes strive for income via extortion, but are able to levy the burden equally on all private parties. Governments threaten inefficient regulation, but these are avoided by payments from private parties. Thanks to this negotiation process, inefficient regulation is commonly avoided. A strong principal will also prevent individual corrupt departments from "overgrazing" the market, because he monopolizes it for corrupt income.

Clearly, avoiding these distortions requires a corrupt government to be particularly strong. This type of a system is commonly termed a "kleptocracy" (Grossman 1995). The ruler is sometimes referred to as a "stationary bandit." Such a government is in a prime position to acquire large bribes, but it is controversial whether this goes along with negative welfare effects. On the contrary, McGuire and Olson (1996) argue that self-serving rulers with complete coercive power want to exercise this power consistently with the interests of society.

An illustrative example of such consistency took place in Indonesia. One of the grandchildren of President Suharto attempted to make a cut from taxes on beer that was collected by his private company. But as a result, tourism in Bali was suffering from a shortage of beer and inflated prices, forcing President Suharto to withdraw the tax.[8] The reputable weekly *Economist* presumed that probably some of his relatives were strong in the hotel business. This argument illustrates vividly the "encompassing interest" of a strong ruler, who comes to consider how inefficient solutions in one sector spill over to other parts of the economy. Provided with sufficient power, a ruler will avoid such undesired consequences. He will keep subordinates from overgrazing the market by taxing excessively and even provide public goods so as to increase future tax income. So, why should we be worried about kleptocrats? One first argument relates to inequality of income.

Whether or not reasonable limits exist on the taxes squeezed out by a predatory regime depends crucially on the elasticity of the tax base. Marcoullier and Young (1995) argue that this elasticity is rather low so that predatory regimes can always rake off a surplus by increasing the rate of taxation. They conclude that this provides reason for predatory regimes to squeeze their citizens without pity. Income will be reallocated in favor of those holding power. Indeed, empirical studies are supportive of a positive correlation between corruption and inequality; see Box 20.

Box 20 Corruption and inequality

Gupta *et al.* (2002) investigate the impact of corruption on income inequality, as measured by the Gini coefficient. They find a significant positive impact of corruption on inequality in a cross section of thirty-seven countries, while taking into account various other exogenous variables. When controlling for GDP per head, this impact remains significant at a 10 percent level. The authors test various instrumental variables to ascertain that the causality runs from corruption to inequality and not vice versa. The authors find further evidence that corruption increases inequality in education and land distribution. Since these variables contribute to income inequality (and are controlled in the first regression) the

[8] *The Economist*, February 10, 1996, "Indonesia. When trouble brewd."

Box 20 (*Cont.*)

overall impact of corruption on income inequality is likely to be even stronger. An impact of corruption on the inequality of income is also found by Gymiah-Brempong (2002) for a sample of African countries. Also, Li *et al.* (2000) find corruption to increase inequality. They show that this effect is even stronger at higher levels of corruption. Unfortunately, they base their finding on the data by PRS – the usual caveats apply.

Gupta *et al.* (2002) also investigate the income growth of the bottom 20 percent of society. Controlling for various influences, they report that increases in corruption exert a significant and negative impact on this variable. However, research on actual trends in levels of corruption has not really started yet and the current perceptions data may not relate well to changes in real levels. In this perspective, the results might be taken with some skepticism.

But whether or not the causality actually moves in a direction from corruption to inequality is questioned by Husted (1999: 342–343), who argues that inequality also contributes to high levels of corruption. This is also suggested by Swamy *et al.* (2001). Moreover, both variables might be driven by cultural determinants. Acceptance of authority and low accessibility of people higher in hierarchy may increase inequality and corruption at the same time (Husted 1999).

You and Khagram (2005) provide evidence for reverse causality. They argue that the poor are not able to monitor and hold the rich and the powerful accountable, enabling the latter to misuse their position. The authors convincingly argue that a large fraction of inhabitants between forty and fifty-nine is a good instrument for inequality. People at that age tend to obtain the largest wages. The higher their share among the population, the more equal is income. The reason is that "fat cohorts" tend to get low rewards, because increased supply on the labor market drives down wages. When these fat cohorts lie at the top of the age-earnings curve, earnings inequality is reduced. The authors show that inequality, as instrumented by this variable, increases corruption. This effect is found to be stronger in democracies: the rich and the powerful can oppress the poor in autocratic regimes, while in the context of democracy they must employ corruption when seeking to maximize their wealth. Their results hold controlling for a battery of control variables. Considering both well-established effects, that is, corruption increasing inequality and inequality escalating corruption, the authors conclude that societies can fall into vicious circles of inequality and corruption. One part of this vicious circle also relates to social norms and intolerance toward corruption. A country's level of inequality increases the likelihood that respondents to the World Values Survey regard cheating on taxes and accepting bribes as justifiable types of behavior.

But, apart from aspects of equality, are there reasons to be concerned about the kleptocrat? Certainly, there are reasons why a predatory regime may fail to allocate resources efficiently. Even the most powerful kleptocrats have to share power with their subordinates and the resulting coordination problems may produce inefficient outcomes. Kleptocrats may have to assign property rights in exchange for peace with potential contestants, that is, for buying off competing factions, and clearly, these property rights need not end up at the hands of those who put it to the most productive uses (North 1981: 28). Even a flourishing economy may threaten a principal's power, because it can provide potential competitors with resources to overthrow the ruler (North 1993: 14). In an attempt to avoid this, a ruler may encourage wasteful competition among lobbies, thriftless contests between political factions, or violence between ethnic groups as a means to divide and conquer, and to bolster his own sway. If the ruler does not have the power to eliminate freelance banditry, or collect taxes from bandits, his extortionate taxation imposed on producers will lower welfare by making banditry more attractive than production (Moselle and Polak 2001). Inefficiency may also result when a ruler has a short-time horizon (McGuire and Olson 1996). The permanent cabinet reshuffles in Zaire, for example, induced ministers to "run with the loot while they can" and to distort decisions in favor of projects with short-term kickback potential (Harden 1993: 52).

The chances for a ruler to avoid welfare losses crucially depend on the assumption of his perfect control. But a principal with full control is a utopian assumption that has been subject to criticism

(Moe 1984: 765–772). One reason for existing constraints is the competition for the principal's position created by potential entrants. The principal must fear being ousted, be it through election, coups, revolution, or by powerful rival factions within the government.[9] Those holding official positions are faced with competition and must exert efforts to remain in power and seek support from outside. This type of competition imposes important constraints on the principal's actions.

These caveats imply that a perfectly strong and corrupt government is utopian. But the resulting conclusions with regard to public welfare remain ambiguous, because losses of public welfare could be traced to the self-serving attitude of rulers as well as to the constraints faced by the principal. Cynics would conclude that public welfare does not suffer from the principal's corrupt intention but rather from his deficient powers. In their view, problems do not reside with governments being corrupt but with the fact that governments are permanently contested. Society would not have problems with bandits per se except for the case where they are insufficiently stationary and where they lack power. Cynics may thus argue that corruption should not be fought; on the contrary, it should be perfected. Along this line, Murphy *et al.* (1993: 413) argue that the problems with corruption are mitigated when corrupt rulers can collect bribes efficiently. But this chapter argues that such cynical conclusions are easily overemphasized.

First, given the ruler's precedent, lower levels in the hierarchy may be motivated to seek extra-legal income for themselves instead of being loyal to higher ranks (Rose-Ackerman 1999: 114–7). Second, citizens will attempt to circumvent the extortionate corruption of the principal. They will invest in techniques to conceal their income and to lower the contribution they must provide to the principal (Choi and Thum 2005). While this type of tax evasion is not peculiar to a kleptocracy, the corruption of the principal can provide legitimacy to these actions and enhance civic antiprincipal cooperation. One result of this behavior can be an increase of the unofficial economy; see Box 21.

[9] While this is a realistic assumption, it is largely alien to the agency approach, which assumes the existence of an uncontested principal who has full control over government operations (Kofman and Lawaree 1996; Laffont and Tirole 1993; Olsen and Torsvik 1998; Strausz 1995).

Box 21 Corruption and the underground economy

Johnson *et al.* (1998: 391) show that corruption increases the underground economy. Friedman *et al.* (2000: 480) run various regressions on corruption and the shadow economy and conclude that "In summary, the relationship between the share of the unofficial economy and ... corruption ... is strong and consistent across eight measures provided by six distinct organizations. All eight of the indices suggest that countries with more corruption have a higher share of the unofficial economy." More recently, Goel and Nelson (2005) report a positive impact of an index of the black market on corruption. This index by the Heritage Foundation embraces activities such as smuggling, piracy of intellectual property, and the presence of black market transactions. While theoretical reasons for this impact are abundant, we may also encounter the reverse causality, for example because corruption in the form of overinvoicing in public procurement is easier in countries where official prices depart from those on the black market.

Another related consequence of corruption is reduced government revenues. Tanzi and Davoodi (1997), Johnson *et al.* (1998), and Friedman *et al.* (2000) provide evidence that countries with high levels of corruption tend to have a lower collection of tax revenues in relation to GDP, controlling the regressions for some standard explanatory variables.

This evidence is further investigated in Tanzi and Davoodi (2001) with a focus on the composition of tax revenues, assuming that different types of taxes respond differently to corruption. They claim that a 1 point increase in corruption is associated with a 1.5 percentage point decline in total revenue relative to GDP and a 2.7 percentage point decline in the ratio of taxes to GDP. Direct taxes suffer more from corruption than indirect taxes, suggesting that countries with high levels of corruption should rely more on indirect taxation – a feature that seems to be in line with current practice. Ghura (2002) supports this finding for thirty-nine countries in sub-Saharan Africa. He controls his regressions for a variety of explanatory variables, differences in the tax base being one of them. Given his usage of the data on corruption by PRS, however, the usual

Box 21 (*Cont.*)

caveats apply. Hwang (2002) supports the evidence for corruption to lower domestic tax revenue as well as total government revenue as a ratio of GDP. In contrast to this, he finds that corruption increases the proportion of government revenues that is obtained from taxes on international trade, such as import and export duties. He suggests that this may relate to corruption increasing with protectionist policies and to an overall increase in tariffs.

Building on the insight that corruption increases the size of the unofficial economy, Al-Marhubi (2000) argues that the optimal level of inflation should increase with corruption, because the larger the size of the unofficial economy, the easier it is to raise government revenue by increasing the money stock (seignorage) rather than by distortionary taxation. He provides evidence for corruption increasing inflation for a cross section of countries for a variety of specifications. Braun and Di Tella (2000), however, argue in favor of reverse causality: they suggest that inflation tends to go along with a higher price variation. This increases the costs for monitoring agents, suggesting that moderate levels of agent's corruption will be condoned. As a result, inflation increases corruption. The authors provide empirical evidence, however, only for the PRS data. Gerring and Thacker (2005) support this finding with more valid data. Also Goel and Nelson (2005) support a positive association between inflation and corruption. They argue that inflation lowers public salaries and increases the need for supplementary income. Overall, the association appears strong, while issues of causality remain difficult to ascertain.

An even more cogent argument in favor of the inefficiency hypothesis arises when considering that the strong, corrupt regime faces a credibility problem, a point that will now be discussed.

4.4. The credibility problem

The most crucial problem with a strong self-serving principal is that he will not be able to commit himself credibly to policies.[10]

[10] Such credibility issues have been dealt with in New Institutional Economics (Klein *et al.* 1978; Wiggins 1991; Williamson 1985). This analysis was applied fruitfully to

Any policy enacted by the principal will suffer from the enforcement problems that were expounded in the first chapters of this book. Given that the corrupt principal is above the law, there is no legal enforcement available for his deals and investors are not provided with necessary guarantees.

Investments usually require sunk costs. Once sunk, such resources cannot be transferred or assigned to different tasks. Railroads cannot be removed, power plants cannot be relocated to different countries, and technical know-how cannot easily be used for other purposes. Thus, investors become locked into a particular usage of resources, and being limited in their power to protect their property against rival attacks, they must fear for the expropriation of their rents. Investments are particularly at risk where there is corruption, because self-serving rulers are neither motivated, nor sufficiently constrained to honor their commitments (Ades and Di Tella 1997: 1026; Henisz 2000; Mauro 1995; Murphy *et al.* 1993: 413).

The credibility problem resulting from corruption can already be observed with regard to lower-level public servants. Corrupt tax collectors can impose capricious tax burdens on investors, corrupt bureaucrats may threaten an arbitrary application of law, and corrupt customs authorities can randomly apply trade regulations. All these actors may be in a position to demand a bribe, while at the same time an investor has lost the outside option of withdrawing the investment decision, having already sunk too many irretrievable assets into the project. Corrupt judges are another issue at hand. Predictable laws are necessary to defend investments against rival attacks and to make contracts between private parties enforceable. But corrupt courts will not necessarily enforce these contracts and may favor the party that offers the largest bribe. This implies that corruption also inhibits the enforcement of contracts between private parties, discouraging investments that are specific to a private party (Acemoglu and Verdier 1998).

In a survey of business people in Karnataka, India, it was found out that the high level of corruption among the local administration affected the software industry less than other industries. This results from the minor role of immovable assets for the software industry, at least as compared with the construction and manufacturing

the operation of political institutions and the political economy of dictatorship (North 1993; Stiglitz 1998b: 8–11; Weingast 1993; Wintrobe 1998b: 24–33 and 38–39).

industries. This lower dependency seems to have reduced extortionate demands for bribes among public officials and rendered aspects of credibility less pressing.[11]

Problems of poor credibility are likely to multiply when not only bureaucrats but also all in government ranks are self-serving. In case of extortion among lower ranks an effective reaction by private parties would be to complain to those higher up in the hierarchy. But if extortion becomes the actual object of government, superiors will not discipline their subordinates but rather choose to optimize a corrupt system so as to benefit themselves. Effective complaint mechanisms would not be in place. There would also be no legal recourse available to investors.

It is precisely this environment where the principal will fail in making credible commitments. As argued by North and Weingast (1989: 803–4),

> The more likely it is that the sovereign will alter property rights for his or her own benefit, the lower the expected returns from investment and the lower in turn the incentive to invest. For economic growth to occur the sovereign or government must not merely establish the relevant set or rights, but must make a credible commitment to them. A ruler can establish such commitment in two ways. One is by setting a precedent of "responsible behavior," appearing to be committed to a set of rules that he or she will consistently enforce. The second is by being constrained to obey a set of rules that do not permit leeway for violating commitments.

In order for commitments to be credible, the respective person must be motivated or forced to honor them (North 1993: 13). But a corrupt ruler is devoted primarily to personal enrichment and lacks the motivation to honor commitments (Rose-Ackerman 1999: 118). Corruption implies that a government is unscrupulous when it comes to taking advantage of arising opportunities. On the other hand, the (utopian) autocrat with full control faces no legal restrictions and can quickly overturn constitutional obstacles if this becomes favorable to his corrupt goals, eliminating any external constraints. While such a principal may be in a position to avoid some of the inefficiencies mentioned earlier, he has lost the option to commit himself to

[11] See *The Hindu*, January 10, 2000, "Investors See Red in Karnataka," *Times of India*, March 28, 2001, "Bribes Are a Big Barrier for Investors."

Figure 4.1. Wizard of ID, Parker and Hart, March 11, 2001 (© By permission of John L. Hart FLP, and Creators Syndicate Inc.)

trustworthy policies. A government's strength helps in avoiding some inefficiency. But, such a strong government can quickly confiscate the wealth of its citizens. Thus, a kleptocrat cannot avoid welfare losses, even when these threaten his income.[12]

A strong kleptocrat is depicted skillfully by the cartoon; see Figure 4.1. As can be easily imagined, such a principal is not trustworthy when inviting investors and promising them fair treatment. The common approach to overcome the credibility problem is to constrain the principal.[13] As soon as such restrictions are

[12] One may conjecture that adverse effects on public welfare can temporarily be eliminated when a kleptocrat finds a credible means of sharing power with bribe-paying investors. This may be what Wedeman (1997) has in mind when he argues that the "rent-sharing" type of corruption that he observes in South Korea has been less detrimental to development than the "looting" type that prevailed in former Zaire. Indeed, if such means of sharing power can be found, this type of corruption may provide fertile ground for large-scale investments. But unless some benevolence exists among the principal, conditions for less powerful investors and innovators may even deteriorate further owing to the strong position of a leading industry that takes over the principal's role (Murphy *et al.* 1993: 413).

Another conjecture could be that the fear of losing one's reputation might effectively induce a kleptocrat to honor sunk investments. But it seems unlikely that investors provide unconstrained kleptocrats with the possibility to establish such a reputation in the first place.

[13] A strong parliament can effectively limit the powers of kings or presidents, as was the case with the 1688 English revolution, limiting the Crown's legislative and judicial powers and disallowing a "confiscatory government" (North and Weingast 1989). A strong high court can provide limitations to a principal and enforce previous political commitments (Landes and Posner 1975). Another of the many possibilities for restricting the power of principals is by delegating decisions to autonomous bureaucrats (Furubotn and Richter 1998: 421). The requirements within a principal–agent model

imposed, the credibility problem will be overcome. But constraining a self-serving principal also disallows a perfect system of bribery, bringing about the other forms of welfare loss described previously. There emerges a trade-off where welfare losses are inescapable.

4.5. Empirical evidence

A standard assumption would be to assume that countries with a better investment climate achieve higher ratios of investment to GDP. An adverse effect of corruption on this variable is found throughout a variety of studies, in line with our expectations (Brunetti and Weder 1998: 526–8; Brunetti *et al.* 1998: 369; Campos *et al.* 1999; Gymiah-Brempong 2002; Knack and Keefer 1995; Mauro 1995; 1997a; Rock and Bonnett 2004). Criticism has been voiced, however, as to whether the ratio of investment to GDP validly depicts the attractiveness of the overall investment climate. The problem might be that domestic investments are less productive in countries with high levels of corruption, bringing about a higher output. This would suggest that the ratio of investment to GDP may increase rather than decrease in response to increased corruption (Lambsdorff 2003b). A better measure for a country's attractiveness can be taken from foreign direct investments (FDI). This and related empirical evidence are reported in Box 22.

Box 22 Corruption and investments

In an early study, Wheeler and Mody (1992) did not find a significant correlation between the size of FDI and the host country's risk factor – which includes corruption among other variables and is highly correlated with corruption. Another insignificant finding is reported by Alesina and Weder (1999), however, the authors make use of the variable by PRS – the usual caveats apply. The data on FDI refer to 1970–1995. But awareness toward corruption and levels of FDI increased considerably after 1995. The insignificant finding should thus not be overrated. Equally inconclusive are regressions provided by Okeahalam and Bah (1998) and Davidson (1999), but for a small sample of countries. Méon and Sekkat

would be to insulate agents from the principal's direct orders. Agents must be required to respect the law and not to follow the opportunistic interests of the principal.

(2004) obtain no significant impact of corruption on inflowing FDI for a small sample of Middle Eastern countries.

More recent studies provide evidence in favor of corruption deterring foreign investors. Focusing on bilateral flows between fourteen source and forty-five host countries in 1990 and 1991, Wei (2000b) detects a significant negative impact of corruption on FDI. He finds that an increase in the corruption level from that of Singapore to that of Mexico is equivalent to raising the tax rate by over twenty percentage points.[14] Aizenman and Spiegel (2003) reveal a negative impact of corruption, measured by the BI-data, on the ratio of FDI to total capital accumulation for a variety of regressions. The coefficient is robust to the inclusion of further independent variables. Lambsdorff and Cornelius (2000) show an adverse impact of corruption on FDI for African countries. Abed and Davoodi (2002: 523) obtain a negative impact of corruption on the US-dollar per capita value of FDI for a cross section of twenty-four transition countries. Doh and Teegen (2003) show that investments in the telecommunications industry (as reported in the World Bank's Private Participation in Infrastructure database, PPI) are adversely affected by the extent of corruption. Smarzynska and Wei (2000) provide evidence for corruption to reduce firm-level assessments of FDI in Eastern Europe and the former Soviet Union. An increase in corruption from the (low) level in Estonia to the (high) level in Azerbaijan would reduce the probability of foreign investment by fifteen percentage points.

[14] In a further contribution, Wei (1997) argues that in addition to the overall level of corruption it is arbitrariness that harms capital inflows. As those who pay bribes have no legal recourse, contracts obtained through bribery cannot be enforced. That is why corruption, while not necessarily more expensive, is more harmful than taxes. Wei derives a measure of arbitrariness from the survey by WEF. While the question posed relates to the overall level of corruption, Wei argues that the variance in the replies represents a form of arbitrariness. This can be considered valid if the insecurity among respondents about the true costs of bribes is reflected in the variance. Arbitrariness, thus defined, significantly enters into the regressions on FDI. But it has been questioned whether arbitrariness is adequately measured by this variable. Particularly, the variance among respondents could also reflect heterogeneous conditions in a country or be related to subjective difficulties among respondents in judging the right score on the questionnaire. Arbitrariness may be better measured by the predictability of corruption, for example as determined by World Bank/University of Basel (WB/UB).

Box 22 (*Cont.*)

Henisz (2000), who uses the Conference Board Manufacturers database, provides a similar result. This database is a collection of data on foreign market entry for more than 1,000 US corporations. Henisz finds that a variable on "unexpected" corruption deters market entry. The variable on "unexpected" corruption is the difference between "actual" corruption as measured by PRS/ICRG and expected corruption as determined by data on the political system. Given the problems with the PRS data on corruption, the results must be taken with some skepticism.

Habib and Zurawicki (2001; 2002) also provide evidence in the line of corruption deterring FDI. They find the impact of corruption on FDI to be larger than that on local investment. They conclude that foreign investors are more sensitive to corruption than their local counterparts. In sum, the evidence of an impact of corruption on FDI now appears sufficiently well established to argue in favor of a significant negative effect.

Fons (1999) reports a significant correlation between the TI CPI and Moody's country ceiling ratings. The latter variable relates to the default risk for debt obligations issued by a national government. Fons argues that poor transparency and high levels of corruption increase credit risks. In a more systematic investigation, Ciocchini *et al.* (2003) show that countries perceived as more corrupt pay a higher risk premium when issuing bonds. Hall and Yago (2000) provide evidence for a small sample of countries that corruption increases sovereign bond spreads, making it more costly for countries with high levels of corruption to obtain loans. Wei and Sievers (1999) report a correlation between corruption and weak bank supervision. Those holding deposits or granting loans to banks are likely to react to allegations of corruption and withdraw their engagement. As a consequence of these findings a negative impact of corruption on a country's capital inflows becomes likely.

The impact of corruption on total net capital imports is shown in Lambsdorff (2003b). In a cross section of sixty-four countries, corruption is shown to decrease capital inflows at a high confidence

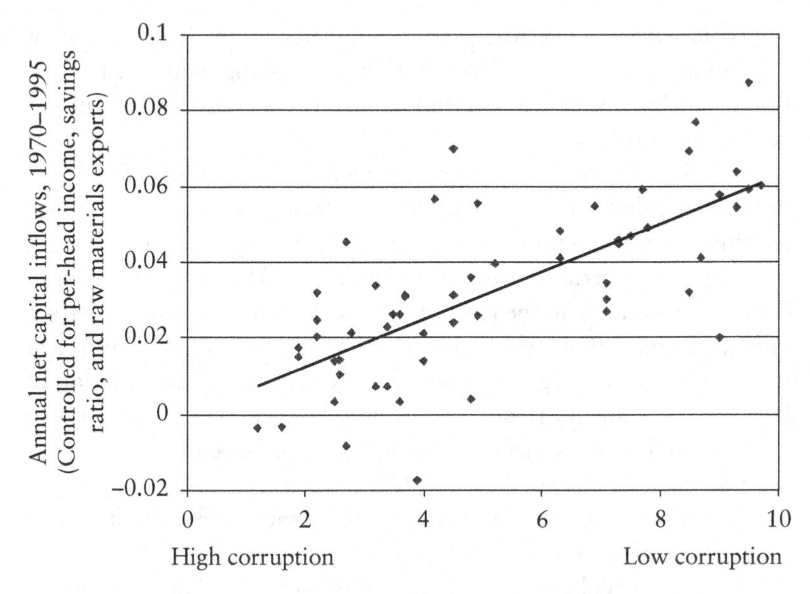

Figure 4.2. Corruption and capital inflows

level, controlling for various explanatory variables such as GDP per head, domestic savings rates, and raw material exports. These results are robust to the use of alternative indices of corruption, tests of linearity, and issues of sample selection. An increase in Tanzania's level of integrity to that of the United Kingdom is found to increase net annual capital inflows by 3 percent of GDP. This coefficient falls when controlling for an index depicting countries' traditions of law and order. This variable by ICRG measures the soundness of political institutions, the strength of the court system, and whether provisions are in place for an orderly succession of power. The results suggest that investors are deterred because corruption undermines a country's legal tradition. Such a tradition otherwise provides investors with the confidence that the political elite would not exploit arising opportunities after investors have entered a country. See Figure 4.2 for a graphical illustration.

In a more recent update of this study, rather than the legal tradition it is the extent of civil liberties that explains part of the impact of corruption. This index by Freedom House embraces freedom of expression and belief, personal autonomy as well as human and economic rights. Investors avoid countries with high levels of corruption, partly because corruption goes along with weak civil liberties such as excessive government intervention and little chance to voice complaints.

According to these estimates, an increase in corruption by one point on a scale from 10 (highly clean) to 0 (highly corrupt) decreases net annual capital inflows by 0.5 per cent of GDP. An improvement with regard to corruption by six points of the TI CPI – for example, Tanzania improving to the level of the United Kingdom – increases net annual capital inflows by 3 percent of GDP. Overall, the empirical finding is robust throughout a variety of studies. While the reaction of domestic investments is difficult to ascertain because of theoretical reasons, foreign investments are significantly deterred by corruption, and this impact is large in magnitude.

Apart from an impact on the total investment volumes, it is also revealing to observe that some types of investment suffer more than others. It is particularly the long-term commitments that are involved in FDI that suffer, while other more volatile types of investment may be less affected by corruption. This exposes corrupt countries to more pronounced fluctuations in response to external shocks. The related evidence is reported in Box 23.

Box 23 Corruption and the composition of investments

Wei (2000c) and Wei and Wu (2001) also hint at corruption reducing FDIs. Interestingly enough, they argue that an impact of corruption on incoming bank loans cannot be obtained. Countries affected by high levels of corruption are thus more reliant on bank loans. Similar findings are reported by Straub (2003). This distortion might reduce economic welfare, because loans can be withdrawn more easily in case of economic problems. This makes corrupt countries more vulnerable to currency crises.

Another strand of research is concerned with a firm's entry-mode decision. Smarzynska and Wei (2000) observe an impact of corruption. Being faced with corrupt requests, investors prefer a joint venture with a local partner to a wholly owned subsidiary because a local partner might be better acquainted with local (corrupt) practice. This effect prevails where a simple production technology is employed. In case of a more sophisticated technology, investors would fear for the leakage of technological know-how to opportunistic local partners. In line with this reasoning, the preference for joint ventures in corrupt countries is not obtained if firms operate with sophisticated technologies.

Uhlenbruck *et al.* (2006) investigate data for the telecommunications industry (as reported in the World Bank's Private Participation in Infrastructure (PPI) database). They show for a sample of 220 telecommunications development projects in sixty-four emerging economies that firms adapt to a country's level of corruption by avoiding the holding of equity and preferring to merely partner with local firms or by entering a country on a short-term basis. The authors do not find a significant difference between joint ventures and wholly owned subsidiaries. By employing the findings by Smarzynska and Wei (2000) we could conclude that this might be due to the high level of technological sophistication prevalent in the telecommunications industry.

Different types of corruption may lead to different outcomes. In addition to an overall level of corruption, its predictability and absence of opportunism was also determined. This embraced, first, whether the costs of corruption are known in advance and, second, whether after making the payment the service is delivered as promised. The resulting impact of these variables on the ratio of investment to GDP was investigated by the World Bank (1997). Further evidence on this matter is provided in Box 24. However, as expounded repeatedly in this book, the good thing about unpredictability and opportunism might be that it acts as a deterrent to corruption. Reform approaches that attempt to divest corruption of its unpredictability are therefore easily misguided because increased levels of corruption might result where promises of corrupt reciprocity become credible.

Box 24 Different types of corruption and investment

For a sample of thirty-nine industrial and developing countries, the World Bank (1997) shows that, for a given level of corruption, countries with more predictable and less opportunistic corruption have higher investment rates. This approach is extended and elaborated further by Campos *et al.* (1999), who make use of the

Box 24 (*Cont.*)

same data by WB/UB in a cross section of fifty-nine countries. While controlling for GDP per head and secondary school enrollment, the authors find that low predictability, high opportunism, and the overall level of corruption reduce the ratio of investment to GDP. The authors conclude that the nature of corruption is also crucial to its economic effects.

Similar to Campos *et al.* (1999), Uhlenbruck *et al.* (2006) also investigate the impact of arbitrariness on the entry mode chosen by the telecommunication industry; see Box 23 for a description of their data. They provide evidence that firms prefer joint ventures to wholly owned subsidiaries in reaction to low levels of predictability, the likely reason being that local partners have an edge over their international competitors in monitoring local office holders and exploiting trusted local relationships. Their results are robust to the inclusion of crucial explanatory variables.

In Lambsdorff (2005a) I employ seven subcomponents of corruption for a sample of 102 countries that appear in the 2003 Global Competitiveness Report of the WEF. The second principal component of this data depicts a grand, political type, embracing corruption in government policy-making and in judicial decisions as opposed to a petty type of corruption that can be found in public utilities and loan applications. It is shown that grand corruption less deters foreign investors. This might relate to smaller organizational effort, investors' feelings of belonging to an inner circle of insiders that can profit from hidden arrangements, or from high-ranking politicians acting as guarantors to the enforcement of grand corrupt deals. The study claims that investors are less deterred by the unpredictability of corruption; it is the petty type of corruption that investors dislike because it goes along with time-consuming negotiations with low-level bureaucrats. Certainly, investors' preference for grand corruption is not necessarily in the public interest.

In sum, there is widespread evidence for the adverse impact of corruption. Our theoretical elaborations suggested that this could be related to corrupt politicians being unable to credibly commit themselves. Corruption therefore deters investors because it goes along with disrespect for law. Whether it is truly this impact that is at play has been investigated in Lambsdorff (2003b). An indicator on "law and order" is added to standard regressions on FDI and corruption. Once included, the coefficient for corruption drops. This reveals that the impact of corruption on FDI is related to its association with a poor legal tradition. Other governance indicators such as the quality of bureaucracy or political stability are insignificant and without impact on the regressions. These do not seem to impact on investor's calculus.[15]

4.6. Conclusions

A constrained principal who seeks corrupt income is likely to produce a plethora of welfare losses. He may allow his agents to get away with shirking, self-serving behavior, and petty corruption. He may distort allocation by promoting sectors with increased secrecy. He may exchange favors with powerful lobbies, inducing wasteful competition for preferential treatment. But there is no shortcut to avoiding these deficiencies. Increasing the power of rulers would get away with the aforementioned problems. But a new problem emerges that has been overlooked by some scholars.

A self-serving principal may attempt to design a perfect bribery system that operates as smoothly as a tax. But in order to do so, he must be able to set aside constitutional and legal restrictions. But this cripples his chances to make believable commitments to long-term policies. The private sector will not risk bearing the initial sunk costs of an investment where corrupt governments do not commit themselves to honoring and defending property rights. Potential investors will justifiably fear opportunism and governments will be unable to attract investors and private capital. The welfare effect will largely be felt by investors who are discouraged from an investment, leading to reduced capital accumulation.

Corruption can be fought in a top–down manner – mainly by reducing bureaucratic corruption and increasing the strength, expertise, and integrity of low-level public servants. A grassroots

[15] In more recent investigations, an index of civil liberties is found to lower the impact of corruption on FDI. The reason for this would be similar: in countries without civil liberties, such as the freedom of expression, investors cannot address the public with their complaints about extortion among the political elite.

approach to reform puts emphasis on improved civil liberties, such as the freedom of expression and human rights. Both these approaches appear feasible – a comprehensive reform strategy would embrace both. Notwithstanding the success that a top–down approach to reform may have, in the long term constraining the political elite's zeal with the help of improved civil liberties and a respected legal tradition appears to be a vital part of reform.

5 Corruption and transactions costs: The rent-seeking perspective

5.1. Introduction

> Corruption is bad not because money and benefits change hands, and not because of the motives of participants, but because it privatizes valuable aspects of public life, bypassing processes of representation, debate, and choice.
>
> (Thompson 1993)

Should corruption be facilitated or impeded? At the core of this book is the idea that we should make corruption as arduous as possible. The downside effects should be felt strongly by those willing to take bribes and embezzle public funds. But some theorists were busy arguing in favor of the opposite. They claimed that corruption should be facilitated because otherwise lobbying for preferential treatment would generate wasteful competition. I show that this conclusion is misguided – our effort must be directed toward increasing the transaction costs of corruption.

As we have argued in Chapter 4, some concept of public interest may be at the center of definitions of political corruption. Therefore, welfare economics can be a starting point for analyzing corruption because it allows for a distinction to be made between useful and wasteful political actions. An early approach in this vein has been presented by the traditional rent-seeking theory. This approach considers various forms of seeking preferential treatment in the realm of public decision-making, for example, through competitive lobbying and corruption. Based on welfare economics, this approach provides a normative framework to determine what type of policy should be implemented. By applying this theory to the actions of decision-makers, traditional

A related version of this chapter was originally published as "Corruption and Rent-Seeking," *Public Choice*, 2002, Vol. 113: (1/2), October, 97–125.

rent-seeking theory focuses on the resulting deviations from optimality. This chapter follows the traditional rent-seeking theory in viewing corruption as a particular type of rent-seeking activity. This viewpoint has gained wide recognition (Cartier-Bresson 1997: 152–3; Rose-Ackerman 1999). But as this chapter demonstrates, the traditional rent-seeking theory by and large fails to compare corruption adequately with alternative forms of rent-seeking.

Section 5.2 describes the traditional rent-seeking theory. Its application to an investigation of corruption is demonstrated in Section 5.3, which also explains to what extent and why traditional rent-seeking theory favors corruption to competitive lobbying. Section 5.4 criticizes the traditional rent-seeking approach to corruption, particularly the welfare implications. Traditional rent-seeking theory fails to identify the impact of a corrupt monopoly on the size of a rent, the role of corruption in motivating the supply of preferential treatment, and the involvement of interests in cases of corruption that are even narrower than those in cases of competitive lobbying. Once these factors are taken into account, the opposite argument is put forward, as in the concluding Section 5.6: corruption has worse welfare implications than organized lobbying. We are well advised to impede corruption and organize a more transparent type of lobbyism instead. High transaction costs of corruption are a good thing because they suggest that those who seek influence prefer open competition rather than obscure and restricted access to politicians.

5.2. The traditional rent-seeking approach

One of the pillars of the traditional rent-seeking theory is the identification of transaction costs (Tullock 1967; 1971).[1] This approach departed from orthodox welfare economics and claimed that welfare losses as a result of monopolization are much larger than the classical Harberger triangle. This triangle is a classical welfare concept, sometimes also called the dead-weight-loss. This loss arises because profitable exchange does not take place as a result of a monopolist's attempt to squeeze prices above their competitive level. The additional transaction costs are associated with costs for transferring income.

[1] What we call transaction costs here was called transfer costs by most rent-seeking theorists – with practically the same meaning.

Transaction costs

As far as efficiency is concerned, it appears irrelevant to whom a given stream of income accrues and how given rents are divided. This is a problem of distribution and not one related to economic efficiency. This changes as soon as transfers are costly to make. Tullock (1967) argues, for example, that taxation and tariffs as a means to shift part of consumers' rent to the state require further administrative costs. These transaction costs arise in the form of salaries for tax inspectors or customs officials as well as public costs for containing smuggling and tax evasion. Such costs lower welfare and must be added to the Harberger triangle.

Transfer of income from consumers to producers invokes costs comparable with those of theft. Primarily, theft represents a mere shift of assets without any consequences for economic efficiency, just like a lump sum tax. There is no inefficiency and no Harberger triangle associated with it. There are welfare losses nonetheless (Tullock 1971). These occur if investments are made to avoid and to facilitate theft at the same time: investments into locks and picklocks, safes and dynamite, fingerprint identification techniques and gloves. Expenses for such investments do not raise welfare and should be regarded as a form of waste.

A similar problem emerges in the case of subsidies and charities. Recipients may invest in becoming a potential recipient of aid. Self-mutilation by beggars may improve their position as a recipient of charity but hardly adds to overall welfare. Tullock (1975) reports that some towns in the United States were entitled to obtain subsidies from their states for the maintenance of roads. But since the poor condition of roads was emphasized as the reason for subsidies, there was incentive to allow roads to become dilapidated in order to obtain larger subsidies. Else the struggle for obtaining subsidies may require costly political campaigns intended to prevent the resources being allocated to other uses. Any of the resources used for or against such campaigns represent pure waste, which neither raises production nor bears any other fruit for third parties. Even if no administrative costs arise for making a transfer, Tullock (1971: 642) argues: "The transfer itself may be costless, but the prospect of the transfer leads individuals and groups to invest resources in either attempting to obtain a transfer or to resist a transfer away from themselves." Expenses for enacting regulation in industry are another example for transaction costs, including salaries to lawyers and lobbyists. Such transaction costs link distributional problems to efficiency considerations as the existence of rents brings about costly investments into mechanisms for transferring payments, including costs associated with competing for the revenues. The resulting type of competition has been a major concern of the traditional rent-seeking approach.

Competition for rents

Costly transfers should be particularly an issue in the case of a monopoly. As monopolies give rise to rents, these incite disputes regarding their distribution. Shareholders, consumers, competitors, and even the state may all engage in attempts to obtain some part of the producer's rent. Investments will be undertaken that are aimed at obtaining or increasing one's share of the producer's rent. Comparable with the case of theft mentioned above, such investments are a part of the transaction costs and represent a form of waste. They are not aimed at increasing production or lowering costs – the standard motivation for making investments. They do not aim at maximizing profit by pleasing consumers with a better or cheaper product. Any revenues that accrue as a result of such activities directly lower revenues of other actors. This type of behavior has therefore been called rent-seeking as opposed to profit-seeking, where investments into production bring about profit only if someone else is better off buying the resulting product (Buchanan 1980).

Crucial to the rent-seeking approach is the particular marketplace under consideration. Ordinary products or services are not the ones under scrutiny. The focus of rent-seeking is on the interaction between the state and private parties, where the state has the monopoly on allocating property rights, be it by certain laws, regulations, subsidies, taxes, tariffs, import quotas, or by awarding contracts in public procurement. Such activities usually entail a certain distribution or redistribution of income. Private firms will try to influence the decision to favor their own benefit. The result of the aforementioned activities is a marketplace where the state offers a certain right or preferential treatment and firms compete against each other in their demand for this.

This view adds another dimension to the usual market competition: firms' ability to use state intervention for their own purposes. The state can be a supplier of physical or financial factors to firms (e.g. in the case of subsidies or licenses) or demand the firms' products (in the case of public procurement). The actions of the state can give rise to shortages, market disruptions, or prices that deviate from competitive prices. This initiates disputes over rents and induces firms to compete for preferential treatment.

Maximizing social welfare may not be the objective of the state. Instead, decision-making will largely be the result of, or at least be heavily influenced by, those seeking rents that arise as a consequence of state intervention. Market restrictions can be offered to those best able to influence decision-makers. Tullock (1967: 228) writes: "Generally governments do not impose protective tariffs on their own. They have to be lobbied or pressured into doing so by the expenditure of resources in political activity." This provides an explanation for the evolution of monopolies, one that differs from the traditional explanations. Monopolies can emerge as a result of state intervention. Monopolies may come into existence, if public decision-makers are in a position to support a monopoly, and impede competition by imposing the respective laws and regulations. The producer's rent in a monopoly is therefore not the result of, for example, economies of scale, voluntary cartelization, or the ousting of competitors by superior products. The welfare effects of such a monopoly must be seen in the light of this struggle required to obtain the monopolistic position (Bartsch and Thomas 1993).

Monopolies require investments for politically defending their position. Potential entrants must be fought with regulation and laws in favor of the monopolist, and costs arise as decision-makers must be influenced accordingly. Furthermore, potential entrants may try to influence decision-makers and allocate resources for this purpose. Consumers may try to break up a monopoly in an attempt to obtain a part of the producer's rent, providing them with a willingness to pay for political decisions. All these expenses for preferential treatment do not add to total production or welfare. Instead, they must be regarded as wasteful.

5.3. The traditional rent-seeking approach to corruption

From the outset, corruption has been considered as one form of rent-seeking. It was viewed as a special means by which private parties may seek to pursue their interests in the competition for preferential treatment. Just like other forms of rent-seeking, corruption represents a way to escape the invisible hand of the market and influence policies to one's own advantage.[2]

There are different approaches for distinguishing corruption from alternative forms of rent-seeking. Two ideas have been emphasized by the protagonists of the traditional rent-seeking theory. First, corruption differs from other types of rent-seeking in the form of transfers involved. Second, corruption differs from other types of rent-seeking in the extent of competition for rents.

Transaction costs of corruption

Traditional rent-seeking theory differentiates between corruption and lobbying as forms of rent-seeking. One apparent difference between these activities relates to the question of how decision-makers are influenced. If money is given to politicians or public servants, this should represent a clear case of corruption. But if rent-seeking is carried out by starting political campaigns, engaging lawyers and public relation agencies, or by public advertising, most observers would not regard the decision-makers thus influenced as corrupt.

These two alternatives involve different welfare implications. Particularly, the question of whether a bribe represents a form of waste has been the cause of some debate. Krueger (1974: 292–3) suggests that bribes create rents for government officials and that a wasteful competition for public jobs may thus develop. This position is not clearly supported by Posner (1975: 812), who argues that initially bribes represent pure transfers. A lobby may choose between paying bribes and starting a political campaign. It is a straightforward assumption that the first alternative benefits the recipient, while the latter may involve annoying phone calls and influence-peddlers

[2] While Mbaku (1998: 197) largely supports the argument that corruption is a form of rent-seeking, he points out that some forms of corruption may not be rent-seeking. He mentions the embezzlement by public servants as an example. But, this type of behavior should also be regarded as a form of rent-seeking. Public servants must lobby for administrative positions that provide opportunities for embezzlement – giving rise to competitive rent-seeking. And even if no competition for such opportunities takes place, this simply represents a monopolistic form of rent-seeking.

squandering politicians' time and effort.[3] It is therefore only political campaigning that can easily be equated with some form of waste, while bribery is certainly closer to a pure transfer.[4] Corruption therefore appears to be the less wasteful alternative for seeking rents (Wintrobe 1998a: 26). Similarly, Tullock (1980a: 21–3) considers the selling of government positions, which can just be another type of corruption, to be a pure transfer of assets, which is not equivalent to waste, since the money increases utility or production elsewhere. Stiff lobbying rules are assumed to increase transaction costs.[5] This leads Wellisz and Findlay (1984: 149) to conclude that: "Paradoxically, maximum waste is likely to occur if the licensing system is absolutely 'fair' and if it brings no benefits to the licensor .... Graft and corruption reduce economic costs."

Corruption versus competition

Another suggestion for differentiating between lobbying and corruption has been put forward by Jain (1998: 16). He argues that corruption differs from legitimate lobbying in the level of competition. Corrupt rent-seeking is a parochial form that does not allow potential entrants in the political competition to enter into the bidding process. In contrast, legitimate lobbying is open to everybody and provides clear and transparent rules for participation. Restricted competition can be regarded as a form of favoritism and nepotism,

[3] Bhagwati (1982) coined the term "directly unproductive profit-seeking (DUP) activities" for such actions.

[4] One may assume that transfer costs arise for two reasons: first, a valuation of a gift by the recipient that falls short of its costs and, second, the transaction costs that are required to make the payment. The idea that cash payments can be made without transaction costs is a strong assumption. As expounded in this book, corruption can go along with considerable transaction costs. One may therefore assume that $c > 0$ in case of bribery. But the assumption of c being larger in case of lobbying can still be defended, because in addition to the transaction costs the recipient's lower valuation of the gift increases c.

[5] In a recent empirical investigation, Stratmann (2003) constructs an index on the strictness of campaign financing rules in fourteen countries and observes that strictness goes along with higher levels of corruption. This finding would be in line with some thoughts of the rent-seeking approach. However, it is surprising to most observers and may relate to endogeneity and the lack of control variables: high levels of corruption being caused by other variables may lead to the adoption of contribution limits so as to operate as a remedy. The finding should thus not discourage the implementation of campaign financing rules.

terms that are apparently close in meaning to corruption. This provides sufficient reason to regard monopolistic forms of rent-seeking as closely related to corruption, a view that is also suggested by the traditional rent-seeking literature.

While at first glance such competition sounds preferable, from the traditional rent-seeking point of view it is not. Since competition for rents increases the expenses for rent-seeking and subsequently for waste, monopolistic forms of political competition are regarded as less wasteful. Viewing corruption as a monopolistic form of seeking preferential treatment suggests that traditional rent-seeking should give preference to this type of rent-seeking over more competitive forms. And indeed, this consequence has been clearly spelled out by advocates of the traditional rent-seeking approach. Krueger (1974: 302) labels less-competitive forms of rent-seeking "favoritism" and argues:

> If [governments] do restrict entry [into competition over rents] they are clearly 'showing favoritism' to one group in society and choosing an unequal distribution of income. If, instead, competition for the rents is allowed (or cannot be prevented), income distribution may be less unequal, and certainly there will be less appearance of favoring special groups, although the economic costs associated with quantitative restriction will be higher.

Similarly, Tullock (1980b: 109–11) argues in favor of biased decision-making. The implication is that discrimination against certain groups of people can be advantageous. Denying certain lobbies access to competition over rents is regarded to be beneficial. Nepotism as a form of corruption has been addressed and advocated by Tullock (1980b: 103–4):

> It would appear that if one is going to distribute rents, nepotism is a good thing because it reduces the number of players and, therefore, the total investment [into rent-seeking]. This is one of the classical arguments for hereditary monarchies ...
>
> Thus, if [a] mayor ... had confined all of the more lucrative appointments to his close relatives, the social savings might have been considerable ... it is better if the political appointments of corrupt governments are made quickly and rather arbitrarily, so that not so many resources are invested in rent seeking.

Also Buchanan (1980: 12) argues in this spirit by suggesting that lobbies should not challenge income distribution because they would otherwise waste resources for the resulting contests. In this sense, traditional rent-seeking theory does not encourage competition against leading politicians. Ultimately, this implies that privileged interest groups should enjoy their loot even if they have paid bribes in exchange.

5.4. A critique

There has been a wide range of criticisms of the traditional rent-seeking approach (Bhagwati and Srinivasan 1980: 1086; Bhagwati *et al.* 1984: 30; Magee 1984: 51; North 1984: 39; Wintrobe 1998a: 28). But the difference drawn between corruption and lobbying has not been sufficiently addressed.[6]

The traditional rent-seeking theory fails to identify adequately the welfare implications of corruption. First, the conclusion that a monopolistic form of rent-seeking is preferable to competitive forms must be rejected on theoretical grounds. Second, the idea that transaction costs of rent-seeking increase waste does not survive scrutiny. Third, other distinctions exist between corruption and rent-seeking: corruption implies a more active, self-seeking role of the state than the one assumed by other forms of rent-seeking. Finally, the interests pursued by corrupt behavior are narrower than the more broadly defined interests of other rent-seeking activities.

Endogenous rents

The first problem with traditional rent-seeking theory arises with the frequent assumption that the size of the rent is exogenous. This shortcoming of the traditional rent-seeking theory, as presented by the

[6] Some academics even fail to differentiate between lobbying and corruption and assume that the adverse welfare conclusions of lobbying as derived by traditional rent-seeking theory are equally applicable to corruption; see, for example, Mauro (1997b) and Klitgaard (1988: 43). This clearly simplifies the core spirit of the rent-seeking theory. To be fair here, most protagonists of the traditional rent-seeking theory admit that corruption has further adverse effects, for example by undermining the legitimacy of government (Krueger 1990: 18). But when it comes to utilizing economic tools, the verdict of traditional rent-seeking theory, as described by the multitude of citations presented in this study, is clearly unambiguous.

formal model in the appendix to this chapter, has long been identified and addressed. Models were developed where tariffs and rents are determined endogenously.[7] A variety of factors may impact on the size of the rent. But, it has largely been ignored that competition is one of them.

When public decision-makers create rents, lowering public welfare, they may suffer from disutilities.[8] Public opinion will commonly be in favor of first-best solutions (Findlay and Wellisz 1984: 94–5). This will impact on politicians' behavior via voting (McChesney 1997: 136). If a public decision-maker excessively creates rents instead of serving the public, former allies may revoke their political support, prospects for the next election may be threatened, and the general public may find various forms of expressing dismay. The disutility associated with creating rents is likely to increase with the size of the rent and the welfare losses imposed on third parties. Inducing politicians to take that burden therefore comes at a price, and politicians will choose an optimum between creating rents and avoiding the resulting disutility.

For competing firms, the overall size of the rent is a public good that they will hardly lobby for. They would rather seek to increase their share and their individual probability of being successful. In contrast, for a monopolist the total rent is not a public good but his own private good. A monopolist may thus be willing to devote resources to rent-seeking activities. Otherwise, the total rent he can capture may turn out to be suboptimal, since decision-makers are not sufficiently induced to maximize rents. Posner (1974: 349) touches on this aspect when he writes: "even a naturally monopolistic industry would gain from legislation that increased the demand for its product." As a result, total rent-seeking expenses may increase, or decrease, with competition. If rent-seeking expenses have a strong impact on the size of the rent, this effect can outweigh the one outlined by the traditional model: monopolists may spend more on

[7] See, for example, Brock and Magee (1978); Findlay and Wellisz (1984); Magee (1984); and Bhagwati *et al.* (1984).

[8] This is a common assumption made in public-choice theory. Appelbaum and Katz (1987) and McChesney (1987) introduced such public-choice elements into formal models similar to the one provided in the appendix to this chapter. However, they failed to observe that this results in competition having an impact on the size of the rent.

rent-seeking than competing firms, and monopolies could be more wasteful than competitive firms in a market for preferential treatment.[9] See the appendix to this chapter for a formal proof.

Apart from the size of existing rents, it is also the creation of new rents that monopolistic firms or lobbies may be devoted to. This is the view particularly embraced by the economic theory of regulation (Peltzman 1976; Posner 1974; Stigler 1971). Competitive firms do not engage equally in influencing public decision-makers so as to create regulations, tariffs, quotas, subsidies, and the like. The reason is that after devoting resources to influencing politicians to enact the desired laws and regulations, a company has no guarantee that revenues thus created will accrue to it. Rent-seekers may be unwilling to invest in lobbying to create rents if they believe that they will have to expend additional resources to compete for these rents once they are created (Mbaku 1992: 249). While this argument is straightforward, it seems to have been largely overlooked in the traditional rent-seeking literature.

Furthermore, Wintrobe (1998a: 28–30) suggests another aspect in favor of competition. The crucial shortcoming of traditional rent-seeking theory is that according to this theory it makes no difference who wins the contest, and consequently no social benefit results from the bidding process. As competitors should be assumed to differ from one another in their product and their rent-seeking skills, such considerations become important. Each new competitor introduces the possibility of a better product or service being selected in the resulting bidding process. Benefits are not likely to result if competitors are picked at random but only if some rationality guides the tendering procedure. This implies another advantage of competition.

Further advantages from competition arise with an information-theoretic point of view. Private firms are the best informed parties

[9] This argument must be modified considering that monopolies may have further means to influence public decision-makers. As compared to competitive lobbies they might be in a stronger bargaining position. Also, inside information from past deals could provide them with the possibility of extorting favors from public decision-makers. This results in monopolists having recourse to further cost-effective means of influencing public decision-makers. Monopolists can in this case better influence the creation of rents but may not have to increase the overall rent-seeking expenses to reach this goal. The resulting total welfare loss then consists of a large Harberger triangle due to an increased creation of rents, along with less waste in the form of rent-seeking expenses. The overall welfare effects of increased bargaining power appear to be ambiguous.

about their own level of efficiency, making it difficult to set the right prices in public procurement. With the help of a public tender, competitors are forced to reveal some of this information about their degree of efficiency, and they are provided with incentives to improve their productivity. In contrast, it is arduous to induce monopolists to adopt this type of behavior.

Another point in favor of corruption over lobbying has been that bribes increase the utility of the recipient, while lobbying does not provide an equal benefit but rather constitutes a form of waste. This argument alone is certainly not strong enough to tip the balance in favor of corruption, just as any type of prohibition is not necessarily in contrast to welfare. The purpose of prohibition would be to change behavior in a desired direction.

When transaction costs are large it becomes arduous for politicians to profit from an exchange with lobbies. Politicians then consider it unattractive to distort markets, harass their voters, and create artificial rents. Instead, they prefer legal perspectives for their career, where they exhibit a commitment to serve the public. The presence of potential waste does not suggest that lobbyism is worse than corruption – just as prohibition would not be rejected on the grounds that it hurts the criminal. See the appendix for a formal treatment of this argument.

Supplying rents

> In Nigeria, corruption isn't part of government, it's the object of government.
>
> Anonymous Nigerian political scientist,
> Washington Post, April 9, 1998

Another related criticism of the traditional rent-seeking approach refers to the role of the state and the incentives of decision-makers to supply the rents that are demanded by private interest groups. As argued by Tullock (1967: 228, citation on p. 113) the government itself is not the one seeking rents or motivated to impose restrictions. It is lobbied into these actions by private firms. For Krueger (1990: 10, 14) corruption emerges as a "by-product" of policy distortions or "inevitably accompanies a set of controls." This leads Tullock (1993: 26) to summarize that "politicians are modelled as providing a brokering function in the political model for wealth transfers." What is missing in this context is an adequate description of what actually causes policy distortions and creates rents. For Buchanan (1980: 8) some flattery or persuasion may be sufficient to induce a political leader to provide monopoly rights to someone. Such explanations invite criticism. McChesney (1987: 102) noted that traditional rent-seeking theory describes a politician as the "passive broker among competing private rent seekers." According to Tollison (1982: 592) the role of politicians remains that of a "mystery actor." Wintrobe (1998a: 25) even considers the role assigned to politicians by traditional rent-seeking theory to be irrational.

Again, to be fair here, protagonists of the traditional rent-seeking theory have elaborated on the causes of rents, the process of rent-creation; for example, Krueger (1990: 19) and the various contributions by Tullock cited in this chapter. It should not be overlooked that rent-seeking theory was much inspired by public choice theory (Buchanan and Tullock 1962; Downs 1957; Niskanen 1971) and the economic theory of regulation (Peltzman 1976; Posner 1974; Stigler 1971), which put clear emphasis on the motivation of politicians, characterizing actions by politicians and public servants as the result of maximizing behavior. However, it is predominantly assumed that this relates to the maximization of an agency's budget or the number of votes a politician can obtain. This viewpoint has been criticized by Hirshleifer (1976) and Peltzman (1989: 7) and elaborated in McChesney (1997: 17–18, 133–55), who point out that public servants and politicians should be treated as wealth maximizers instead.

Particularly, what has been disregarded by traditional rent-seeking theory is how far corruption, as opposed to lobbying, may impact on the process of rent-creation. Corrupt politicians and public servants need not be pushed by private businessmen to take regulatory action but have a motivation of their own to do so. Corruption motivates politicians and public servants to impose (or threaten to impose) market restrictions so as to maximize the resulting rents and the bribes paid in connection with them.

The chief shortcoming of traditional rent-seeking theory can be illustrated with the help of an example by Buchanan (1980: 12–13). He describes a taxi market where the municipal government limited the number of licenses required for taxis, for "whatever reason." He continues to describe how the resulting rents may later be captured by political entrepreneurs. While this is a possible sequence of actions, there is no convincing reason why the causality should not just work the other way round: very good reasons existed for limiting entry into the taxi market; politicians and administrators may have limited the access for taxi drivers so as to sell the valuable licenses and to pocket parts of the rents they were creating. This type of causality appears less logical for the case of lobbying, where public decision-makers are exposed to harassment by interest-seekers and have few prospects of extracting some profit for themselves. Lacking these prospects for self-enrichment, this type of rent-seeking is less attractive to public decision-makers. In contrast to lobbying, corruption reverses the causality. It is a force motivating the creation of rents.

That corruption can motivate the creation of monopolies and regulations so as to obtain bribes can be illustrated with the help of some recent case studies. The dramatic downturn of the economy in Georgia has been blamed on mismanagement and corruption. International investors have complained of capricious tax officials and a bewildering system of licensing businesses, which, some of them say, is designed to squeeze cash out of entrepreneurs for personal gain.[10] Another case took place in Pakistan, where Benazir Bhutto sold the monopoly right to import gold; see p. 9. A further illustrating example comes from Nigeria. The Abacha family was behind the operations of the firm Delta Prospectors Ltd., which mines barite, a mineral that is an essential material for oil production. In spring 1998, shortly after Delta's operations had reached full production, General Abacha banned the import of barite. This turned the company into a monopoly provider for the large Nigerian oil industry.[11] Rose-Ackerman (1999: 37) provides further examples where market concentration has been increased as a result of corruption, even when the respective firms have been privatized.

Also some empirical evidence reported in Box 18 is supportive of corruption giving rise to artificial restrictions. For example, Faccio and Parsley (2006) show that the value of political connections is higher in corrupt countries, making it more likely that firms invest in such connections as a way of increasing profits. Policy distortions may

[10] See Reuters, July 27, 1998, "Georgian Leader Forces Government to Quit."
[11] See *Washington Post*, June 9, 1998; "Corruption Flourished In Abacha's Regime. Leader Linked To Broad Plunder."

be the result of corruption, and not the other way round. This idea has also been spelled out explicitly by Bardhan (1997: 1323): "The distortions are not exogenous to the system and are instead often part of the built-in corrupt practices of a patron-client political system." As an example in this respect, Myrdal (1968) cites the 1964 Santhanam Committee on the Prevention of Corruption appointed by the Government of India. He argues that corrupt officials may, instead of speeding up, actually cause administrative delays in order to attract more bribes. A similar proposition is put forward by Rose-Ackerman (1978: 90), citing Gardiner and Olson (1974: 196): "bureaucratic personnel may deliberately slow down service after the initial payoff and create more red tape in order to establish additional inducements for others to make payments or to raise the ante."

Similar to bureaucrats, politicians can also engage in such tactics, for example, by imposing or threatening troublesome regulation so as to extort donations from the private sector, (McChesney 1997: 3). Also Tullock (1989: 659) in his more recent work argues on behalf of this type of causality: "once corruption becomes established in a government, laws may be enacted for the specific purpose of maximizing the bribes available for permitting people to avoid them."

Coolidge and Rose-Ackerman (1997: 4) point to the fact that, particularly in the case of rent-seeking among the top of a country's hierarchy, "the search for personal gain can itself importantly influence the level and type of government intervention in the economy." Opportunities for rent-seeking emerge as a result of officials' desire for personal financial gain. Imperfections in government in this case are the result of optimizing behavior and not of laziness or incompetence. Bribes paid under such circumstances do not help to circumvent bothersome regulation, but are a source of inefficiency on their own. The authors provide case studies to support their argument. Also the investigation of excessive bureaucratic regulation in De Soto (1989) leads the author to conclude that they were largely motivated by the desire to generate corrupt revenues. It has therefore been suggested that corruption might be distinguished from lobbying by focusing on the endogeneity of legislation and regulation. Corruption differs from lobbying insofar as artificially created rents by public decision-makers are the result of rent-seeking and not its cause (Pritzl 1995).

The active role of creating rents is sometimes ascribed only to public servants and politicians, for example, by McChesney (1997). But, businesspeople can also be central players. This has already been illustrated by the case study from Pakistan on p. 9. Another illustrative case stems from Saudi Arabia. Allegations were made concerning a son of the Interior minister via the Internet in Saudi Arabia. It was suggested that he had established a chain of body shops for car repairs. Afterwards, he engaged his father to obtain a decree by the king, imposing a requirement for the annual inspection of all five million cars registered in Saudi Arabia in a licensed car repair shop. His chain was the first to obtain the license. To the best of my knowledge, no evidence has been produced to substantiate the claims. But the existing rumors are helpful in illustrating the point being raised here. While the creation of rents commonly involves public and private actors, responsibility for the resulting inefficiencies cannot be assigned *ex-ante* to either side. Some cases exist where private parties are clearly the cause of rent-creation, for example, when politicians are lobbied into regulation that hampers competing companies or when the police is bribed to harass a rival (Rose-Ackerman 1999: 24–5). Extreme examples are organized criminal groups that obtain preferential treatment from public servants through extortion.

This is certainly not to say that rents created by public decision-makers are always caused by corruption. A multitude of other reasons may be thought of for political interference in the market. But even when market restrictions occur for "whatever reason," corruption often acts as a motivating force to ensure market restrictions in the future. For example, South Africa had a twin currency system for a while. This was aimed at providing foreign currency to investors for most-needed investments at below market rates while impeding purchase of less-needed import goods that had to be purchased for the higher exchange rate. But the parliamentary commission entitled to distribute the cheaper currencies was said to request favors in exchange. As a result, currencies were awarded to those providing favors rather than to the salient investments. Abolishing this system was long impeded by the commission's influence on parliament.[12] In Nigeria, in the early 1980s free trade

[12] See *Financial Times*, March 14, 1995, "Strong Debut for Unified Rand" and (Rose-Ackerman 1999: 11).

reforms were favored by the IMF, but were not carried out, because the import licensing system was a major source of payoffs. When the system was finally abolished in the late 1980s the state quickly introduced other new rent-seeking opportunities (Rose-Ackerman 1999: 11). Corruption can motivate the extortion of bribes when inefficient rules provide bureaucrats with a high level of discretion. According to a survey of businesspeople in Karnataka, India, an outmoded regulatory mechanism was used by the middle- and lower-level bureaucrats to harass investors and extort bribes.[13] Reforming regulation is in this case commonly impeded by those who intend to preserve their level of discretion.

The fact that the active, self-seeking role of governments has often not been clearly addressed may be related to political caution rather than to lack of sophistication. Obfuscating the actual causes for rents may present a less controversial way to criticize: in 1993 the World Bank noted the emergence of conglomerates in Indonesia that seek "to capture rents created by policy-created market distortions." In reality, this description meant that Suharto-crony businesses were given government-issued licenses to control various parts of the economy, that is, corruption motivated the creation of monopoly positions for Suharto relatives.[14]

For many years, multilateral donor agencies were reluctant to openly address the problem of corruption. They spoke of "market distortions" and "red tape," but their causes, that is, the corrupt incomes these distortions were intended to generate, were not addressed publicly. This has changed recently (Rose-Ackerman 1999: xi–xii). Still, the cautious wording in such contexts should not mislead the reader as to the corrupt motivation that often lies behind the initiating and supporting of market distortions.

Narrow interests

Seeking preferential treatment by public decision-makers includes a wide range of different actions. Imagine that a manager of a construction company considers engaging in rent-seeking. This may include such diverse activities as, first, bribing in order to obtain a

[13] See *The Hindu*, January 10, 2000, "Investors See Red in Karnataka."
[14] See the *Wall Street Journal*, July 14, 1998, "Speak No Evil: Why the World Bank Failed to Anticipate Indonesia's Deep Crisis."

contract in public procurement; second, organizing a lobby aimed at increased spending for public construction; or third, campaigning jointly with other interest groups to increase public spending.

While all these activities are commonly regarded as forms of rent-seeking, traditional rent-seeking theory does not distinguish clearly between them. All of these activities are potentially beneficial to the construction company and may bring about competition for the rents as other companies or lobbies also try to capture similar privileges. Rent-seeking theory thus appears applicable. But a more interesting issue is to what extent these actions *differ* from each other with respect to their welfare implications.

For this purpose it is crucial to identify the *interaction* with other rent-seekers. It is the interests involved and the type of good being exchanged that distinguish one rent-seeking activity from another. One such approach has been suggested by Olson (1982); see also MacGuire and Olson (1996) and Pryor (1984). The idea elaborated there is that interest groups that embrace larger segments of the economy will take the macroeconomic impact of their actions into account when trying to maximize the income of their members. This considerably reduces the ill-effects of rent-seeking, as the larger lobbies have an "encompassing interest" in creating welfare-enhancing policies. As a result, large interest groups are less detrimental to economic development than smaller ones. In the utopian case of a lobby consisting of everybody in the society, the interests pursued are public interests (Posner 1974: 350). An organized political campaign for higher public spending is unlikely to disregard the broader economic effects and more complicated repercussions of its actions. It is therefore closer to promoting a first-best solution. In contrast to this, lobbies that campaign for larger expenses in public construction may not care about other sectors' performance and promote policies that are more harmful to the economy.

With respect to smaller interest groups, Olson (1982) argues that the thicket of special interest groups in any society chokes off innovation and dampens economic growth. This argument is plausible in the comparison of smaller interest groups with those who have a broad encompassing interest. But it may not be valid when comparing smaller interest groups with individuals who separately engage in rent-seeking. Individuals would strive to maximize a very narrow range of self-interest, while smaller groups may be the first step to broadening the interests involved. This idea was advanced by Putnam (1993), who defends the contribution of smaller groups in building society and helping democracy at the same time. Smaller groups are shown to form horizontal networks of civic engagement, improving the effectiveness and responsiveness of regional governments (Putnam 1993: 176, 229). See the appendix for a formal treatment.

Firms can be better off if they unite their rent-seeking activity by forming a lobby. Jointly and publicly, firms may favor the establishment of rules for decent competition, contracts being awarded to the best qualified and adequate tendering procedures being set up to guarantee such an outcome. But individually, they would strive to undermine this by paying bribes and increasing total rent-seeking expenses. It is still not the macro economy that such a lobby becomes concerned about but the well-being of a whole sector. As the interests involved are broadened the welfare losses diminish.[15]

This differentiation between narrow and broad interests is also tackled by Stiglitz (1998a: 16), when he argues that a distinction between rent-seeking interest groups and voice-conveying citizens must be drawn, even if this may be difficult in practice. He argues that: "increasing the numbers of participants and degree of competition would ensure more balanced signals of societal preferences." To sum up, the crucial difference between the three actions mentioned above is the *type of interest involved* and the *type of good* being exchanged. The first transaction includes the payment of a bribe by a single company to a single public servant to obtain a single contract. As this action is based on very narrow interests, it does not take into account the negative externality this imposes on other construction companies. The narrow interest of the actors corresponds to a product that provides a special privilege to its recipient. Such a type of rent-seeking is particularly harmful, because the incentives for creating market distortions are strong. In the second transaction the scope of interest is broadened to

[15] Forming lobbies not only aims at broadening the interests involved but also aims at obtaining a better bargaining position. Vis-à-vis a corrupt bureaucrat or political leader, individuals may come to realize that paying bribes is too costly. Uniting their interests by forming a cartel, they may attempt to redistribute rents on their behalf. In public procurement they can form a cartel that hands out small bribes to a public servant for awarding contracts and then determines the actual contractor according to some prespecified rules. Something similar may happen to lobbies that cooperate only with the intention of increasing their rents at the expense of a corrupt public sector.

include other companies. The goods being exchanged do not include special treatment to individuals but to larger groups. This may go along with a less ad hoc and arbitrary administrative or political decision. Such a type of rent-seeking is less harmful. As negative externalities are partly internalized, total expenses for rent-seeking diminish and the incentives for creating rents are lowered. Still, the interests involved remain limited, as negative externalities to other sectors are not taken into account. As the encompassing interest is further broadened in the third transaction, the resultant rent-seeking gets closer to yielding the first-best solution. The larger lobby will internalize most of the externalities and will rather avoid large rent-seeking expenses and large rents to be created by public decision-makers via imposing market restrictions.

5.5. Two applications

Browning (1974), based on the work by Olson (1965), investigates the organizational difficulties faced by lobbies. He assumes that in order to grasp the rents offered by the government individuals must organize their interests and form a lobby. They must convince public decision-makers of the necessary intervention and would fail if they act independently. But establishing a lobby brings about organizational problems that are best described by the classical prisoner's dilemma: when noncooperative behavior is preferable from an individual's perspective, maximization of individual utility disregards others' utility and brings about a suboptimal solution for all actors. This dilemma also exists for a lobby. Engaging in a lobby imposes costs on the individual, but the benefits of the lobbying activity accrue also to those who do not devote time and effort. The preferable strategy is therefore free–riding: not investing individual costs while still profiting from the efforts devoted by other members. With this being the preferable strategy, it is possible that the lobby cannot be formed at all, although its actions are advantageous to the group of beneficiaries.

It is commonly argued that the larger the potential group of beneficiaries, the less likely it is that lobbies can be formed. Browning argues, there are hardly any groups that campaign for broad topics such as the progression of income taxes.[16] Lobbies can form most

[16] Posner (1974) and Stigler (1971) have pointed out that this relationship may be countered by another aspect: seeking to build a cartel, large lobbies consisting

easily when they fight for rather narrow interests and when those who benefit from their actions can be clearly identified. For Browning (1974: 374) this prisoner's dilemma is welfare-enhancing as it impedes the creation of lobbies. He bases his conclusion on the results of the traditional rent-seeking theory that claims largest welfare losses for wasteful lobby activities.

Based on the previous analysis we must reject Browning's conclusion. Lobbies are a first step away from narrow interests, balancing the various interests of their members to form a broader interest. This can be helpful, as bribery by their individual members, for example firms within a certain sector, is abandoned in favor of maximizing a common goal. Therefore, the difficulties lobbies encounter in their formation are not a good thing. Instead, lobbies should be assisted in becoming more representative of society at large rather than being impeded so that only the obscure and narrow-interest-seeking ones survive.

Another application of the traditional rent-seeking theory relates to the role of legislation and the judiciary. According to the rent-seeking approach, "legislation is 'sold' by the legislature and 'bought' by the beneficiaries of the legislation." Landes and Posner (1975: 877) investigate the role of an independent judiciary and the Supreme Court in their impact on rent-seeking behavior. These institutions have some discretionary power in interpreting the law, in checking the consistency of laws against older legislation and the constitution, and in setting preferences in case of conflict. They may have the power to reject the enforcement of new laws. This restricts the parliament in its potential to "sell" new laws that are in conflict with older laws and introduces continuity in the otherwise unbound and potentially arbitrary laws enacted by parliament. Laws, once passed, assign long-term income sources to those who are able to influence legislation in their favor, because the judiciary helps to enforce the "deals" made by effective interest groups with earlier legislatures. This raises the rent associated with a certain law and consequently the rent-seeking related to it (Tullock 1993: 59–60). A similar role is assigned to the veto power of the president by Crain and Tollison (1979).

of many producers may have a larger demand for state intervention as compared with groups of few producers who may be able to overcome free-riding behavior privately.

But to derive adverse welfare implications from this would be misleading. Such institutional devices are likely to change the product that is being exchanged through rent-seeking and the interests that are involved. Laws apply to a large and anonymous group of private parties, while ad hoc decisions give preferential treatment to individuals or small groups. Therefore, lobbies, which promote broader interests, will be fighting for laws that are valid over a longer period. Rapidly changing laws and ad hoc decisions are lobbied for by those striving for narrow interests. This can more easily result in outright bribery. Restricting legislation to durable laws will therefore help countries move closer to an open debate where public opinion has a chance to make a difference.

5.6. Conclusions

In comparison with lobbying, corruption is commonly described as the more monopolistic form of rent-seeking. Rent-seeking is called corruption when competition for preferential treatment is restricted to a few insiders and when rent-seeking expenses entail benefits to the recipient.

But traditional rent-seeking theory largely failed to identify correctly the resulting welfare effects of corruption. It failed to understand that corruption motivates the creation of inefficient rules that generate rents. It failed to notice that the size of the rent a public decision-maker controls will commonly increase with the extent of corruption and that corruption involves interests that are narrower than those involved in competitive lobbying. In contrast to the traditional rent-seeking theory, it was argued that corruption has worse welfare implications than alternative rent-seeking activities. Since corruption impedes the organization of broad interests, it goes hand in hand with larger expenses for rent-seeking and higher inducements for public decision-makers to create market distortions. If rent-seeking involves transaction costs, this is welfare-enhancing because it assures that resources are spent for production of goods and services rather than for seeking preferential treatment.

These transaction costs were assumed to arise particularly in case of lobbyism while they were absent in case of bribery. This was a strong simplification. For various reasons there exist also transaction costs where partners corruptly exchange favors. Moreover, efforts can be made to increase these transaction costs. Chapter 6 elaborates on these issues. From the current chapter we have learned that increasing transaction costs of corruption and lobbyism does not adversely impact on welfare – the opposite is more likely.

Appendix: A formal model

It is rational to invest in rent-seeking as long as the marginal input is smaller than the potential output it generates [Tullock 1980b]. The resulting market equilibrium can be determined by a formal model.[17] Assume that firms compete for a monopolistic position created by the state. It is a standard assumption (but questionable as we will see later) that all firms take the total rent (R) to be given exogenously. The probability for winning the competition (p_i) is proportional to a firm's investments into rent-seeking (x_i). Since this applies to all firms equally and all probabilities must add up to one, a single firm's probability decreases with the investments undertaken by its competitors. In case of n firms, this results in

$$p_i = \frac{x_i}{\sum_j x_j}, \qquad i,j = 1,\ldots,n,$$

with x_i being the expenses for rent-seeking of firm i. The resulting equilibrium can easily be determined once assumptions are introduced that firms are risk-neutral, act symmetrically, and are unable to influence their competitors' level of rent-seeking x_j. Maximizing the expected profit, $E(p_i R - x_i)$, then requires

$$\frac{d(p_i R - x_i)}{dx_i} = \frac{d\left(Rx_i / \sum x_j - x_j\right)}{dx_i} = \frac{R}{\sum x_j} - \frac{Rx_i}{(\sum x_j)^2} - 1 = 0. \qquad (1)$$

Function (1) can be solved by introducing symmetry, $x_i = x_j = x$. This brings about the Cournot–Nash-equilibrium and the following optimal level of rent-seeking:

$$\frac{R}{nx} - \frac{Rx}{n^2x^2} = 1 \Leftrightarrow nR - R = n^2x \Leftrightarrow x = \frac{n-1}{n^2}R.$$

[17] See, for example, Tullock (1967; 1980b); Krueger (1974); Posner (1974 1975); Bhagwati and Srinivasan (1980); Congleton (1980); Hillman and Katz (1984); Appelbaum and Katz (1987); and Bartsch and Thomas (1995).

Total expenses (S) for rent-seeking then sum up to

$$S = nx = \frac{n-1}{n}R. \tag{2}$$

As more firms (n) enter into the competition over monopolistic rents, more resources (S) are devoted to wasteful lobbying. This implies that competition increases waste. If only a single monopolist competes for the rent, that is $n=1$, no expenses are allocated for rent-seeking purposes, $S=0$. In the extreme case of perfect competition over monopolistic rents with n approaching infinity, the waste equals the rent ($S=R$). This implies that the total welfare loss consists not only of the classical Harberger triangle, but also of the total producers' rent.

This finding must be modified when considering that the size of the rent should be positively dependent on the total rent-seeking expenses:

$$R = R(S), \quad \text{with } R' > 0. \tag{3}$$

The larger the size of the rent (R) that private parties seek to obtain, the larger the total expenses for rent-seeking (S) required to induce the requested preferential treatment. Equation (3) can be introduced in the formal model. Since $R(s) = R(\sum x_j)$, equation (1) can be rewritten:

$$\frac{d(R(\sum x_j)x_i/\sum x_j - x_i)}{dx_i} = \frac{R'x_i}{\sum x_j} + \frac{R}{\sum x_j} - \frac{Rx_i}{(\sum x_j)^2} - 1 = 0. \tag{1'}$$

In case of symmetry, $x_i = x_j = x$, the Cournot–Nash-equilibrium is

$$\frac{R'x}{nx} + \frac{R}{nx} - \frac{Rx}{n^2x^2} = 1 \Leftrightarrow nR - R = nx(n - R') \Leftrightarrow x = \frac{n-1}{n(n-R')}R.$$

Waste as measured by the total rent-seeking expenses is now given by

$$S = nx = \frac{n-1}{n-R'}R. \tag{2'}$$

A positive impact of the number of competitors (n) on rent-seeking expenses (S) is no longer warranted. If R' is larger (smaller) than 1, S is larger (smaller) than R, and an increase in the number of competitors (n) will decrease (increase) the total expenses for rent-seeking. This shows that the classical assumption of rents dissipating through competition reemerges. In normal product markets, producers' rents dissipate through competition. As rents attract new entry into the market, the increasing production level drives down prices and reduces rents. In the traditional case of rent-seeking for preferential treatment, the rents were assumed to be given exogenously and not to dissipate (Buchanan 1980: 6–11; Flowers 1987). But as soon as rents are seen to depend on rent-seeking expenses, the classical advantage of competition reemerges. Economically, this relates to the fact that the positive impact of rent-seeking expenses (S) on the rent (R) will be felt more when few competitors exist.

The idea that transaction costs are higher for lobbying is taken up by Wellisz and Findlay (1984: 148–9) and similarly by Appelbaum and Katz (1987: 687). They provide a lobby's expenditure function of the form

$$z = (1 - c)x, \quad 0 \leq c \leq 1,$$

where x is the expenditure for rent-seeking purposes, and z the recipient's valuation. The parameter c relates to the transaction costs with $c = 0$ if cash is given and $c = 1$ if those gifts legally permitted (and actually given) are valueless to the recipient. In the latter case, stiff lobbying rules increase transaction costs (c) and increase the extent to which lobbying is wasteful.

It appears plausible to assume that it is not rent-seeking expenses per se that are crucial to influencing a politician's behavior but his valuation of these expenses. This suggests a modified rent-creation function:

$$R = R((1 - c)S), \quad \text{with } R' > 0. \tag{3'}$$

Introducing this function into the formal model brings about the following function for a firm's rent-seeking expenses (x):

$$x = \frac{n - 1}{n(n - (1 - c)R')}R.$$

Total waste would no longer be depicted by S, because part of the rent-seeking expenses is not wasteful but mere transfers. Waste is rather depicted by cS, that is, total expenses multiplied by the transaction costs that arise for rent-seeking expenses. Total waste is therefore given by

$$cS = \frac{c(n - 1)}{n - (1 - c)R'}R. \tag{2''}$$

As can be shown by differentiation, an increase of the transfer cost c raises waste only if $R' < n$, and lowers waste otherwise. Large transaction costs of rent-seeking reduce the possibilities for inducing politicians to create rents, that is, S decreases with c. This, in turn, helps in avoiding rent-seeking activities and the resulting waste. The conclusions with respect to the total welfare losses are even stronger. These consist not only of waste (cS) but also the classical Harberger triangle. Since the latter is positively dependent on the rent (R) and this strictly decreases with the transaction costs (c), there exists a negative impact of the transaction costs on the allocative welfare losses. This implies that it becomes even more likely that high transaction costs of rent-seeking are beneficial to the economy.

The argument that lobbies that embrace larger segments of society are less detrimental to welfare can be proven with the help of the formal model. Lobbies may be able to internalize the negative externalities that rent-seeking by one party imposes on other parties. For example, those participating in a public tender impose a negative externality on their competitors by paying bribes, but a joint lobby would take this effect into account. Another example of negative externalities relates to industrial groups that lobby for restrictions on market entry on behalf of their members, inducing higher prices for their products. These impose negative externalities on those who buy their product. In case a larger lobby is formed, which also includes industrial sectors that purchase the product, the negative externality will partly be taken into account. Let us assume that the total losses imposed on others as a result of the rent are proportional to the size of the rent: qR. These losses consist of welfare losses and transfers, for example from consumers' to producers' rent or from one producer who pays increased prices for input factors to those who artificially increased prices with the help of rent-seeking. Owing to the welfare losses, q should be assumed to be greater than 1. Let t be the extent to which the externality is internalized by a lobby. The fraction $(1 - t)$ of the negative externality is carried by parties not represented by the lobby. While the expected gain from rent-seeking for the individual firm has been determined to be $E(p_iR - x_i)$, that for the organized lobby turns out to be $E(p_iR(1 - qt) - x_i)$. Introducing this modification into the basic model, the Cournot–Nash equilibrium can be shown to yield the following optimal level of rent-seeking:

$$x = \frac{n-1}{n^2} R(1 - qt).$$

Total expenses (S) for rent-seeking then sum up to

$$S = nx = \frac{n-1}{n} R(1 - qt). \qquad (2''')$$

The more lobbies are able to internalize the negative externality, that is, the larger t, the lower the resulting total expenses for rent-seeking. Assuming that the rent is positively dependent on total expenses for rent-seeking, like in equation (3), a lower rent will equally result.

6 Making corrupt deals: contracting in the shadow of the law

6.1. Introduction

Hindustan Times, New Delhi, October 1985,
Astrological Section, Virgo:
All round improvement but not without strings, which you must be able to recognize and accept ... If paying a bribe to anyone, see that the job is done.[1]

How can we make corruption as arduous as possible? How can we increase the transaction costs of corrupt deals? These questions are at the core of this chapter, which will employ new institutional economic thinking for an analysis of the microeconomic determinants of corrupt transactions. In spite of a growing interest in the economics of corruption, the tools of New Institutional Economics have hardly been applied to this topic. Noteworthy early exceptions are Husted (1994), Lambsdorff (1999), Lambsdorff *et al.* (2004), della Porta and Vanucci (1999), Vanucci (2000), and Rose-Ackerman (1999: 91–110).

This chapter argues that an institutional viewpoint can enrich our understanding of corrupt agreements. Central to the analysis are transaction costs, including the costs of searching for partners, determining contract conditions, and enforcing contract terms. Transaction costs of corrupt agreements differ from those of legal deals, because there is a need for camouflage and because partners in such a deal end up with potentially damaging information about each other. For these reasons, corrupt agreements are more likely to employ middlemen or come about as a by-product of legal exchange and social structures.

A related version of this chapter was originally published in *Journal of Economic Behavior and Organization*, 2002, Vol. 48 (3), 221–41.

[1] Cited from Oldenburg (1987: 508).

Two different forms of corruption should be distinguished: *market corruption* and *parochial corruption* (Husted 1994; Scott 1972). Market corruption is defined as a competitive type of corruption with a high degree of transparency. As far as this type of corruption is concerned, the identity of the partner in a corrupt exchange is irrelevant. Such market relationships can indeed occur, particularly in the case of petty corruption, for example, the issuance of driver's licenses and permits for village market stalls, or the acquisition of seats or freight space on railway cars (Husted 1994: 20). Also illustrative of the concept of market corruption is a multitude of "coyotes," who wait outside the department of motor vehicles in Mexico to expedite the processing of a driver's license, along with the payment of speed money (Husted 1994: 21). A similar case is reported from El Salvador, where "tramitadores" can be hired to deal with cumbersome bureaucracies and pay "additional fees" when required.[2] Those demanding illegal services are confronted with a transparent price system and the opportunity to choose from different suppliers for the required service.

Parochial corruption, on the other hand, is defined as a corrupt transaction with few potential contractors, and, thus, restricted competition. Owing to limited entry and exit, the identity of partners can matter. Crucial to the difference between these two types of corruption are transaction costs. As market opportunities are investigated, typically, the total transaction costs arising as a result of exchanging goods or services increase with the total number of potential contractors sought. This increase results from the efforts required to search for potential contractors and evaluate the quality and adequacy of each of their products as well as their individual capacity and willingness to comply with corrupt contracts. The number of contractors sought can be assumed to be optimal, once the marginal transaction costs of searching for another partner are equal to the expected gains resulting from a potentially better deal with another competitor. Taking this into account, it becomes evident that the higher the (marginal) transaction costs the fewer potential partners are sought.

[2] See taz, die Tageszeitung, Berlin, Germany, July 12, 1999: "Die diskrete Kunst der Korruption. Warum 'tramitadores' ewig leben". Other cases of market corruption are reported by Rose-Ackerman (1999: 15–16).

In reality, transaction costs of corruption are high, making parochial corruption the dominant form of corruption. Examples of *market corruption* must then be regarded as exceptions (Cartier-Bresson 1997). They require that prosecuting authorities either abstain from investigation, reflecting public approval, or at least assume a broadly permissive attitude toward corruption. Alternatively, the market may already have developed certain institutional mechanisms that help in lowering transaction costs, as in the case of the "coyotes," and the "tramitadores." The German Federal Bureau of Criminal Investigations reports that in only 20 percent of revealed cases of corruption the relationship was shorter than one month. This compares with 54 percent of cases where the contact between briber and bribee had lasted longer than three years (Bundeskriminalamt 2004: 37).

This chapter argues that in most cases corrupt agreements are characterized by a high degree of secrecy, little transparency, and limited participation. Various costs arise concerning the exchange of corrupt services. For example, bureaucrats may expend resources so as to have sufficient discretion for illegal activities. But such types of costs should rather be regarded as production costs. Since they do not arise as a matter of exchange, they will not be investigated further here. Similarly, this chapter will not elaborate on aspects of cooperation between suppliers of corrupt services. Such cooperation can at times be necessary, particularly to bypass controls and overcome barriers imposed as a result of a division of responsibilities.

Transaction costs of a corrupt agreement can be categorized according to the sequence in which they arise. Usually, the exchange of services and the returns do not take place simultaneously. As resources are usually invested into the relationship before the collection of the return, there are three stages where transaction costs can arise. First, in order to initiate a contract, information with respect to the required service and the appropriate partner must be gathered and contracts must be specified. This will be dealt with further in Section 6.2. Second, since the proceeds cannot be collected at the moment when resources are committed, strategies must be developed to enforce contracts and avoid opportunism. Section 6.3 investigates this. Third, after finalizing the exchange, corrupt agreements differ from legal contracts, because the partners have placed themselves at the mercy of each other. Both end up in possession of information that can potentially be damaging for the counterpart; their relationship is not terminated with the exchange of service and return. This situation will be studied in Section 6.4. Section 6.5 concludes and indicates avenues for future research.

Theoretical considerations introduced here are illustrated further by the help of case studies. Because the evidence from academic papers is still scarce, these are partly taken from the international media. As newspapers tend to scandalize more than report trustworthy details, several thousand articles from various press archives had to be screened over a period of four years to arrive at the few case studies that provided sufficient details to allow for theoretical conclusions. Reports were cross-checked against reports from other newspapers, and whenever cases did not end in convictions, it is made clear that these represent allegations.

6.2. Contract initiation

Seeking the partner

Seeking a corrupt service requires information with respect to the capability of the potential partner to actually provide the required service. Corruption provides opportunities for fraudulent offers. For example, avoiding the payment of speeding tickets by offering bribes often results in people pretending to be policemen, seeking bribes without having the authority to give speeding tickets. Such cases are numerous in many less-developed countries.

In the event that a partner with the capacity to provide the service is found, it must be discovered whether she is also willing to do so and whether her criminal capabilities are sufficient to provide the requested service in return for a favor. Direct inquiry can be dangerous, since potential counterparts who are not inclined to corruption may prefer to denounce the request. Take the example of an employee at a police station in Germany who was in charge of processing speeding tickets and was alleged to have offered to suppress such tickets in exchange for a bribe. The deal was offered to drivers via middlemen. Two drivers reported the case to the prosecutor's office, which arrested a middleman when he attempted to pocket the bribe.[3]

[3] See *Kölnische Rundschau*, January 20, 1998: "Im Kreishaus Anzeigen entwendet und an die Temposünder verkauft".

Endeavors by prosecuting authorities or internal audit controls may further threaten those who are seeking corrupt partners. Such institutions may employ an "Agent Provocateur," someone who only pretends to offer a bribe, but is in fact seeking to compromise the counterpart. This appears to be a common practice of the FBI.[4]

Public advertisement cannot be used as a means to announce the sale of corrupt services. Those seeking or spreading such pieces of information cannot rely on regular sources such as the media or written advertising material. Information on corrupt opportunities is not exchanged in the setting of a transparent market where comparisons between potential partners can easily be made. Instead, other means for exchanging information must be sought: first, by attempting some public distribution of the relevant information in a disguised form; second, by organizing "advertisement" via middlemen; or, finally, by providing the information only to well-acquainted business partners.

Of course, in the case of a public distribution of information, it is evident that the likelihood of detection is drastically increased (Alam 1990: 90; Borner and Schwyzer 1999: 32; Rose-Ackerman 1998: 97). One way of overcoming this problem is to spread the information in a disguised form, for example, via rumors about the potential corruptibility of oneself. Such rumors should be understood by potential partners as an offer. A lavish lifestyle can be one way to spread such rumors, since living beyond the official sources of income is an apparent hint for one's corruptibility (della Porta and Vanucci 1999: 56–9). Advertising corrupt services by spreading rumors is also described by Heymann (1995: 51), formerly the deputy attorney general of the United States. But he stresses that such rumors can also be interpreted as worthwhile hints of actual corruption for prosecuting authorities.

Another means of spreading information is to engage a broker, who may not have to fear sanctions for publicly advertising the corrupt service.[5] She then serves as a front for those who offer their

[4] See *Chicago Sun*, December 9, 1997: "Ald. Frias Plans to Argue Entrapment at Bribe Trial"; December 12, 1997: "Tape Shows Frias Approved Payoff," and the *Associated Press*, July 30, 1998: "Securities Lawyer Convicted of Wire Fraud and Bribery."

[5] This is particularly the case if the expected penalty for middlemen is relatively low. Either their activity may not be the subject of legal sanctions in the first place or they may be more mobile so as to escape prosecution.

services. This seems to be the case with operations of Nigeria's state oil company. Each contract specified a "commission" to be paid to a specific beneficiary. Traders had noted that sometimes the beneficiary was a well-known Nigerian, and at other times was a completely unknown person who, traders believed, was fronting for someone else.[6] The advantage of making use of such a front is obvious – while the actual supplier of corrupt services cannot be identified, the service can be offered to a larger audience.

Even in cases where the distribution of information on corrupt services cannot be organized, this does not spell the end for corruption. Corrupt opportunities can still be encountered at random. The most obvious opportunities arise between business partners with established legal relationships (Rose-Ackerman 1999: 12). As their relationship deepens, they may encounter the opportunity to collude at the expense of their firms or departments (Wintrobe and Breton 1986). In this case, corruption emerges as already existing relationships deteriorate into illegal relationships. To be precise, it is not corruption that brings people together in the first place. The exchange turns out to be parochial, excluding those without existing legal ties. Legality and corruption cease to be two opposing forms of relationships. Instead, a legal relationship represents a vehicle for establishing a corrupt relationship and the latter is parasitically linked to the former.

Determining contract conditions

Offering a bribe is a risky undertaking, because a public official might refuse either on moral grounds or simply because of insufficient criminal capacity. But even those who are potentially corrupt can at times prefer to denounce their counterpart in order to win public approval for their alleged dislike of corruption. Such cases can occur, particularly, if the bribe offered is worth less than the reputational gains from denunciation (della Porta and Vanucci 1999: 195). This raises concern about how to determine the appropriate value of a bribe. The risk of denunciation must be weighed against the risk of paying more than necessary for the requested service.

[6] See *Washington Post*, June 9, 1998: "Corruption Flourished in Abacha's Regime – Leader Linked to Broad Plunder."

Negotiating a corrupt agreement also requires consent with respect to the type of return. Instead of monetary inducements, partners may prefer gifts or favors whose connection with corrupt services may be difficult to detect for the prosecution authorities. The public may perceive such favors to be less of a bribe than a direct monetary payment. Invitations to a lavish dinner, as in Japan, may appear to be a regular means of exchange and not an illegitimate inducement. Paying for the tuition fees of the daughter of a foreign politician may be seen as a way to promote cultural exchange rather than outright bribery. But the disadvantages of in-kind exchanges rest with the difficulty of matching mutual desires and the indivisibility of the media of exchange – standard arguments that brought about the evolution of money.

The risks involved in a corrupt deal may be amplified if the conditions of a corrupt deal are not sufficiently specified at the beginning. Partners in a corrupt transaction may avoid precision as to the quid pro quo of their exchange. The partners' advantage of less precision is to better excuse illegal behavior, for example, by suggesting that their deal is nothing else but an exchange of gifts between friends. On p. 156 an example is given where insufficient specification of contract conditions lead to dispute and denunciation afterwards.

Partners may also conceal payments. Substituting a bribe for a loan can provide a legal appearance to a payment. The actual bribe is then hidden in the lack of repayment or in favorable conditions associated with it. A bribe can also be concealed by burying it in a different transaction, for example, the exchange of a commodity at a price above or below its market value. A case study at hand relates to a Russian finance minister and three of his employees who were suspected of having obtained a royalty for their book on the history of privatization in Russia. The excessive magnitude of the payment was seen in connection with the preferential treatment the publisher received from the ministry during the privatization process.[7] In Miami, it was alleged that employees of the port authority illegitimately used public resources to provide funding to a political

[7] See *Die Welt*, November 17, 1997: "Jelzin hält trotz Affäre an Tschubais fest;" *Los Angeles Times*, November 16, 1997: "2 More Yeltsin Aides Fired in Bribery Scandal;" Der Spiegel, 48/1997, "Der letzte Fehler;" and *The New York Times*, November 23, 1998: "Gore Rejected C.I.A. Evidence of Russian Corruption."

party. Almost US$200,000 were paid to the "Democratic National Committee" by a private firm who, in exchange, was not charged for the use of the port's cranes.[8] Instead of making outright monetary payments, the Dutch telecommunications company KPN incurred a financial risk to reciprocate a favor in 1996. In exchange for being sold a 17 percent stake of Telkomsel, an Indonesian state-owned telecommunications concern, the Dutch firm provided a free put option to Mr. Djody, a friend of (and presumably a broker for) the Suharto family. KPN guaranteed a US$91 million bank loan for Mr. Djody to purchase another 5 percent share of Telkomsel and provided him with the option to return either the loan or the shares in 2001.[9]

Disguising the nature of the return is instrumental in a corrupt deal but it goes along with transaction costs. The last case illustrates this. The market value of the put option is roughly US$30 million. Usually, exchanging such an option makes sense if the recipient values it higher than the issuer. These differences in valuation can occur if the issuer can hedge the risk by another open position, or because asymmetric information puts him at an advantage in evaluating a firm's true value. Neither of these arguments fits the above case. Since exchanging the option, valued by itself, may not have been beneficial to the partners, it represents a cost that is related to the disguise of the corrupt nature of the arrangement: the Indonesian side may have preferred a simple, say, US$15 million bribe while the Dutch valued the risks associated with the option much higher.

Linking the return of a favor to a different (legal) transaction also has further disadvantages. While the legal transaction will be enforceable by courts, this may not be the case for the corrupt side of the deal. This aspect carries over to opportunism and contract enforcement, to be investigated in the next section.

[8] See Reuters, June 4, 1998: "ex-Miami Port Chief Charged with Embezzling." It was later ruled, however, that the revenues from the ports accrued to a private firm, which paid a fixed franchise fee to the county, so that the defendants were acquitted of misusing public funds; Reuters, June 7 1999: "Defendants Cleared in Miami Port Corruption Trial."

[9] See *Wall Street Journal*, March 31, 1999: "KPN Arranged Loan to Gain Telecom Stake." A more detailed description was presented by the Dutch television station KRO and a political magazine named *Netwerk*, March 28, 1999 and June 23, 1999. KPN largely admitted the charges.

6.3. Contract enforcement

Formal models of corrupt behavior usually assume that contracts can be enforced, requiring no further costs. This assumption appears realistic only in the rare case of market corruption, where a face-to-face exchange of bribes and favors renders opportunism unlikely. Usually, the corrupt deal entails the necessity of one partner in the transaction providing the service before the return is obtained – or obtaining the return before the service is delivered. This is the rule in larger transactions, where the corrupt service is too complex to be provided at once. A corrupt service may require the manipulation of tendering procedures or steady lobbying for certain decisions – actions that take place over a fairly long period of time. Such cases give one partner the possibility of reneging on the deal (Rose-Ackerman 1999: 17, 98). After obtaining the corrupt service, she may refuse to provide the return, or after obtaining a bribe, she may defect on the delivery of the negotiated service (Boycko *et al.*, 1995). She may also raise the price of the service later, or simply demand another payment. Alternatively, she may sell secrets about competitors' bids in a public tender to many competitors at the same time, each time invalidating the previously sold information.

The World Bank (1997: 34) cites a businessman accordingly: "there are two kinds of corruption. The first is one where you pay the regular price and you get what you want. The second is one where you pay what you have agreed to pay and you go home and lie awake every night worrying whether you will get it or if somebody is going to blackmail you instead." This brings forward the necessity of investigating potential mechanisms to secure corrupt agreements, that is, to guarantee the delivery of what was negotiated. A variety of such mechanisms and their value for corrupt agreements will be discussed in the following subsections.

Legal enforcement

The first question with respect to enforcement is to what extent legal institutions (such as courts) can be engaged to resolve conflicts in corrupt agreements. The first obstacle arises because of the fear of prosecution. Once evidence is provided in civil proceedings it may be used also for criminal investigations. If immunity from prosecution is granted, such concern may not be relevant. Such immunity from prosecution may arise particularly when bribe-takers are foreign public servants, since such cases have in the past not been prosecuted in OECD countries.[10] Further problems arise with the necessity to produce evidence that is needed for legal resolution. Those making corrupt deals may abstain on purpose from the production of such evidence so as to avoid unintended leakage of information. Written contracts, receipts, support by witnesses, and similar instruments of authentication are often "not available."

Yet, even in cases where sufficient evidence can be provided to allow for third-party resolution, legal enforcement of corrupt contracts is usually not possible. In Germany, §138 of the Civil Code, Bürgerliches Gesetzbuch (BGB) declares transactions that conflict with public morals void (German: sittenwidrig). According to current jurisdiction, corrupt agreements are interpreted in this sense, which prohibits legal enforcement of claims resulting from corrupt agreements. §817 (2) BGB denies those involved the right to reclaim their payments (bribes) or favors. Those who operate outside the law cannot claim the law's protection[11] Similar regulation exists in other countries.[12] It is, therefore, commonly acknowledged that corrupt deals are not legally enforceable (Dick 1995: 26; Rose-Ackerman 1999: 92, 96).

However, such regulation can be circumvented by making use of middlemen. The idea would be to pay a "regular commission" to such middlemen who then undertake the "dirty work," that is, the payment of bribes. Payments to such middlemen can be based upon

[10] This situation has changed lately; see Wiehen (1996: 116) and Chapter 7 of this book. However, even though OECD countries made the bribing of foreign officials a legal offence, still no cases of conviction, let alone of prosecution, have been recorded.

[11] There is a noteworthy difference between the usual arguments regarding the lack of legal enforcement and those brought forward here. Lacking possibilities for legal enforcement commonly result from excessive complexity of contracts and the impossibility of measuring the relevant item, leading to nonverifiability of contractual specifications (Hart 1987: 168; 1991). In the case of corruption, it is the explicit decision of the judiciary not to enforce such contracts. The idea behind this is that improper contractual relations should not be supported by legal enforceability. In this context, courts take it consciously into account that the proceeds of an improper contractual relation are randomly divided between the corrupt partners (Fikentscher 1987: 89).

[12] Influence peddling for public contracts and the resulting claims by such lobbyists are considered void under French law (Jarvin 1986: 31).

written contracts and appear to be legal. Such a middleman can pay out bribes and arrange deals, and after providing the corrupt service she can claim the promised return or, if rejected, threaten to use legal recourse. Alternatively, such a middleman can work as an *intervening purchaser*, acquiring contracts for herself by means of bribery and passing them on to her own clientele. In such a case, contracts can easily prespecify prices and conditions between the firm and the middleman, containing a compensation for the required bribe payments.[13]

In the past, such arrangements often failed. First, the risk of contract enforcement is merely shifted from the private firm and the service provider to the relationship between the middleman and the service provider. The middleman bears the risk that after payment the corrupt service may not be delivered. Enforceability, therefore, remains a problem. Second, the contract between the firm and the middleman is not necessarily legally enforceable: if it is apparent that the commission to the broker was mainly for the payment of bribes, the contract may not be enforced by courts.

For example, in Germany, a supplier of brewery equipment was sued by a British broker for the payment of commission for arranging contracts with a Nigerian local government. The claimant declared she had arranged the payments of bribes totaling DM300,000. The claim was rejected by the German High Court (Bundesgerichtshof) in 1985, since the contract violated §138 of the Civil Code. It was argued that the main job of the broker was the arrangement of bribe payments with local public servants and that payment for this service was the basis of the commission (Fikentscher 1987: 86). A similar decision was made by the Arbitration Council of the International Chamber of Commerce (ICC) in 1982, case 3916 (Jarvin 1986: 31). An Iranian broker arranged various contracts between Iranian authorities and a Greek firm with a written agreement that he would receive at least 2 percent of the total value of the contracts. After the Iranian revolution put an end to this business deal, the Greek firm still owed some commissions and refused payment. The Iranian broker brought the case to the Arbitration Council. The arbitrator

[13] See della Porta and Vanucci (1999: 156–65) and the *Wall Street Journal*, September 29, 1995: "Greasing Wheels – How U.S. Concerns Compete in Countries Where Bribes Flourish". Reselling of contracts and subcontracting in public procurement, is therefore, often prohibited. In Singapore, private firms that engage in such deals face a five-year ban on public contracts.

concluded that the claimant's activity was primarily the "influencing" of public officials. This was sufficient to declare the contract void and reject the claim by the Iranian broker.

Based on such court decisions, lately, many private firms have refused to pay commissions that they owed to middlemen, claiming a violation of moral codes of conduct – after having received the promised service (Knapp 1986: 999). As a result, middlemen are unlikely to make upfront bribe payments and usually request their commission simultaneously with making illegal payments. The companies are then still faced with the problems of enforceability, and the inclusion of middlemen may not contribute to the solution of this problem.

Hostages

Lacking legal ways of enforcing a corrupt agreement, partners must seek private alternatives, (Klein 1996; Klein *et al.*, 1978: 303; Williamson 1985: 163–205). Contracts must be written in a manner that guarantees cooperative behavior at all stages of contract fulfillment, that is, contracts must be *self-enforcing*. This is usually achieved by credibly threatening premature contract cancellation in case the partner does not fulfill her part of the bargain. Alongside such retaliatory action, partners must weigh whether their costs, for example, in the form of lost opportunities for future profits, will be higher than the possible gains from opportunistic behavior.

Usually, corrupt agreements are not self-enforcing in and of themselves. Special mechanisms are required to achieve their enforcement. One potential instrument is the use of "hostages" (Wiggins 1991: 640; Williamson 1983). Much like the concept of collateral, this is a valuable asset given by someone who might profit from opportunism to those on the other side of the contractual agreement, who are in a position to be harmed by opportunistic behavior. In case of nondelivery of the proposed service, keeping the hostage is an obvious threat. With respect to corrupt agreements, such a hostage can be provided in the form of a down payment. Public servants who fear that a promised bribe might not be paid after service delivery will demand parts of the bribe in advance (Moody-Stuart 1994: 15). Such payments must be well balanced, since excessive amounts may provoke opportunism from the other side. Service delivery and payment schemes must be synchronized in such a way that the risks and costs of premature contract cancellation are reduced to a minimum (Rose-Ackerman 1999: 35).

While such payment schemes can be found in any kind of contractual relationship, in the special case of corrupt agreements another option can be observed: the corrupt agreement can be linked to a legal agreement in such a way that the latter provides safeguards against opportunism in the former. Resources owned by someone else (e.g. the state in the case of public procurement) can be used to serve as an enforcement device for corrupt contracts. This can be illustrated by the following case study. Submarines manufactured by the Howaldtswerke Deutsche Werft AG (HDW) were ordered by the Persian government in 1978. The total value exceeded DM1 billion, of which the Shah claimed a commission of DM109 million for himself. The deal was arranged by letting the Persian government make an advance payment of DM231 million to HDW from which the requested commission could be passed on to the Shah's Swiss bank account.[14]

The idea in this case was to allocate third-party funds, that is, those of the Persian government, to the enforcement of the corrupt agreement. If the Shah were to renege on the contract, HDW could threaten to keep the down payment. Similarly, there was no risk on the Shah's side since he was paid in advance. The whole risk of contract enforcement was borne by someone not at all profiting from the corrupt agreement: the Persian government, which might have lost its outlay in the event of conflict. While this strategy appears to be workable in general, it was not successful in this case. The Iranian revolution put an end to the Shah regime, and the new leaders canceled the above-mentioned purchase of the submarines, claiming back the deposit. HDW rejected the claim, arguing that the down payment had already been used for necessary investments. In 1991, the case was brought to the arbitration council of the ICC in Paris. It was decided that only expenses directly related to the deal could be kept by the HDW, but the commission to the Shah could not be considered such an expense. The commission had to be paid back to the Persian government. And, of course, HDW could not reclaim the money from the Shah. In case third parties whose assets were misused as enforcement devices by corrupt partners are able to reclaim their

[14] See *Focus*, 1995, Germany, Vol. 44: 65.

property, the risk associated with nonenforceable contracts remains with the corrupt partners.

Reputation

Another potential enforcement device for corrupt agreements is to establish a reputation (Kreps 1990; Kreps and Wilson 1982; Rose-Ackerman 1999: 99–102; Williamson 1985: 260 and 375–7). If advantage was not taken of opportunistic self-enrichment in the past, this may signal a preference for honesty over profit to third parties. Past actions in this case reveal an individual moral attitude – and can certainly turn out to be profitable in the long run.

Corrupt public servants who behaved opportunistically in the past may risk developing a bad reputation (Bardhan 1997: 1324). Based on past experience, potential partners may reject future collaboration. Maintaining a good reputation turns out to be profitable, along the lines of a popular joke: "I am a man of principle. Once bought, I stay bought."[15] Ironically, being corrupt does not imply being dishonest. Establishing a reputation for being honest and virtuous is not alien to corrupt partners (Husted 1994: 24). On the contrary, disputes regarding legal agreements can be settled through recourse to the law and depend less on the mutual trust than do corrupt agreements.

Dishonesty, broadly defined, is sometimes seen to cause corruption. It induces public servants to pocket a bribe instead of serving the public. But any argument along this line must better define the moral attitudes involved. Preference for honesty can have a rather ambiguous effect on corruption. It may restrict the inclination to become involved in corruption, but it can also help in enforcing corrupt contracts. A negative attitude toward opportunism and a positive attitude toward reciprocity could promote corruption more than it helps in inhibiting it. In a survey of the general public in Bulgaria, it was asked in 1998, "in case someone has successfully used his contacts, do you think that he/she would feel obliged to give a present to the person that helped him?" Sixty percent of the respondents approved of this proposition (Center for the Study of

[15] This joke among politicians in the United States has been reproduced in Drew (1983: 97).

Democracy 1998). Feeling obliged under such circumstances is certainly an aid in enforcing corrupt agreements.

A reputation does not become public knowledge on its own. It requires some mechanism to process and deliver the respective pieces of information. As in legal markets, suppliers of corrupt services must find ways to advertise their honesty. But in contrast to legal markets, the information should be withheld from prosecutors, which prohibits their public delivery. Establishing a good reputation is particularly an option for middlemen, emphasizing again this institutional device for corrupt agreements. Unlike the actual supplier of a corrupt service, a broker may be in a position to publicly disclose her past record and establish a reputation for dealing honestly. Reneging on an agreement would result in disreputable news about the broker, preventing such a behavior in the first place. This provides a clear advantage for middlemen in arranging a corrupt agreement as opposed to the actual partners. A middleman can thus act as a guarantor of a corrupt deal, someone who links up the parties involved (della Porta and Vanucci 1999: 46). Oldenburg (1987: 522) provides an example of middlemen who offered to use their connections at the land consolidation department in India on behalf of their clients. They sometimes provided a "money-back" guarantee to farmers, who were seeking nothing but fair treatment at the department. This announcement may not be so astonishing, but it is certainly surprising that farmers believed it. According to della Porta and Vanucci (1999: 61), the importance of one's reputation has been stressed by a broker for corrupt transactions: "Above all, if you want to have a minimum of credit as a corrupter, it is necessary to honor commitments and be as precise as a Swiss watch. If 10 million must be paid at 10 o'clock on the 10th of November you have to be there five minutes early with not a sixpence less than the sum agreed."

Repetition

There are economies of scale in setting up corrupt relationships. As new opportunities for corruption arise, it is preferable to deal with old partners. One reason for this is that the expectation of future deals provides a leverage to avoid current malfeasance. Threatening to reject cooperation in succeeding deals can be sufficient to serve as a deterrent against opportunism in current transactions. Control over future deals can be used to retaliate.

That repetitive games can result in cooperation has already been shown in the seminal contribution by Axelrod (1984). An application to corruption within a principal–agent framework has been undertaken by Pechlivanos (1998; 2004).[16] He investigates the impact of repetitive collusive opportunities on agents' behavior and argues that collusion is sustainable only when nonconforming behavior can be punished by way of canceling future business. The following case study illustrates the function of repetition as an enforcement device. Allegedly, the German firm Avia obtained oil from Saudi Arabia at a price below market prices and paid US$378,000 to a German and a Lebanese agent every two weeks. The agents "arranged" the contract with Saudi-Arabian public servants. The profitability of this arrangement secured the loyalty of all partners. When serious disputes arose about how to share the proceeds, they were settled, owing to the fear that these might threaten future business.[17]

The threat of losing future business is not only valid for future corrupt agreements but also for succeeding legal ones. Partners in a legal relationship can use their already existing ties as an enforcement mechanism for the corrupt side-contract. Opportunistic behavior within the corrupt agreement can now be deterred by threatening cancellation of the legal market relationship. This threat may not be effective, given strong competition in the legal market: other competitors can be sought, and cancellation of market exchange would not necessarily invoke huge and irrecoverable losses. But when competition is limited, and the legal relationship is based on trust between partners, threats to end a longstanding exchange impose serious damage on both sides. Such threats, which are typically used for the smooth functioning of legal agreements, can also be misused for securing a corrupt agreement. This consideration works in favor of the argument that corrupt deals can be a by-product of legal agreements.

[16] In contrast to Pechlivanos (1998; 2004) most principal–agent models neglect the existence of transaction costs, for example, Kofman and Lawaree (1996: 390), Laffont and Tirole (1993: 478), and Olsen and Torsvik (1998: 433).

[17] See *Der Spiegel*, 1984, Germany, Vol. 18: 79. A related case study from Italy is provided by della Porta and Vanucci (1999: 129–31).

Also with regard to government regulation, corruption may emerge as a by-product. Regulation often requires repeated control, for example, monitoring the fulfillment of pollution requirements, probation orders, or entitlements to subsidies. Regular contacts can help lower the transaction costs for arranging corrupt agreements, rendering some public servants particularly apt to take bribes. For example, Borner and Schwyzer (1999) argue that policemen can lower the transaction costs of corrupt agreements with criminals by regularly controlling the activities of such people.

Vertical integration

Another way of securing corrupt contracts can be designed by common ownership (Klein *et al.*, 1978; Wiggins 1991: 607; Williamson 1985). This is a standard instrument to provide incentives to comply with the original terms of a contract. Those who deliver and those who receive services or goods integrate vertically to form a new company under common ownership and control. Raising the profit of the firm is now in the self-interest of each partner.

This type of arrangement can also be used for corrupt agreements. A political decision, for example, the construction of an infrastructure project, can be "bought" by founding a joint-venture and giving free shares to the respective politicians. Or a public servant may be given an option to buy shares of the joint-venture. The advantage of this kind of arrangement is obvious: the recipient of the favor obtains some legal documentation of her property and is simultaneously provided with an incentive to comply with the terms of the contract. A failure to deliver the corrupt service will result in worthless shares. The actual bribe payment then takes place in the form of entitlements with respect to future profits of the joint-venture.

Allegedly, former President Suharto of Indonesia and many of his friends and relatives possess shares in a variety of joint-ventures in Indonesia's airline, power utility, and oil and gas industries. Reportedly, these shares were not obtained in exchange for cash but rather in return for government licenses and contracts.[18] Another case from Indonesia is similar to the one reported on p. 143. The US

[18] See the *Financial Times*, November 2, 1998: "Indonesia: Companies Try to Buy Suharto Stakes."

mining company, Freeport, found large deposits of copper, silver, and gold in Irian Jaya, Indonesia. In 1991, Freeport claimed more time and area for exploration. In exchange, the Indonesian government required that Freeport should incorporate its local subsidiary in Indonesia and sell a 10 percent stake of this subsidiary to a "local interest." Only one bid was provided – by Indonesia's Bakrie Group, run by a friend of the minister of mines and energy. The shares were bought via a Virgin Islands company, and it was alleged that high-ranking politicians had a stake in this company.[19] Politicians with such a stake have an incentive to provide the concessions for exploration to Freeport and are unlikely to behave opportunistically.

Another possibility to integrate vertically is by giving hierarchical control rights to the provider of corrupt services. Refusal to provide the promised payment becomes improbable because of its direct and unpleasant impact on the future cooperation with somebody holding control rights. One way of doing this can be to award a public servant with a position on a firm's board (Jagannathan 1986).

Social embeddedness

Institutions can be designed so as to safeguard against opportunism and help in enforcing contracts. In this case, social relationships are influenced by individualistic optimization and the resulting desire to economize on transaction costs. But quite often the causality can be reverse: corrupt relationships can be set up with partners with whom some kind of organizational link already exists. For example, someone seeking a corrupt partner may prefer to strike a corrupt deal with a fellow board member, since opportunism becomes more unlikely the more the partners are obligated to any type of future cooperation. Similarly, politicians can easily lobby for contracts to be awarded to companies in which they already have a stake themselves. This results in

[19] See *MSNBC*, November 15, 1998: "The Price for a Pot of Gold;" the *Washington Post*, November 30, 1998: "Mining Company Fills a Hole;" and the *Wall Street Journal*, September 30, 1998: "Hand in Glove. How Suharto's Circle and a Mining Firm Did So Well Together." It is not apparent at first sight that a favor was provided by Freeport to the Indonesian side. But, it was argued that the price for the shares was by far too low, and that the Bakrie Group hardly incurred a financial risk because a US$173 million bank loan to finance the US$212.5 million purchase was guaranteed by Freeport.

corrupt agreements emerging as a by-product of already existing legal relationships. Hierarchical relationships and existing ownership structures serve as a safeguard against opportunism.

Preexisting social relationships can lay the foundation stone for economic exchange by providing the required safeguards against opportunism. Economic exchange is thus facilitated by being embedded in a social structure (Granovetter 1992). For members of a social structure, the advantages to be gained in the long run from benefiting another member may regularly outweigh the motivation to behave opportunistically or to denounce another member. Such social structures can easily be used to facilitate the sealing of a corrupt contract (Cartier-Bresson 1997: 163; Rose-Ackerman 1999: 98). A large variety of potential social structures come into question, for example, relationships such as kinship or belonging to the same ethnic or cultural group. Other types of social relationships include secret societies or criminal organizations, particularly when they establish rules of reciprocity (Anderson 1995: 42–7; Gambetta 1998: 59; Schrag and Scotchmer 1997). Their capability to use violence against people can provide them with a prime position to prevent opportunism. In case they are perceived to settle disputes impartially, they can also offer their service as middlemen to third parties (della Porta and Vanucci 1999: 221–31). Political parties can also assume the role of a guarantor of corrupt agreements (della Porta and Vanucci 1999: 103–9, 122–3). Social structures may also be helpful in spreading information on corrupt opportunities. Group members can be entrusted with delicate pieces of information that should not be spread outside the group. In this respect, they are preferred over markets, where anonymous recipients of information may deliberately cooperate with law-enforcement authorities.

6.4. The aftermath

"I took my first bribe in my second term on the city commission ... It's a terrible thing, like cheating on your wife for the first time."[20]

[20] This impression was voiced by a former mayor of Miami Beach, who accepted a monthly bribe of US$1000 from a banker and was sentenced in 1992 to seventeen months imprisonment for tax evasion and taking bribes; see *USA Today*, April 22, 1998: "Miami's Corruption Endemic, Brazen."

Typically, contracts are assumed to end with the exchange of services and return. Contractual problems, as they are typically discussed, are those associated with securing and arranging the actual exchange. After the fulfillment of mutual claims, it is assumed that there are no further problems associated with a contractual relationship. While this may be true of legal contracts, corrupt agreements may have further repercussions, owing to the fact that each partner has the option of denouncing the corrupt agreement. Both have locked themselves into mutual dependence, and the corrupt agreement has a binding impact upon the partners even after the contract has been fulfilled. Having the means to impose harm on his counterpart, one partner in a corrupt contract can attempt to extort the other by threatening exposure.

In fact, information obtained from people who have themselves been involved in corrupt dealings is quite often an important source of information for prosecuting authorities (Anderson 1995; Rose-Ackerman 1999: 53). The public prosecutor specializing in organized criminal activities in Frankfurt am Main in Germany, W. Schaupensteiner, declared that the major sources of information used by prosecuting authorities: "were often insiders. Their information is usually obtained anonymously. The salient cases in recent years were started by such anonymous tip-offs."[21] Similar experience is reported by G. Colombo, public prosecutor in Milan, Italy, and part of the "Clean Hands" Movement (Colombo 1995).

Denunciation and extortion

Miscellaneous motivations exist for denunciation. We know from a multitude of experimental studies that actors tend to "do bad to those who did them bad." This reaction even takes place if penalizing others is costly to oneself. Penalizing is an action chosen even where it contradicts game theoretic expectations. This type of "negative reciprocity," as this behavior is labeled, may be particularly relevant when conflict arises among those who are in a corrupt relationship.

The largest company in France, Elf Aquitaine, allegedly set up an internal financial network aimed at providing funding for corrupt

[21] See *Frankfurter Neue Presse*, April 14, 1998: "Korruption: Der Appetit kommt beim Essen," own translation.

political purposes. This so-called "Investment Board" consisted of relatives and friends of the chairman of the board. This institution was well established, and succeeded for a while, but the booting out of one member put an end to its operation. The outcast took his revenge and denounced operations of the network.[22] Clearly, some type of conflict can motivate one party to take revenge or to prefer honesty to involvement in illegal transactions.

Apart from collaborators, conflict can also arise with well-informed people who were not part of the corrupt deal. Insiders privy to corrupt agreements may denounce particularly if they need not fear prosecution. This puts them in a prime position to extort hush-money. This appeared to be the case with the Christian Democratic Party in Hesse, Germany. A staff member in the party's office was alleged to have embezzled DM1 million of party funds. But he was given impunity owing to fears that he may denounce the party's illegal hidden accounts, and even some of his debt was paid by the party, raising allegations that these payments represent a form of hush-money.[23] Another case of hush-money was reported from Vietnam, where citizens posing as reporters used a hidden camera to try to extort money from border police whom they filmed taking bribes from drivers in exchange for turning a blind eye on lacking licenses.[24]

As argued on p. 142, corrupt agreements are particularly likely to breed conflict, because the initial conditions of the deal are often insufficiently specified. One case involved allegations against the former Israeli Prime Minister Netanyahu and his wife, who were suspected of accepting free moving and cleaning services. In return, the contractor Yaakov Amedi was allegedly slated to receive a government contract after election. But after Netanyahu was defeated in the election, and Amedi did not get the government contract, he submitted a US$110,000 bill to Netanyahu. Since Netanyahu rejected payment, the case was brought to court and became public.[25] The partners apparently forgot to specify whether the favor was supposed

[22] See *Rheinischer Merkur* November 27, 1997: "Schmutzige Geschäfte."
[23] See *Süddeutsche Zeitung*, February 4, 2000: "Hessische CDU zahlte angeblich Schweigegeld."
[24] See *South China Morning Post*, July 13, 2000: "Cameras Turned on Corrupt Police."
[25] See the *Associated Press*, March 28, 2000: "Police: Book Bibi!"

to be reciprocated at any rate or only in the case of successful reelection.[26]

Another motive for providing information on illegal transactions may also result from monetary inducements by third parties. While prosecutors may offer crown witnesses a reward in exchange for inside information, private agents may also bid on such information, for example as a means to regain access to markets lost to corrupt competitors (Rose-Ackerman 1999: 56). For the media, it is common practice to pay for tip-offs, enabling them to report on political scandals. Crucial information about corruption by Benazir Bhutto and her husband in Pakistan was obtained from a collaborator in London. Pakistani prosecutors obtained these pieces of information in exchange for a payment of US$1 million.[27] As people can profit from obtaining such information for a variety of reasons, and may be willing to pay a price, a market has emerged for inside information on corrupt agreements.

As pointed out by Rose-Ackerman (1999: 53), penalties imposed on payers and recipients of bribes are often asymmetric. Assume that an entrepreneur can somehow escape prosecution, but the public official bribed could be heavily penalized if detected. Payment of the immune witness or any other nonmonetary benefit gained from taking revenge can easily provide an incentive for denunciation. The immune entrepreneur can use this situation to blackmail the public servant. This raises classical questions as to whether or not extortion works. Commonly, such a threat is ineffective if the blackmailer cannot convincingly assure his victim that she will be safe if she pays. However, if there is some chance that the partners may repeat a corrupt agreement sometime in the future, such threats may turn out to be effective. As long as future business is sufficiently profitable, the entrepreneur does not have an incentive to denounce the public servant. This forces the public servant to seal future corrupt

[26] Interestingly, in the laboratory experiment by Abbink *et al.* (2000) described on p. 55 two different treatments were carried out, one without communication and another one where participants were given the possibility to explicitly negotiate the terms of their (nonbinding) exchange. Trust was partly higher in the second treatment. This suggests that the less explicit a corrupt agreement the more vulnerable it is to opportunism.

[27] See the *Straits Times*, Singapore February 1, 1998: "Paper Trail Points to Illicit Bhutto Hoard."

agreements with the entrepreneur so as to maintain the latter's incentive not to expose him.

Above that, profit-sharing rules will change. While the division of proceeds during the first corrupt agreement was characterized by the risk that a failure to cooperate would result in zero profit for both sides, failure to cooperate now induces the entrepreneur to denounce the public servant. The entrepreneur is thus in a much stronger position. At a court in Bochum, Germany, an employee of the road-construction authority confessed to accepting bribes for contracts relating to marking roads. Beginning in 1987, and lacking business experience, he passed on names of competing firms in a public tender. After this incident, he received an envelope filled with DM2000 from the private firm who obtained the favor. "Suddenly I knew that I had begun to be at his mercy," was the explication given in court and the justification for why he afterwards became entrapped in this corrupt relationship.[28]

Resulting contract design

Anticipating such dependence, public servants may prefer not to start with corrupt agreements in the first place. At the same time, those entrepreneurs who need not fear prosecution – for whatever reason – may appear very generous when it comes to granting a first favor. This phenomenon has also been described as a kind of "feeding," that is, giving favors in order to place the other side at one's mercy. This may include gifts without requesting any return in the beginning. Yet, acceptance of the gift becomes the first step to dependence. Some time afterwards, rejecting a genuinely corrupt agreement suddenly becomes more difficult since declaring acceptance of earlier gifts may be troublesome and give rise to suspicion of more severe misconduct. The resulting relationship has been described by Galeotti and Merlo (1994: 14) in the case of Italian ministers: "once the first transaction has been accomplished, the equilibrium pay-off share of the minister has to decrease as his bargaining power decreases. In other words, acceptance of the first offer brings about fairer gain shares in future transactions as the partners come to be 'hostages' to

[28] See Westdeutsche Allgemeine Zeitung/Cityweb, February 10, 1998: "Mit jedem Gefallen tiefer in den Sumpf."

each other." If the proceeds from corruption do not accrue to public decision-makers but to the department or political party they work for, rotating personnel can be a helpful means to increase bribes. New public servants or politicians can demand higher bribes than their predecessors who live at the mercy of others. Galeotti and Merlo (1994: 14) and della Porta and Vanucci (1999: 43) suggest the presence of this type of organization for the Italian government, where former ministers had been captured by private parties and a change of ministers was intended to increase the payoffs ministers collected for their political parties.

There are two noteworthy effects of the risk of exposure after a corrupt contract has been fulfilled. The first one involves the consequences of increasing penalties. Typically, economists suggest that criminals regard penalties as a form of cost (Becker 1968; Becker and Stigler 1974). Increased penalties are then passed on to the recipients of their services in the form of higher bribes.[29] But this suggestion is not without strings. Particularly, for the case of public servants who live at the mercy of immune entrepreneurs higher penalties for public servants increase their dependence on the entrepreneur. This lowers their bargaining position and thus reduces the level of bribes.

The second side-effect involves problems in enforcing corrupt contracts. Anticipating the risks of exposure can serve as a mechanism to enforce the corrupt agreement. This is illustrated by the following case. In a recent case against India's former Prime Minister, Narasimha Rao, a London-based trader in herbs claimed that, in 1983, Rao had promised him preferential treatment in public procurement in exchange for a bribe of US$100,000. Yet, after the payment was made, the favor was never provided in exchange, which motivated the trader to bring the case to court in 1997.[30] Another

[29] See Rose-Ackerman (1978: 121; 1975: 189); Andvig and Moene (1990); Neugebauer (1978: 15); Mookherjee and Png (1995: 150) and Gupta and Chaudhuri (1997: 333). Rasmusen and Ramseyer (1994) report discrepancies between costs and proceeds of such activities. This is also described as the "Tullock Paradox" (Bardhan 1997: 1326; Rasmusen and Ramseyer 1994; Tullock 1980a).

[30] See the *Straits Times*, Singapore November 9, 1997: "Rao's Reforms Found More Favour with Foreigners" and CNN, November 4, 1997: "Former India Premier's Bribery Case Opens."

related case is provided in the concluding chapter of this book, on p. 226.

In these cases, corrupt deals led to opportunism on one side of the agreement. The case was brought to court. In contrast to legal enforcement as described earlier, the function of the court was not to resolve the conflict – which it may have rejected. Instead, the court was used in order to draw public attention to the partner in the corrupt agreement and expose him – less to prosecution than to public disdain. In this way, one partner made use of the fact that he could easily escape prosecution while his counterpart would suffer from public exposure. Such denunciation can help in countering opportunism and enforcing the initial corrupt agreement. The expected penalties become a means of securing the corrupt deal and stabilizing an illegitimate relationship.

Partners who face little harm or love to take risks may be in a good position to extort their counterpart. A corrupt agreement, therefore, requires that each partner must equally value the losses resulting from denunciation and thus refrain from such actions. Another solution can again be to engage middlemen. One of their obligations may be to remain silent about the identity of their clients, preventing partners from being in a position to blackmail each other afterwards. Such brokers then act as a "fall guy," someone who takes the responsibility or blame for another's dereliction or delinquency, a scapegoat, serving as a firewall to absorb the risks that otherwise may harm their client. Such a person acts as a front and is expected to keep silent with respect to the identity of her client, even after arranging the contract and exchanging service and return. In case the counterpart then denounces the deal afterwards, the broker must be willing, whether paid or forced, to take the full blame.[31] One possibility in this respect is available to managers who employ company members lower down in the hierarchy. Such persons can be assigned the task of arranging corrupt agreements. Their silence can be ensured, for example, by threatening to fire them. Company boards may deliberately encourage employees to pay bribes as long as they can deny any involvement

[31] This proposes the existence of different forms of middlemen as suggested by Oldenburg (1987: 531). Brokers who advertise a corrupt service and build up a reputation of honesty should be sufficiently independent from their client so as to avoid any apparent link. This contrasts to brokers who are closely controlled by their client so as to guarantee their long-term discretion.

afterwards. In Japan, such persons are called "Yogore Yaku," a well-paid lower-level employee with special benefits given to his family in case of conviction. Another means of control is available to clients in possession of compromising information about their middlemen, della Porta and Vanucci (1999: 56).

6.5. Conclusions

The smoke screens and concealment required for corrupt agreements largely increases the costs arising from the transaction. The need to develop private mechanisms for enforcement is another costly factor of a corrupt deal. Furthermore, threats of denunciation lock in partners of corrupt agreements even after contracts have been fulfilled.

In order to economize on transaction costs, various types of brokers can be employed to act as facilitators, guarantors, and "fall guys." Another conclusion of this chapter is that corruption often takes place as a by-product of other relationships. These relationships may be characterized by a market exchange based on trust, hierarchical relationships, or social structures. Such structures help economize costs of searching and spreading information, facilitate the disguise of a favor, support contract enforcement, and avoid extortion or exposure.

There has been debate with respect to the welfare effects of corruption. Some authors suggested that corruption might help to reestablish the efficiency of market exchange where excessive bureaucracy and regulation impedes economic activity. For a review on these issues, see Bardhan (1997: 1322) and Andvig (1991). The existence of large transaction costs adds another dimension to this controversy. It limits entry and exit in corrupt markets, restrains exchange to insiders, converts corrupt deals into long-term relationships, and restricts competition (Rose-Ackerman 1999: 30). Parochial corruption becomes the dominant form of corruption. As a result, corruption can at best replace politically motivated inefficiencies with those inefficiencies associated with the lack of competition.

Corruption is sometimes associated with moral decay. But transaction cost analysis presents a challenge to this viewpoint: individual moral attitudes can actually be a useful instrument for partners in corrupt agreements, since they can serve to guarantee contract fulfillment (Rose-Ackerman 1999: 97–9). Even the common notion that the penalizing of individuals is crucial to contain and fight corruption is challenged by transaction cost analysis. This chapter suggests that under certain conditions penalties imposed on individuals can help secure corrupt agreements and stabilize corrupt relationships. If corruption emerges as a by-product of market exchange, it must be considered to what extent this exchange can be penalized, for example by blacklisting firms, and thus excluding them from future public contracts. Once hierarchical relationships have been used to facilitate corruption the responsibility for malfeasance rests primarily with a firm and less with its employees. This calls for corporate criminal liability as a way of imposing penalties on the offending organizations and not just on the individuals who might be "fall guys" or public servants entrapped into corruption after a minor misconduct.[32]

Since Tullock (1971), transaction costs are commonly assumed to lower welfare. In the case of transaction costs *of corrupt* agreements this argument does not hold (Lambsdorff 2002b; Chapter 5 of this book). Since corruption is detrimental to economic development, associated transaction costs may help contain the level of corruption and therefore operate in favor of increasing public welfare (Gambetta 1998: 59). Our observations indicate methods for fighting corruption by restricting the smooth operation of institutions that are used to facilitate corruption, hence increasing transaction costs of corrupt agreements. The actions of brokers deserve scrutiny in this respect, and discussions should focus on methods to sanction them, for example by imposing penalties, or requiring registration and improved accountability. For example, in Nigeria, crude oil was formerly sold to cronies of the military regime who acted as middlemen. New regulation was designed to cut out middlemen and sell crude oil only to end users who own a refinery or to globally recognized traders.[33]

[32] Arlen (1994) remarks that corporate criminal liability may decrease corporate enforcement expenditures and monitoring systems so that firms avoid the discovery of charges for which they would be held liable. But she points out that these shortcomings can be overcome if corporate penalties take into account whether firms took "due care" of their employees or whether information disclosed by a corporation cannot be used against it in criminal litigation.

[33] See Transparency International (1999: 7) and the *Financial Times*, August 18, 1999: "Oil: Nigeria Awards Licenses."

Research into the causes of corruption may profit from taking the role of transaction costs into account. The role of the judiciary in increasing the value of enforceable contracts is interesting in this connection. Social structures, in their tendency to favor reciprocity at the expense of the general social good, could well contribute to opportunities for corruption. Investigating organizational structures and firms in their propensity to facilitate corruption is another worthwhile avenue for future research. Survey work focusing on such aspects, such as the one presented from Bulgaria, are likely to contribute to the understanding of corruption. And, finally, cross-country investigations into the causes of corruption may discover appropriate instruments to observe to what extent institutional facilitators actually contribute to a country's overall level of corruption.

7 *Exporters' ethics and the art of bribery*

7.1. Introduction

> The Apostle of Allah (peace be upon him) cursed the one who bribes as well as one who takes bribe.
>
> Sunan Abu-Dawud: Book 24, Number 3573

As shown in previous chapters, the willingness to take bribes brings about disadvantages to the corrupt actors themselves. Public servants become useless to those who would like to entrust them with tasks that require integrity. They remain dubious to their corrupt counterparts who would steadily expect to be cheated. Neither task, legal or illegal, may be delegated to them. The willingness to take bribes backfires. I call this the principle of the invisible foot, helping good governance even in the absence of good intentions. But can the power of this principle survive? While the standard invisible hand of competition brings about good markets, does it destroy good governance? Would competition undermine the principle of the invisible foot? I argue that this is not the case. Ethical behavior survives market pressure for various reasons.

In November 1986, Masupha Ephraim Sole was appointed Chief Executive of the Lesotho Highlands Development Authority (LHDA), which was in charge of the Lesotho Water Highlands Project, a system of dams and tunnels that would provide water for South Africa and electricity for Lesotho. A large number of transnational corporations, among them the Canadian company Acres, which provided qualified professional staff to the LHDA, had engaged an intermediary, Mr. Bam. The prosecution was successful in producing evidence that between June 1991 and January 1998 Acres had paid Can $493,061.60 to Mr. Bam, who transferred portions of that sum to Mr. Sole's account. During the same period, Can $180,825.48 were transferred by Acres into the Swiss bank account of Mrs. Bam, who then transferred the money to Mr. Sole's account (Darroch 2004). A contract had been signed that Mr. Bam would receive 3.6 percent of the net value of LHDA's contract with Acres. In exchange, Mr. Sole had failed to follow the correct procedures for the award of the service contract that was signed with Acres.

However, Acres argued that payments to Mr. Bam were legal, that they needed a qualified representative in the occasionally fraught and volatile political climate of Lesotho, and what Mr. Bam might do with the money thereafter was a matter for him. The prosecutors, on the other hand, turned in circumstantial evidence, revealing that Acres was not in need of such representation and that Mr. Bam did not deliver the contracted services (Darroch 2004). The judge, Mr. Justice Mahapela Lehohla, took the view that "it defied common sense that Acres should pay so much money as it did consistently over a period spanning the duration of this practice, without knowing that its money was being used through their agent to pay the Chief Executive of an organization in which they had a direct interest." He also regarded the secrecy of the payments as an indicator that the payments were a vehicle for bribery (Darroch 2004: 21–2). Based on this body of circumstantial evidence, the Mr. Lehohla decided to hold Acres liable for corruption.

This case is representative of many other illegal deals. It shows how corruption involves both those who take and those who give, and sheds a light on the struggle over who bears most of the responsibility for malfeasance. In a seminal contribution, Friedman (1970) argued that the sole responsibility of business is to increase its profits. Consequently, if one looks for the "sinners" in the case of corruption, it would be ethically misleading to point to businesspeople.[1] Alongside the description of human beings as wealth maximizers, economists have tended to regard businesspeople as largely reacting to a given environment, to the market distortions and opportunities for corruption created by the state. Brunner and Meckling (1977: 82–4) explicitly assign responsibility to those who take bribes and shape

[1] While Friedman also tends to accept that laws should be obeyed and that business should not engage in fraud, he does not solve the puzzle that emerges when laws and profits are in conflict, which is commonly the case with corruption. His argument can also be extended to a more unscrupulous position, where legal restrictions should only be obeyed when effective sanctions are in place.

government and administration, while those who give bribes are assumed to take passively the institutional environment as given and react accordingly. In a similar spirit, Becker (1968: 176) writes:

> The approach taken here follows the economists' usual analysis of choice and assumes that a person commits an offense if the expected utility to him exceeds the utility he could get by using his time and other resources at other activities. Some persons become "criminals," therefore, not because their basic motivation differs from that of other persons, but because their benefits and costs differ.

In a world where paying bribes to foreign officials has not been penalized until recently (except in the United States), there should be no substantial costs of bribery, while the benefits might be similar to all businesspeople. A corollary of this ethical viewpoint should be that all businesspeople behave equally, devoted only to the interests of their firms' shareholders. Opportunities for corruption should depend only on those who take bribes. The conflict between profit and morality is well described by Kapstein (2001): "Today most companies have internal codes against making payoffs to government officials. But how do these same firms respond when they are competing with others which engage in corrupt practices? Is it the bottom line or the moral code that wins out?"

Economists tend to argue that businesspeople should not and do not take ethical aspects into consideration. Even when they attempt to do so this behavior cannot survive market pressure. The reverse hypothesis would state that ethics plays a crucial role in businesspeople's behavior and renders some more inclined than others to pay bribes. Whether ethics can survive market pressure is investigated here. This debate has been topical for at least the last ten years.

7.2. Corruption as an art

Given the global character of corruption, reform has often focused on requests to include all global players. Poor developing countries, while often being primarily affected by high levels of corruption, may not have the capacity to contain corruption by themselves. Sometimes, their local efforts are impeded even further, if multinational firms and donor institutions do not fight corruption sufficiently within their own ranks and tolerate bribery in less-developed countries. With a variety of international agreements the industrial countries have come to accept their responsibility. An OECD convention signed by all member countries in 1997 prohibits the payment of bribes to foreign public officials and prevents such payments from being tax deductible. One of the goals of the convention is to reduce the level of corruption in international business transactions and to create a level playing field for all exporters.[2]

While these international initiatives have marked a major change to the global recognition of corruption, it remains to be asked how far companies in and of themselves can actively contribute to the fight against corruption. This issue remains at the frontline because laws and international conventions may be skillfully circumvented. Firms may relabel bribes as commissions – continuing to claim tax rebates for these expenses.[3] Instead of handing out bribes, firms may guarantee loans, hand out shares and options, or delegate the dirty business to local agents, subsidiaries, or joint-venture partners (Moran 2006). How far firms remain innovative in circumventing laws will crucially depend on whether corruption continues to be a profitable business.

However, for various reasons private companies may be genuinely willing to stop bribery. First, renouncement of corrupt business methods may not only be due to moral sentiments – it can also emanate from purely economic considerations. Corrupt deals can be risky and may prove unprofitable in the long run. Given the opacity of corrupt deals, a firm's own employees can attempt to divert back part of the bribes into their private accounts (Bannenberg 2002: 142–3). Allowing bribery by one's staff may therefore backfire, turning loyal staff members into employees who seek loopholes and devote their

[2] Apart from governments and companies, international organizations such as the World Bank and the IMF have similarly revised their lending policies so as to inhibit corruption within their own institutions. How far these initiatives are satisfactory is still controversial, and discussion in this regard is likely to continue.

[3] In 1996 the German Chamber of Commerce, Deutsche Industrie- und Handels Kammertag (DIHK), ran a survey of their foreign branches, asking whether ending the tax deductibility of bribes would adversely impact on the company's business. The overall (unpublished) response was that this would have no effect. Apparently, firms would find alternative methods of deducting such expenses from their tax liability.

efforts to defrauding their own firm. For example, the German airport operator Fraport was alleged to have committed bribery to win an order for the modernization of Tashkent airport in Uzbekistan. However, the charges were dropped by the prosecutor, who considered that the employees may have embezzled the money instead.[4] A similar allegation has been made about the French firm Elf Aquitaine for having paid bribes to the Christian Democratic Party in Germany – embezzlement within the firm has been suspected as an alternative explanation for the missing funds.[5] Another, still unpublished, case reported to this author by a staff member of the former German firm Mannesmann relates to the firm's local trade executive in Hong Kong. It must have taken place around 1995. Mannesmann's local executive secured various contracts with mainland China. Each time he reported that 10 percent bribes had to be paid, which was approved by higher authorities within the firm. Revelations circulated later that payments of this size had not been necessary. On average, only 5 percent had to be paid. The local executive had used his Chinese contacts to arrange for amplified bribes and a certain share being paid back to his own Swiss bank account. Mannesmann fired him and intended to pass on the case to prosecution authorities. However, the local executive threatened to reveal publicly the identity of all Chinese bribe-takers, which would have made future business impossible for Mannesmann in the region. The case was settled privately.

As argued by a petroleum company

> companies that participate in corrupted dealings ... do themselves no favours. Although a business deal here or there may be obtained, the cost includes creating a culture of dishonesty within the company. If cheating or bribery or fixing the books are tolerated for certain purposes, a company can never again be sure that these dealings are not tolerated for others. The whole organisation can come to believe that dishonesty is an accepted approach. (OECD 2003: 11)

[4] See Bloomberg ("German Prosecutor Stops Bribery Probe against Fraport Managers;" March 22, 2004).

[5] See *International Herald Tribune* ("Imbroglio over the Elf-Kohl Payoff: Was It a Hoax to Hide Kickbacks?"; October 13, 2000).

A firm engaging in bribery might also be exposed to denunciation and extortion and may have to fear for its reputation. Furthermore, the level of bribes requested may rise with the firm's propensity to pay. A reputation for honesty can constitute a safeguard against excessive demands for bribes by public servants. Therefore, forbidding one's employees to pay bribes may sometimes be in line with profit-maximizing behavior. Such considerations may explain why different strategies – that is, different attitudes towards business bribery – persist in competitive markets. Offering bribes is clearly far from being the natural result of competition.

Box 25 How to fix a football match, by Declan Hill[6]

There are two types of match-fixing in professional football: internal and external. Internal fixes are done by agents within the game (players, managers, coaches, etc.) and are usually arrangements to win matches. Team A might be able to win the championship if they beat Team B. To Team B the game does not mean a great deal. So an arrangement is made between the teams to gift the points to Team A.

However, external fixes are different. They take place when agents from outside the game (gamblers, politicians, or marketers) enter the game and try to ensure that a team loses a match. These fixes present their own organizational difficulties. The foremost is how does an outsider come in and ensure that agents within their own profession subvert their specific codes? Let us start with a case where the fix did not work.

Kenan Erol was a man with a plan. On April 6, 2005, he walked into the Sabatspor football stadium in Northeastern Turkey with a bag full of 500 Euro notes. He was going to try to bribe Hakan Olgun, the goalkeeper for the Turkish Super League. Someone wanted Sabatspor to lose the game and was willing to pay someone a lot of money to make sure that they did. Kenan Erol was their man.

[6] The author is a former investigative journalist for Canadian and American television and for CBC and BBC radio. Currently, he is pursuing his Doctorate of Sociology at the University of Oxford under the supervision of Diego Gambetta.

Box 25 (*Cont.*)

Erol talked to, at least, seven other players on the team, but he needed to make sure the goalie, the player who could save or destroy a team's chances with a couple of mistakes, was on board. Kenan Erol met Hakan Olgun that morning. But it really was not Kenan Erol's day, because Hakan Olgun secretly tape-recorded their conversation. This is an extract from their conversation:

Kenan Erol: *I have spoken to all the other players about this fix. The others know about it.*
Hakan Olgun: *What? The whole team knows?*
Kenan Erol: *Don't worry about it!*
Hakan Olgun: *I don't understand. Do you want me just to leave the goal area and "eat" a goal?*
Kenan Erol: *First half you will be ahead 1–0. But Kayseri should win the game. You should let in 2 or 3 goals in the second half.*
Hakan Olgun: *Can I trust you?*
Kenan Erol: *The money is in the car. Let me show you.*
Hakan Olgun: *You mean it is betting? Or do you have an arrangement with the other team? Does our team management know?*
Kenan Erol: *If you talk about this to your management you won't get a single lira! I'm trying to do you a favour. These guys are trying to bet 500–600 billion Lira. (He shows him the bag with the money inside) There are two hundred thousand Euro in the bag and there will be more. Just get the score we want.*
Hakan Olgun: *Brother! They are all 500 Euro notes. I have never seen that much money in my life! Are you going to give it to me?*
Kenan Erol: *When the match is finished, it will be in your pocket.*
Hakan Olgun: *I have 130–140 billion TL [Turkish Lira] debt. How much will I get?*
Kenan Erol: *At least 75 billion TL. The rest will go to your friends.*

The identity of "these guys," who were purportedly willing to bet 500–600 Turkish lira on the game, has never been publicly revealed. But the transcript did give the Turkish Football Federation an accurate record of what happened. Their administrative board suspended six players for their alleged role in the fix and gave Hakan Olgun €50,000 as a reward for his coming forward. They also invited Kenan Erol to explain his actions before their committee. Perhaps unsurprisingly, Mr. Erol declared that he was unavailable to meet with the committee.

For all the murky circumstances around this fixing attempt, one thing is clear. Kenan Erol is a terrible match-fixer. His bribery attempts were inept and clumsy; his instructions were incompetent. But if he wanted to, how could he improve his performance?

One of the things to understand is how good an external match-fixer must be at their job. Here is an example from Malaysia, which took place in 1994. Following is an extract from the confession of one former national team player about how he was recruited to help fix games.

> The fixer contacted me. He was speaking Tamil on the phone. He wanted me to sell the match. I was scared. He said, "Don't worry. I already control your entire team. … He then asked me to inform XX that if he (XX) does not cooperate, he will break his legs. I told XX. He agreed to fix the match. The fixer then asked me to inform the rest of the group. All of them agreed. They promised us 20,000 RM [Malaysian Ringgit] each to fix the game. We had to lose or draw – make sure we did not win.

In this excerpt, the fixer reveals himself to be a sophisticated strategist. First, he speaks in Tamil, a language in Malaysia that is used only by a small, relatively oppressed working-class community. By speaking in this language the fixer establishes a kind of "us against them" bond with the player. This bond sets the tone for the rest of the conversation.

Second, the fixer is trying to replace the team management and coaches in the player's mind with himself. He wants to ensure that the player does not go to the one set of officials who purportedly have an interest in ensuring that the games are not fixed – the team management. So almost immediately, the fixer psychologically

Box 25 (*Cont.*)

isolates the player by suggesting that the management is on the take. In Turkey, with Kenan Erol's futile attempt at fixing, when the player asked if the management was corrupt, Erol's response was to threaten the player. The Malaysian fixer's approach is far better because if the player does go to his coach to denounce the approach by a fixer, there is a possibility that the coach may tell the fixer. This implied threat is followed by a real one, but not, of course, directed at the player. "Could you tell XX that I will break his legs?" There is nothing to stop the fixer from telling the player directly that he will break his legs but that would destroy the friendliness and confidence that he is trying to establish. After the player tells XX of the threat, he not unsurprisingly joins the fixer's network.

The fixer also gets the player to establish the network with the team. This ensures that there is far less risk for the fixer. He also (although this is not contained in the above extract) pays the players in the network immediately. By paying money immediately, the fixer does two things: first, he establishes trust, a key commodity in a illegal act, and second, he hooks the players. Once they have accepted his money, it will be difficult for them to claim that the money was simply for winning matches.

Match-fixing is a crime wrapped in mystery. Although many people speak of it, few actually understand the dynamics and mechanism at its heart. To properly contain this type of corruption a sophisticated and careful analysis is needed: as sophisticated and careful as the good match-fixers.

Finally, as expounded in previous chapters, corrupt agreements usually cannot be legally enforced. Striking corrupt deals thus imposes substantial risks of nondelivery, of denunciation and extortion. Dealing with this risk requires substantial criminal capacities. Some international traders and investors are insufficiently experienced. This is well documented by the following news headline from news.com.au, April 11, 2001:

For Jakub Bierzynski, the wake-up call was of a personal nature. Head of the Warsaw-based media planning company OMD-Poland, a US–Polish joint venture, Bierzynski was confronted by corruption last year when two big international clients separately demanded bribes of "hundreds of thousands" for two advertising contracts. "It was like a very cold shower. I asked myself if I could do business in a corrupt environment," says Bierzynski, who had incorrectly assumed his firm's US mother company afforded him a degree of protection from kick-backs. The answer was no. ... "Leaving aside the moral connotations (of giving bribes), I have no skills in giving bribes. I have never done it before, I don't know how much, I don't know to whom and I don't know in what situations I'm supposed to give bribes, so I am losing in that competitive field and I am sentenced to death in the business world." Instead, the 34-year-old channelled his outrage into a proposal to launch an anti-corruption business association unprecedented in central and Eastern Europe, in which members would pledge not to offer or receive bribes."

Businesspeople tend to be cautious when entering new markets because potential advantages in "know-how" are easily offset by their ignorance with respect to "know-who." The extent to which corrupt deals require specialized qualifications is well explained in Box 25, relating to match fixing. Those who lack the necessary criminal skills are well advised to abstain from attempting illegal deals. They might be better off with the legal alternatives or even to write off a market that does not provide them with legal access. Empirical investigations reveal how corruption tends to distort the private sector as a result (see Box 26). This chapter intends to provide a comparative assessment of exporters' behavior. A possible approach to assess the behavior of those who give bribes could be to conduct an international survey of business people and construct indices of corruption similar to those who receive bribes. Indeed, such surveys were conducted recently and may adequately describe subjective perceptions of experts. This chapter investigates the results found in Transparency International's Bribe Payers Index (BPI). To what extent such perceptions tell a true story will be discussed. Using alternative methodologies is helpful in assessing the robustness of the outcomes. Such an alternative approach is presented here by focusing on bilateral trade data and relating it to the level of corruption perceived for the importing countries. This makes it possible to differentiate between exporters who trade more with "clean" countries and others who export mainly to "corrupt" countries.

Box 26 Corruption distorting the private sector

Beck *et al.* (1991) investigate whether corruption distorts international trade. They find that corruption had a small negative but significant impact on the export competitiveness of the United States – suggesting that the United States may behave more responsibly in international trade. Similar conclusions are reported by Hines (1995), showing that US aircraft exports after 1977 decreased in countries perceived to be corrupt. He also shows that US investors differed from others in preferring to locate their FDI in less-corrupt countries after 1977. Hines relates this to the imposition of the Foreign Corrupt Practices Act (FCPA). A related effort is undertaken by Wei (2000b) to find out whether Japan has a tendency to invest more in corrupt countries, the implication being a possibly higher Japanese propensity to pay bribes. But the author did not find any differences between the investment pattern of Japan and the United States. Hines' findings would also not suffice to claim a competitive disadvantage of the United States, because they could just as well indicate that competitive advantages in corrupt marketplaces before 1977 had been neutralized thereafter.

Habib and Zurawicki (2001; 2002) investigate whether all investors are deterred equally. Referring to bilateral FDI data, they find that investors coming from countries with a high perceived level of corruption are deterred less when entering a corrupt host country than their clean competitors. Investors from countries with little corruption prefer host countries that also have low levels of corruption. This might relate to the psychological distance separating the home and the host countries. Organizational or moral issues might be at play, because investors who obtained local experience with corruption might know better how to arrange corrupt deals and be less scrupulous.

Alesina and Weder (2002) investigate whether corrupt governments attract or deter aid from OECD countries. The authors make use of a variety of different measures of corruption and investigate different samples of countries. Testing for various specifications of the regressions, they do not find evidence that foreign donors discriminate against corrupt countries. On the contrary, some results suggest that corrupt countries are even more apt to attract foreign aid from OECD countries. Alesina and Weder (2002) also investigate bilateral aid flows. Scandinavian countries and Australia have a significant tendency to avoid providing aid to corrupt countries. At the opposite extreme is the United States, where a significant negative coefficient of the corruption variable indicates that the United States tends to favor corrupt countries in providing aid. Unfortunately, regressions on bilateral aid flows are run using only the corruption variable provided by PRS. The authors did not cross-check their results by employing other indices, leaving a grain of skepticism regarding these controversial insights.

In a similar spirit, Sandholtz and Gray (2003) investigate how corruption affects lending by multilateral donors. They show that IMF credit in the late 1990s is influenced positively by a country's level of corruption. This must certainly not imply negligence towards corruption by the IMF but rather point to the prevalence of payments crises in countries with higher levels of corruption. However, a similar influence is not encountered concerning World Bank loans.

The next section outlines the results from the trade approach developed in Lambsdorff (1998a; 2000). Following this discussion, Section 3 presents the outcomes of the business survey. Section 4 compares the results of the two previous sections. Section 5 provides a critical analysis of the data used for compiling the BPI. Finally, concluding remarks are offered in the last section.

7.3. The trade approach

Bilateral trade data serve as the starting point to measure exporters' propensity to pay bribes. A crucial assumption is that the level of corruption of importing countries significantly affects trade. The most obvious kind of influence relates to goods that are imported by the public sector. The extent of corruption among public officials and politicians influences which competitor is most likely to win a contract. Tendering procedures can be falsified and contracts awarded in favor of those competitors who offer the highest bribes. Also

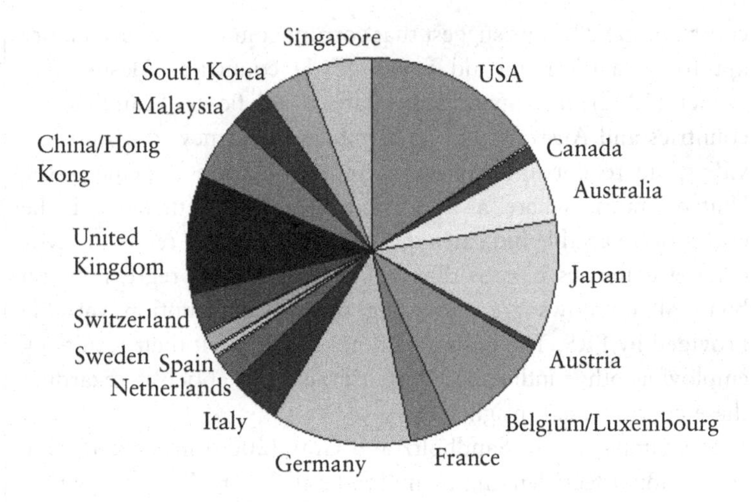

Figure 7.1. Shares of the Indian import market

private sector imports – and even trade between headquarters and subsidiaries of multinational companies – can be influenced by the extent of corruption prevalent in a country. On the one hand, the extent of corruption at all state levels that regulate and control external trade – such as customs, trade ministry, and trade regulation authorities – impact on this kind of business. The crucial hypothesis is that those exporting countries that are prone to offer bribes can secure a competitive edge in corrupt import markets. On the other hand, in case of clean import markets such a competitive advantage cannot be achieved by means of paying bribes.

The subsequent investigation determines the eighteen biggest exporting countries' tendencies to export into corrupt import countries. For this purpose data on bilateral trade flows are taken from the IMF, Directions of Trade. The figures represent the exports between 1993 and 1997 to the 106 largest importing countries, according to their import statistics.

Figure 7.1, showing the shares of the import market of India, is illustrative of the approach taken here. India is perceived to be relatively corrupt. This compares with other countries seen to be less affected by corruption. If exporting countries obtain systematically higher import shares in countries perceived to be corrupt, this serves as an indicator for the willingness to offer bribes. The appendix to this chapter reports technical details to the statistical analysis.

Table 7.1 The impact of lack of corruption on the trade pattern

Country	*Impact: lack of corruption*
Malaysia	0.046**
Australia	0.031**
Sweden	0.027*
Singapore	0.022
Japan	0.010
South Korea	0.001
Canada	−0.001
Spain	−0.003
United Kingdom	−0.003
Austria	−0.004
China/Hong Kong	−0.010
United States	−0.013
Germany	−0.016
Switzerland	−0.017
Netherlands	−0.017
France	−0.024*
Belgium/Luxembourg	−0.031*
Italy	−0.034**

Note: *significant at a 95% level; **significant at a 99% level.

The results of the regression are in Table 7.1. The influence exerted by geographic distance, colonial ties, language, and EU membership are controlled for. The various coefficients for the corruption index are of primary interest. Italy, Belgium/Luxembourg, and France have a significant tendency to export into corrupt markets. The export pattern of Malaysia, Australia, and Sweden is significantly oriented toward markets perceived to be clean.

Since other potential influences had been controlled for, it is concluded that the results relate to the respective exporters' inclination to offer bribes. A coefficient of −0.034 for Italy indicates that with a rise in the corruption index by 1 degree (indicating decreasing corruption) the deviation index will decrease by 0.034. For an import market where the actual market share is close to its target value this is equivalent to a drop of the market share by twice that value, almost 7 percent. For example, if Colombia were to lower corruption to the level of the United Kingdom, for instance, by 6 points in the corruption index, this would reduce the Italian share of the import market by 42 percent, that is, from the current 4 percent to 2.4 percent. The conclusion derived in this context is that this impact should be due to Italian exporters' high propensity to pay bribes, which is less effective when import markets are cleaner.

7.4. Survey results

Another approach to determine which exporters are more prone to pay bribes is to gather subjective assessments from experienced people. In order to develop a feasible methodology to explore this approach, first tests were conducted via Internet at the University of Göttingen. A sample of Internet users with an interest in corruption was surveyed and different questions were tested for appropriateness. Also, the number of replies required for statistical significance could be determined with the help of this test. Further comprehensive work was carried out by Galtung (1999). In 1999, this led to a survey undertaken by Gallup International on behalf of Transparency International and the publication of the "Bribe Payer's Index (BPI)." The results are reported in Table 7.2, including those of a more recent update from 2002, which was carried out with the same methodology.

Businesspeople in fourteen emerging markets were polled: Argentina, Brazil, Colombia, Hungary, India, Indonesia, Morocco, Nigeria, Philippines, Poland, Russia, South Africa, South Korea, and Thailand. The rationale to focus on these countries was due to Transparency International's interest in international corruption and its effect on developing countries. At the same time these countries were picked because of their relatively balanced patterns of trade. Their import markets were not dominated by just one major exporting country. The respondents included executives at major foreign or national companies, chartered accountancies, bi-national chambers of commerce, major commercial banks, and legal practices. The response rate reported in Galtung (1999:12) appears rather low with a value barely above 20 percent. But this value compares the total contacts with the achieved sample. It does not suggest that almost 80 percent of those approached refused to turn in answers to the questionnaire but rather that many contacts had been needed to find respondents willing to devote the necessary time. In this sense, the low response

Table 7.2 The Transparency International Bribe Payers Index

Rank in 1999	*Country*	*Assessments in 1999*	*Score in 1999*	*Score in 2002*
1	Sweden	423	8.3	8.4
2	Australia	371	8.1	8.5
3	Canada	448	8.1	8.1
4	Austria	382	7.8	8.2
5	Switzerland	457	7.7	8.4
6	Netherlands	440	7.4	7.8
7	United Kingdom	479	7.2	6.9
8	Belgium	395	6.8	7.8
9	Germany	493	6.2	6.3
10	United States	523	6.2	5.3
11	Singapore	397	5.7	6.3
12	Spain	426	5.3	5.8
13	France	483	5.2	5.5
14	Japan	472	5.1	5.3
15	Malaysia	375	3.9	4.3
	Hong Kong			4.3
16	Italy	487	3.7	4.1
17	Taiwan	417	3.5	3.8
18	South Korea	418	3.4	3.9
19	China (including Hong Kong in 1999)	456	3.1	3.5
	Russia			3.2

Note: The score ranges between 10 (highly clean exporter) and 0 (highly corrupt exporter).

rate does not suggest that the particular type of survey turned respondents away.

At first, respondents were supposed to assess whether they perceive differences among exporters' propensity to pay bribes: "Are companies from some countries more willing than others to pay bribes to win or retain business in this country? This question may apply equally to competition for public tenders or, for example, to obtain authorisation for new investments." Interestingly enough, from 778 valid responses only 89 replied "no," claiming that all exporters are equal, while 567 responded "yes" (122 replied "did not know"). One can conclude that, as perceived by respondents, the unwillingness to pay bribes can survive market pressure and contribute to observable and different behavior of exporters. In an attempt to assess the nineteen major exporting countries' propensity to pay bribes, the following question was posed subsequently: "In the business sectors with which you are familiar, please indicate whether companies from the following countries are very likely, quite likely or unlikely to pay bribes to win or retain business in this country."

Answers were only processed from the 567 respondents who had responded "yes" to the first question. Apart from an opt-out possibility, three categories (very likely, likely, and unlikely) were provided. The original data (BPI'_i) thus ranged between 1 (unlikely) and 3 (likely). The results were re-scaled according to $BPI_i = 10 + 5 \cdot (1 - BPI'_i)$, so that 10 depicts an exporting country with a high level of ethics while 0 indicates a country that is perceived to be highly prone to offer bribes. Table 7.2 reveals that Sweden, Australia, and Canada have a good reputation while Italy, Taiwan, South Korea, and China/Hong Kong are perceived as most likely to offer bribes.[7]

The results correlate strongly with the level of corruption as perceived within the respective countries, that is, the level of corruption among local politicians and public servants – largely in their dealings with business people. This could indicate that business people behave similarly abroad as they do at home, suggesting a real convergence between the two indices. But it could also imply that respondents did not fully distinguish between these two forms of corruption so that

[7] Another survey was conducted by Bray (2006). Telephone interviews have been conducted, based on a set questionnaire, with 350 business directors of large international companies based in the UK, the United States, Germany, France, the Netherlands, Brazil and Hong Kong. The survey asked respondents to rate companies from the seventeen leading OECD and non-OECD exporters on a four-point scale with regard to compliance to the OECD convention. The responses were denoted as follows: (1) strict compliance, (2) generally high standard of compliance with only occasional lapses, (3) companies would prefer to comply but will pay bribes if competitors are doing so, and (4) companies will always pay bribes if it is customary to do so in the host country. It is interesting to observe that the results correlate strongly with the BPI (with a coefficient of 0.97), providing support for the TI index.

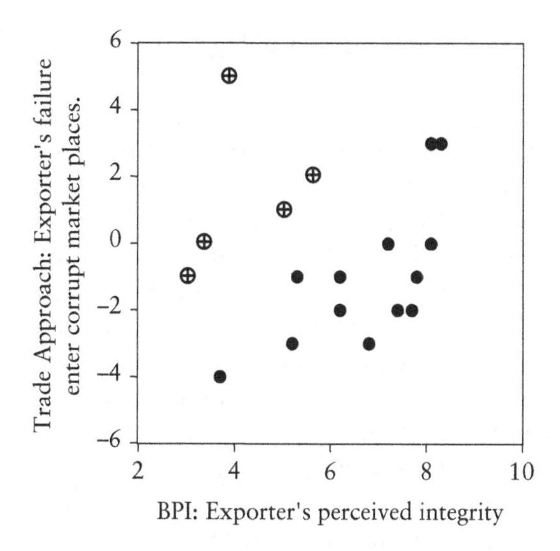

Figure 7.2. Scatterplot: BPI, and trade approach

the overall reputation of the countries in containing corruption at home overshadows their behavior abroad.

7.5. Comparing different approaches

When comparing the results from the trade approach with TI's BPI, one observes some differences. The overall correlation coefficient is only 0.07. For some exporters, however, the results show similarities. While Italy and France are considered to perform poorly, Sweden and Australia are perceived to abstain from paying bribes and obtain only small market shares in countries perceived to be corrupt.

Large differences between these two approaches are obtained for Asian exporters (indicated by the crossed markers in Figure 7.2). Asian countries are rated considerably worse in the BPI than they are in the trade approach. This difference is remarkable and open to various interpretations. Either Asian countries are indeed highly inclined to pay bribes, but unlike their competitors, they are not able to increase their market shares by paying bribes, or perceptions with regard to Asian countries are distorted.

Such a distortion may result from the economic success of Asian countries. These have experienced a vast increase in their exports over the last two decades, whereas traditional exporters lost market shares.

The differences between the trade investigation and the BPI may, thus, be the result of increasing exports.

Two lines of reasoning are at hand to explain this impact. First, in an attempt to enter new import markets, the payment of bribes is not an effective approach because corruption is more helpful in retaining market shares. This argument would favor the BPI results over the trade approach. There are good reasons for assuming that corruption is more effective in retaining business than in opening up new markets. There are transaction costs to be considered that suggest that making corrupt deals is easier when long-standing business relationships have already been developed (Lambsdorff 2002a). Partners in a corrupt relationship cannot assure each other that they will stick to their promises. Instead, they often renege after having obtained a bribe, or ask for a second payment. Legal recourse is commonly not available. Other mechanisms must be used to enforce corrupt contracts. Establishing a reputation of "honesty" among corrupt partners and repetitive business relationships provide safeguards against opportunism. But these are more readily available to those who intend to retain market shares and less to newcomers. Thus, exporters' propensity to pay bribes may not fully be captured by their tendency to export into corrupt markets. If this impact is considered relevant, then the trade approach may provide a distorted picture.

Second, perceptions may be biased. They may relate to pure hearsay, rumors, or gossip, or else they may equally relate to actual experience. In the former case, perceptions are not a good indicator of reality. It is well worth noting at this stage that TI has never explicitly stated that the BPI reflects actual export behavior. What might be relevant is that respondents may have negative opinions about successful competitors. This would introduce a bias with regard to subjective indicators. Businesspeople may have an attitude to denounce competitors' success as the result of unfair practices. For example, a CIA report claimed that between 1994 and 1995 the United States lost $36 billion worth of business deals due to bribery and corruption by its competitors. But it was slandered that the high value may relate more to US businesspeople seeking excuses after having lost market shares. If taken seriously, this argument would classify subjective assessments as inappropriate and lead one to assume that the trade approach is closer to reality.

7.6. Conclusion

The CPI largely describes the level of corruption among those who take bribes. In a sense, this assessment is unfair once international business transactions are taken into consideration. If a western businessperson hands out a bribe to a public servant in a less developed country, such an index behaves unfairly in that it assigns a bad score to the receiving country and not to those who pay bribes. This chapter may serve as a useful complement to the current indices and correct for a politically sensitive misrepresentation. We must contend, however, that an assessment of Asian exporting countries remains controversial.

Several issues for reform emanate from the findings in this chapter. First, while some are artists in playing the corruption game, others have moral scruples. Others again fear for their corporate culture, that employees are misguided to betray their own firm or that formerly honest customers and suppliers want a share of the corrupt cake. There is no race to the bottom where only the lowest code of ethics can survive. There seems to be scope for ethics to survive competition – contrary to some economists' belief. As exporting countries exhibit different patterns of behavior, it can be concluded that they do not simply take the cultural climate as given and adjust their ethical standards accordingly. Insofar as export behavior differs from country to country, the inclination to offer bribes emerges as the sovereign choice of the exporters.

Second, the large differences among exporters signal that these can contribute to anti-corruption. A moral commitment by firms need not be in contrast to their maximizing strategy.

Third, recent research shows how corporations can contribute to anti-corruption. The Business Principles for Countering Bribery developed by Transparency International provide detailed suggestions on how to implement anti-bribery provisions in codes of conduct, whistleblower procedures, and compliance mechanisms. There is recent research on how corporate governance can limit corruption. A total of 1966 international firms have been investigated with respect to the capacity of their corporate governance in containing corruption (EIRIS 2005). There is a strong correlation of the performance of countries, as determined in this chapter, and the findings reported there. Countries hosting companies with good corporate governance are perceived to be less affected by corruption of its exporters and obtain fewer market shares in corrupt import markets. Good corporate governance seems to be effective. There is also evidence that stock markets pay a premium for those firms with strong corporate governance.

As the introductory case study from Lesotho suggests, however, codes of conduct can easily become ineffective if firms are innovative in circumventing them. Employing intermediaries is one such method. While, for example, companies in the defense and aerospace sector are currently busy implementing codes of conduct, much of their bribery appears to be delegated nowadays to local agents or subsidiaries that operate in a less stringent environment.

Reform therefore must address how to deal with intermediaries. Nowadays, these appear to be at the core of arranging corrupt transactions, particularly large international government purchases. One option for reform would be to prohibit intermediaries. As regards public contracts, this is the case in Algeria. Public arms deals in India disallow the payment of any commissions, also serving as an impediment to the operation of intermediaries. But evidence suggests that such prohibitions are often circumvented (Aburish 1985: 29, 105–9). Intermediation services are difficult to define in legal terms and often carried out by expatriates who can easily escape prosecution.

It can be observed that commitment to honesty can be advantageous to some agents. This can be exploited more systematically for anticorruption. Box 27 shows how a voluntary certification of an agent can help in committing to honesty and thus separate the wheat from the chaff.

Box 27 Hindering corrupt intermediaries

Corruption is an art. Given that some firms are not skillful, they attempt to delegate the dirty work to specialists. These operate as intermediaries, exploiting their insider knowledge about the criminal capacities of public servants and, foremost, their repeated exchange with politicians (Hasker and Okten 2004). A middleman can thus act as a guarantor of a corrupt deal, someone who links up the parties involved (della Porta and Vanucci 1999: 46; Vanucci 2000). Fortunately, there is no perfect competition in supplying corrupt intermediary services. This is so because intermediaries often cheat their clients and vice versa, and their contracts cannot be legally enforced. Still, large cases of corruption are often arranged by intermediaries. How can their operation be inhibited?

Corrupt transactions can quickly backfire and destroy the corporate culture of a private firm. Instead of ending corruption, some firms pretend integrity by delegating the job to intermediaries. Legal provisions such as the US FCPA prohibit the payment of bribery irrespective of whether the payment is made directly or via intermediaries. Similar provision is provided by the 1997 OECD convention. One strategy by firms to circumvent this is by rational ignorance. Intermediaries are paid large sums in exchange for contracts, formally requested to sign integrity provisions, and the rest is up to them (Bray 2004; Sayed 2004; Stansbury 2004).

But there exist a variety of "red flags" that make it difficult for firms to deny knowledge. A disproportionate size of the commissions is among them, alongside a request to obtain the payment in cash or to make it to a numbered bank account. Others arise from the intermediaries' need to enforce the corrupt agreement. In order to avoid being cheated by either side, the intermediary needs the commission before paying the bribe. Since such advance payment is contrary to standard business practice it signals to firms the intention of the intermediary. Problems arise also if an intermediary is "recommended" by public servants or politicians, especially if these have an ownership interest in the intermediary's firm. A past record of paying bribes and representation of other companies with a questionable reputation, finally, are indicators of an intermediary's willingness to pay bribes (Bray 2004: 127; Darroch 2004: 50–51).

Stiffer regulation of intermediaries is clearly an option for reform. For example, it might be made a legal offense to pay commissions related to various government functions such as public procurement, extraction concessions, or the granting of subsidies, unless the recipient is registered for this special task. Accounting standards can be made obligatory for these registered intermediaries, including annual audits. If payments to nonregistered intermediaries are related to public contracts and concessions this would invoke criminal liability for the firm and legal unenforceability of the underlying contract. Aburish (1985: 29) reports that seventy intermediaries in Iraq were allowed to legally represent foreign firms and that intermediary operation outside this regulation had been punishable by death.

Box 27 *(Cont.)*

Some honest firms fear a bad reputation or being held liable for the corrupt acts of their intermediaries. Such firms are willing to carry out due diligence in order to ascertain that their intermediaries abstain from paying bribes – if only the administrative costs for due diligence could be reduced to a reasonable level. The public and the courts may also not honor a firm's such efforts because other firms dress up the corrupt relationship to their intermediaries by having similar formal procedures in place that provide an appearance of legality. On the other hand, some intermediaries have an incentive to commit to honesty. Those who dislike corruption or are little skilled in criminal deals can profit from such a commitment. They become trustworthy to the honest firms. Reform should aim at matching honest intermediaries with honest firms.

A feasible approach to reform would be to offer intermediaries a certification. Intermediaries commit to honesty by registering at a specialized agency, adopting anti-bribery policies, and allowing scrutiny and auditing of their regular business.[8] The agency would carry out due diligence and publish whether any red flags have been detected. This agency lowers the administrative costs of due diligence because its assessment of an intermediary can be drawn on by multiple firms. The certificate can also be used to defend a firm's reputation in public and before court as an unbiased signal of a firm's commitment.

Simultaneously, noncertified intermediaries send a signal about their willingness to offer corrupt intermediation services. Corrupt firms can thus more easily identify corrupt intermediaries. If a certified agent would have been available, preference for a non-certified competitor sends a signal to potential whistleblowers, prosecutors, and the public about a lacking commitment to honesty. In light of this, the risk for corrupt firms increases and even those with less stringent ethics may prefer to operate legally.

[8] One such certification agency has recently been founded: TRACE (Transparent Agents and Contracting Entities). The success of its promising approach deserves to be closely monitored.

Appendix: Technical details to the trade-regressions

Figure 7.1 shows the actual import market share obtained by each of eighteen exporters in India. Such market shares are determined for 108 import markets. Before running the regressions, the actual market share is compared with a target value (T_{ij}). This represents the expected market shares as a function of the sectoral distribution of products, that is, the structure of goods produced by a particular exporter is taken into consideration. Ten categories of goods (k) are taken into consideration.

Each of the 18 exporting countries (i) obtains a certain share (M_{ij}) in each of the 106 import markets (j). An example of such shares in the Indian import market is presented in Figure 7.1. This share is compared with a target value (T_{ij}). This represents the expected market shares as a function of the sectoral distribution of products; that is, the structure of goods produced by a particular exporter is taken into consideration. Ten categories of goods (k) are taken into consideration, as determined by the Standard International Trade Classification (SITC). These are, for example, crude materials and fuels, machines and transport equipment, miscellaneous manufactured goods, chemicals or food, and live animals. For exporting country i and all importing countries j, the target value is represented by the following equation:

$$T_{ij} = \sum_{k=0}^{9} \frac{M_{jk}\ X_{ik}}{M_j\ X_k},$$

where Mj represents the dollar value of imports into country j, M_{jk} indicates those of category k, X_{ik} represents country i's exports of category k, and X_k signifies all of the eighteen countries' exports of category k. The equation determines the share of all sectors' exports that country i is able to obtain (X_{ik}/X_k) and multiplies the result with the respective import share of country j (M_{jk}/M_j). The sum of these values gives the expected total market share.[9] A deviation index (D_{ij}) is constructed by comparing actual values and target values:

$$D_{ij} = \frac{M_{ij} - T_{ij}}{M_{ij} + T_{ij}}.$$

[9] Since an appropriate measure of total world exports cannot be derived from bilateral trade data, this formula must be further fine-tuned; see Lambsdorff (2000).

If exporter *i* is able to obtain a market share on import market *j*, which exceeds its target value – based on total export strength and the particular sectoral composition of imports and exports – *Dij* turns out to be positive. Otherwise, a negative value is obtained. This will be the dependent variable entering into the regressions.

A system of multivariate regressions is utilized to observe the impact of explanatory variables. Most important among the explanatory variables is the 1998 Transparency International Corruption Perceptions Index (CPI), which is used for depicting the level of corruption of the importing countries; see Chapter 1 of this book. The presentation by Transparency International (TI) only includes countries for which at least three sources had been available, publicizing only the more reliable figures. This approach would exclude many large importing countries. For the purpose of the regressions, the respective corruption perceptions values for all other countries were also determined. Here I will present the results only for the enlarged set of countries. The results turned out to be robust to different specifications of the regressions; see Lambsdorff (2000). The purpose of including the CPI is to separately determine each exporting country's tendency to export into rather corrupt or rather clean countries.

Naturally, the share of the import market will be lower as the distance to the respective market rises. This suggests the need for a variable of geographic distance, measured as the distance between the demographic centers of the respective countries. Also, a common language may support trade, which was accounted for by the inclusion of a dummy variable. This variable has been assigned the value 1 for countries who share a common language with the exporting country, be it officially or owing to a high representation in the media, business, or education sector.[10] Colonial ties are another important factor to be considered. This is captured by a dummy variable, indicating whether during the last 100 years a country was a colony of the respective exporter whose influence has not been radically overturned by a cultural revolution.

[10] In the case that several languages are found in an exporting country, a composite of the respective dummy variables is determined, according to the importance of the respective languages.

For countries outside the European Union there seem to be trade disadvantages with EU members. This was tested by including a dummy variable taking value 1 for EU member countries.[11] Other political organizations, such as the Commonwealth of Nations or EFTA, were insignificant. Many further variables are tested in the study, such as religious belief, economies of scale in setting up trade relationships, or common borders between trading nations. But these were also found to be insignificant. The final system of regressions is depicted by the following equation:

$$D_{ij} = \mathrm{C1}_i + \mathrm{C2} \times \text{Geographic Distance}_{ij} + \mathrm{C3}_i \times \text{Absence of Corruption}_j + \mathrm{C4} \times \text{Language-Dummy}_{ij} + \mathrm{C5} \times \text{Colonial-Ties}_{ij} + \mathrm{C6}_h \times \text{EU-Dummy}_j$$

The results for colonial ties, EU-dummy, and especially geographic distance were highly significant. The findings for absence of corruption are presented in Table 7.1.

[11] Two coefficients, $(\mathrm{C6}_h)$, $h \in \{0,1\}$ are allowed in the subsequent regression depending on whether the exporting country is an EU member or not.

8 How confidence facilitates illegal transactions

An empirical approach

8.1. Introduction

Since corruption does not allow for legal recourse, corrupt contracts are not legally enforceable. This is why corruption can go hand in hand with opportunism, reneging, and threats of denunciation (della Porta and Vanucci 1999; Husted 1994; Lambsdorff 2002a; Rose-Ackerman 1999: 91–110; Chapter 6 of this book). Corrupt deals can thus go along with low predictability for investors and the absence of confidence regarding mutual promises. There has lately been empirical support that this lack of confidence deters investors.

An important index for the predictability and confidence of corruption was published by the WB/UB in 1997 for a cross section of countries. This data has been fruitfully employed in research. The World Bank (1997: 103, 172) argues that for a given level of corruption in a sample of thirty-nine industrial and developing countries, countries in which corruption functions more predictably have higher investment rates. This approach has been extended and further elaborated by Campos *et al.* (1999), who make use of the same data by the WB/UB in a cross section of fifty-nine countries. Controlling for GDP per head and secondary school enrollment, the authors find that both low predictability and the overall level of corruption reduce the ratio of investment to GDP. The authors conclude that the type of corruption, apart from its level, is crucial to its economic effects. This measure of the predictability of corruption by WB/UB has also been employed by Kaufmann and Wei (1999). The authors provide evidence that not only the level of corruption but also its predictability is a crucial determinant of the time managers must waste negotiating with bureaucrats. Wei (1997) uses the term

A related version of this chapter was originally published in *American Journal of Economics and Sociology*, 2002, Vol. 61 (4): 829–53.

"arbitrariness" to address the same issue, making use of different data from WEF. He argues that arbitrariness of corrupt transactions adversely impacts on capital inflows, justifying the hypothesis that corruption is more harmful than taxes. One conclusion for reform that is derived from these results could be that in order to dampen the adverse effects of corruption one should attempt to make it more predictable. Regulation and jurisdiction may help enforce corrupt deals and thus reestablish investors' confidence. Whether or not this is a sound conclusion will be discussed in this chapter.

Fighting corruption and restoring investors' confidence commonly go hand in hand. But a conflict between these two goals can arise when investors themselves have been paying bribes. Here is one example from the power industry in Pakistan. During the tenure of former Prime Minister Benazir Bhutto, many private power companies were awarded contracts to sell power to the state Water and Power Development Authority. But the government's main anti-corruption arm believed that kickbacks had been paid to bureaucrats and politicians in exchange for these deals. A change of government provided reason for the new government to renegotiate the old contracts and cut the electricity unit rate by 30 percent. But the IMF and the World Bank (whose loans to private power companies would soar in case of a price cut) warned the Pakistani government that unilaterally cutting electricity unit rates would seriously lower investors' confidence. In order to exert pressure on the government, multilateral donors postponed loan agreements.[1]

A related example comes from Indonesia, where, because of charges of corruption, the government's utility authority canceled its contracts to obtain power from large power plants built by joint-ventures with large foreign companies. In this case, relatives of Suharto had been given shares of the operations, raising suspicions of kickbacks and inflated prices for electricity. But foreign delegations of export credit insurers exerted pressure on the Indonesian government to honor the old contracts. It was argued that "[t]he future investment climate will be shaped by a long-term resolution... that protects the fundamental rights of investors. ... [Default] will impair Indonesia

[1] See *Financial Times*, October 29, 1998, "Pakistan: Attempts to Solve the Power Tariff Dispute" and Reuters, April 26, 1998, "Pakistani Power Row seen Scaring Investors."

and our ability to work with you in the future."[2] In both these cases there is a conflict between fighting corruption and honoring (potentially) illegal deals. If corruption is primarily harmful because of its adverse impact on the investor's confidence, reform might focus on restoring and preserving confidence, irrespective of how contracts had been arranged. It would be justified to resort to diplomatic measures and to honor deals, regardless of allegations of corruption. In a similar vein, Murphy *et al.* (1993: 413) propose that, instead of paying bribes, politicians should be given a stake in the operation, because this would restore investors' confidence in politicians' credibility and lower the risk of expropriation.

But, I dare to challenge this proposition. Corruption incurs costs to private parties not only because of the payment of bribes but also as a result of the variety of organizational problems that arise, and result in large transaction costs. Legal recourse is not available to lower these transaction costs. Investors face a trade-off between incurring transaction costs and living with unpredictability. Low transaction costs for corrupt agreements will provide further incentives to engage in corruption. Likewise, if corrupt deals cannot be enforced, this, in itself, can act as a deterrent to corruption. Under such circumstances, honoring corrupt deals is a cause of further entrenched corruption, which is likely to have various detrimental welfare effects besides destroying investors' confidence (Rose-Ackerman 1999). By the same token, large transaction costs of corrupt agreements, while being troublesome to investors, can, in turn, help in decreasing the level of corruption. These costs may render a corrupt transaction too costly and thus induce potential partners of a corrupt transaction to prefer legal alternatives.

So far, little attention has been paid in empirical research to the argument that predictable corruption can be a source of corruption on its own. In a survey in four Eastern European countries (the Czech Republic, Slovakia, Bulgaria, and the Ukraine), the general public was asked in 1998, "In case someone has successfully used his contacts, do you think that he/she would feel obliged to give a present to the person that helped him?" (Miller *et al.* 2001: 99). While 13.7 percent

[2] Citation from the *Far Eastern Economic Review*, October 21, 1999, "Trouble on the Grid." See also the *Financial Times*, March 10, 2000, "Interim Deal in Indonesia Power Dispute."

of the valid responses in the Czech Republic answered "No," only 10.4 percent in Slovakia and Bulgaria rejected the obligation of giving a present. In the Ukraine the value was as low as 8.9 percent.[3] A low percentage of "no" responses indicates that people feel obliged to reward the help of others, even when this may involve questionable and corrupt deals. Likewise, a high percentage of "no" responses indicates a propensity to opportunism. Interestingly, these values correlate with the positions of the four countries in the TI CPI. In 2000, the Czech Republic scored 4.3 and Bulgaria and Slovakia both obtained a score of 3.5, while for the Ukraine a value of 1.5 indicated high levels of corruption. This correlation suggests that feelings of obligations can help the enforcement of corrupt agreements. However, the variation between countries is not very large and, with only four countries included, the argument lacks robustness.

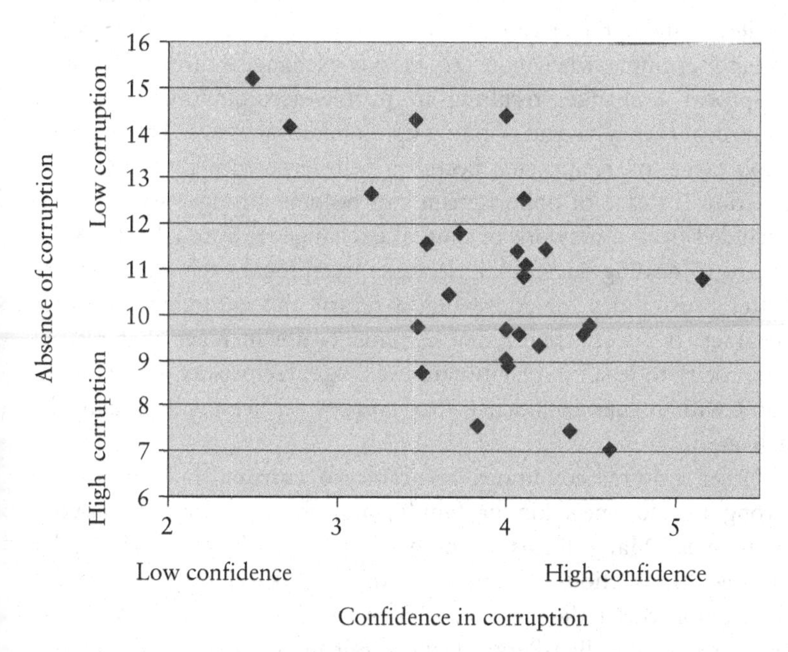

Figure 8.1. Corruption and confidence in twenty-six African countries
Source: Lambsdorff and Cornelius (2000).

[3] The results to this question are not reported in the publication. They were provided to me by W. Miller.

A more reliable link between predictability and corruption requires a larger sample of countries. Such a correlation is reported in Lambsdorff and Cornelius (2000) for a sample of twenty-six African countries (see Figure 8.1). Data has been gathered from African businesspeople as to whether they are confident about the delivery of a corrupt service after an irregular, additional payment has been made. A high level of confidence in the proper delivery of a corrupt service is observed to be highly correlated with an overall high degree of perceived corruption. This chapter will deepen this insight. By employing data from WB/UB, I argue that confidence in corruption contributes to high levels of corruption. I show that these results are robust throughout a variety of specifications and tests of causality.

8.2. Reciprocity, network ties, and corruption

Owing to cultural conditions, some countries are likely to provide more fertile ground to the private enforcement of corruption. This can be the case, for example, when monetary market exchange is rare in relation to reciprocal exchange, resulting in people accumulating rights for reciprocal favors instead of piling up on financial assets. The resulting importance of reciprocity becomes self-perpetuating, because the sanctions in case of opportunism can become stronger when one is excluded from a network of mutual exchange (Kranton 1996). With regard to dealing with public servants, reciprocal exchange provides better possibilities for concealing a return and enforcing a corrupt contract. If no effective moral sentiments are in place that restrict reciprocity to legal and legitimate exchange, reciprocity goes hand in hand with higher confidence that corrupt services will actually be delivered.

Other cultural conditions favorable to corrupt transactions are strong ties to one's kin or family, and the existence of network economies. Many forms of network ties are helpful for regular business transactions. Comparable to reciprocity, they represent a transaction cost reducing approach to enabling economic exchange; see, for example, Ben-Porath (1980). But in doing so, they may also facilitate the sealing of corrupt deals by embedding individuals in trusted social relationships that contain opportunism. Some observers even go as far as equating network ties with corruption and arguing that the different terms relate only to the subjective views held by observers. What is called corruption in one society would then be termed the stable use of networks in another. I do not follow this approach. In fact, the relationship between network ties and corruption is not as straightforward as one may assume. Countries such as Japan, Germany, Switzerland, or the Scandinavian countries are classified as coordinated market economies (CMEs), characterized by a widespread use of network ties (Soskice 1999). But at the same time they are rated largely free of corruption through a variety of subjective indicators. What seems to matter more than the mere existence of networks is whether networks strive largely for the material benefit of their members or, instead, cultivate some type of fairness toward third parties. A classic example with regard to network ties of Protestant sects has been provided by Weber (1920: 207–36). While these sects may sanction malfeasance of their members, it appears that this is less related to the material interests pursued by the network and more related to their members' general virtue. Acting fairly to third parties becomes a crucial consideration of such networks. Aspects of fairness may then be superior to the material interest of the network. Acting against these interests may thus be socially acceptable, particularly when this goes along with avoiding corruption. As soon as such considerations become relevant for networks, there is no simple argument that these necessarily facilitate corrupt agreements. On the other hand, when fairness to third parties is not an issue, kin and network ties may facilitate corrupt deals. For example, the Chinese *guanxi* networks embed individuals in social structures that provide safeguards against opportunism but simultaneously facilitate corrupt transactions (Schramm and Taube 2003).

8.3. The data

One approach to measuring the absence of predictability has been presented by Wei (1997). He derives a measure of arbitrariness from a business survey by the WEF. The question posed relates to the overall level of corruption, but Wei argues that the variance in the replies represents a form of arbitrariness. This argument can be considered valid if the insecurity among respondents about the true spread of bribes is reflected in the variance. Arbitrariness, thus defined, significantly enters into regressions of FDI for a cross section of countries. But, it has been questioned whether or not arbitrariness is adequately measured by this variable. Specifically, the variance among respondents could also reflect heterogeneous conditions in a country or be related to subjective difficulties among respondents in judging the right response on a questionnaire. It is therefore preferable to use data that directly relate to whether investors have confidence in the trustworthiness of corrupt counterparts.

I employ the data from a business survey conducted by WB/UB. Two questions included in the survey relate to a country's overall level of corruption (questions 12n and 14).[4] In addition, respondents were asked to assess three further characteristics of their home country with respect to "irregular additional payments," a term which is sufficiently close to "bribe and corruption": these questions address different aspects of confidence relating to the size of bribes, the possibility of additional requests, and the likeliness of opportunism:

Unpredictable size of bribes. Question 15 of the survey: "Firms in my line of business usually know in advance about how much this 'additional payment' is."

No additional requests. Question 16 of the survey: "Even if a firm has to make an 'additional payment' it always has to fear that it will be asked for more, e.g. by another official."

Level of opportunism. Question 17 of the survey: "If a firm pays the required 'additional payment' the service is usually also delivered as agreed."

The adequacy of these statements was supposed to be assessed on a scale ranging from 1 (always) to 6 (never). Consequently, answer 1 (always) to question 15 and 17 and answer 6 (never) to question 16 should indicate high predictability and high confidence, while answer 6 (never) to question 15 and 17 and answer 1 (always) to question 16 should indicate poor predictability and poor confidence.[5]

[4] These data are described in more detail in Brunetti *et al.* (1997). The data by WB/UB can be obtained from the Internet. www.macro.vwl.uni-mainz.de/ls/ger/94.php

[5] Problems began to emerge with this simple interpretation of the replies. At first, respondents who had basically never observed any additional payments had problems in answering questions 15 and 17. Some of them tended to answer that they never knew the amount of bribes in advance or that the service was never delivered when in fact what they had *wanted* to state was that corruption did not exist at all (Brunetti *et al.* 1997: 31–3). The sample has been truncated by the authors: those responding that no additional payments had to be made were left out. Given this truncation, the data appear acceptable.

Responses to question 16 presented a problem to our analysis, because respondents may not perfectly distinguish this question from an assessment of a country's overall level of corruption. The intention of the question is to determine whether there exist repeated bribes for the same transaction. But, respondents may mix this experience with the perception of a generally high level of corruption and the repeated payment of bribes for various distinguishable transactions.[6] In addition, question 16 could also relate to extortion. Extortion takes place if private parties are not voluntarily seeking preferential treatment by public decision-makers, but are forced to make payments, for example, in exchange for avoiding harassment. Extortion may particularly go along with insecurity concerning when the next payment is due. Respondents confronted with extortion will report a high frequency of additional payments and simultaneously fear that they will have to pay again and again. Since question 16 is overshadowed by these influences, it does not clearly reflect the level of predictability associated with voluntary corrupt agreements. For this reason I will not include it further in the analysis. The same approach was also taken by Campos *et al.* (1999).

Predictability can be so poor that a corrupt transaction is no longer worthwhile carrying out. This in turn can lower a country's level of corruption. Therefore, a testable hypothesis is that poor predictability lowers corruption. As investors have a choice between engaging in corruption and following a legal alternative instead,[7] large transaction costs of corruption will induce them to prefer the latter. But the availability of legal alternatives may vary between countries. Where they are readily available, there is less pressure to engage in corruption. Another subjective indicator from WB/UB can be used to depict the existence of legal alternatives: the availability of complaints mechanisms. This was depicted by question 18 in the survey: "If a government agent acts against the rules I can usually go to another official or to his superior and get the correct treatment."

[6] This association is even stronger, considering that in question 14 the overall level of corruption is determined according to the question: "It is common for firms in my line of business to have to pay some irregular 'additional payments' to get things done." This commonality of bribes should also increase if repeated bribes for the same transaction are required.

[7] Observe that such an alternative is not present in the case of extortion.

This variable will be called "legal alternatives" in the subsequent regressions.

The survey was conducted in seventy-four countries. But some inconsistency in the data emerged for Zimbabwe. Upon request, Beatrice Weder, one of the authors of these data, could not clarify these inconsistencies and, furthermore, warned that data for Brazil were also less reliable. Both these countries were consequently omitted. A description of the data is provided in Tables 8.A1 and 8.A2, Appendix 1. Levels of corruption are determined by questions 12n and 14 from WB/UB. Both variables are directed toward the frequency of corruption and its effect on business conduct. I standardize responses to these questions and take the simple average as an index for the perceived level of corruption.[8] The index is standardized to the mean and standard deviation of the TI CPI. This will simplify comparisons to regressions conducted thereafter. Since 10 indicates a clean country and 0 a high level of corruption, the variable will be called "absence of corruption."

There have already been a variety of investigations determining the causes of corruption. An assessment as to whether transaction costs significantly contribute to the causes of corruption should not disregard the other determinants that have been identified. Specifically, regressions should control for GDP per head (logarithm of the dollar value as determined by the World Development Indicators for 1995), because levels of corruption tend to correlate with a country's level of development. Since GDP per head may also correlate with the transaction costs of corruption, the omission of this variable would introduce an omitted variable bias and the results would risk losing validity. Regressions should also control for the impact of the British colonies, a dummy variable that has been found by Treisman (2000) to exert a positive impact on the absence of corruption.[9] I determine this variable here by assigning the value 1 to countries that were British colonies at some stage during the last one hundred years.

[8] Responses to question 12n had to be multiplied by -1. The results obtained in the regressions also hold taking either question 12n or 14 as the indicator for the level of corruption.

[9] The precise reason for this impact is unclear. Treisman (2000) argues that a pro-British bias in the survey responses is unlikely to be the reason and argues that there might indeed be less corruption in British colonies. The reason could be the common law system and a legal culture left behind in British colonies.

8.4. Regression analysis

As shown in Table 8.A2 in Appendix 1, a strong correlation exists between corruption and the predictability of corrupt transactions as denoted by the correlations between questions 12n, 14, 15, and 17. This correlation is represented by Figures 8.2 and 8.3. Similar low levels of corruption are obtained when public officials act opportunistically and the delivery of the corrupt service is uncertain. This association suggests that confidence in a corrupt system, while lowering the transaction costs for a single operation on the one hand, can itself be a source of corruption on the other hand.

Absence of corruption, certainly, is also driven by many other explanatory variables. Their impact must be controlled in order to arrive at unbiased coefficients. This requires the application of the multivariate regression technique, as shown in Table 8.1. The nonspecialist can quickly understand this table by looking at the (White-corrected) *t*-statistics, which are reported in parenthesis below the coefficients. Values above 2 or below −2 indicate that the coefficient is significant, meaning that it does obtain a noteworthy impact on the level of corruption.

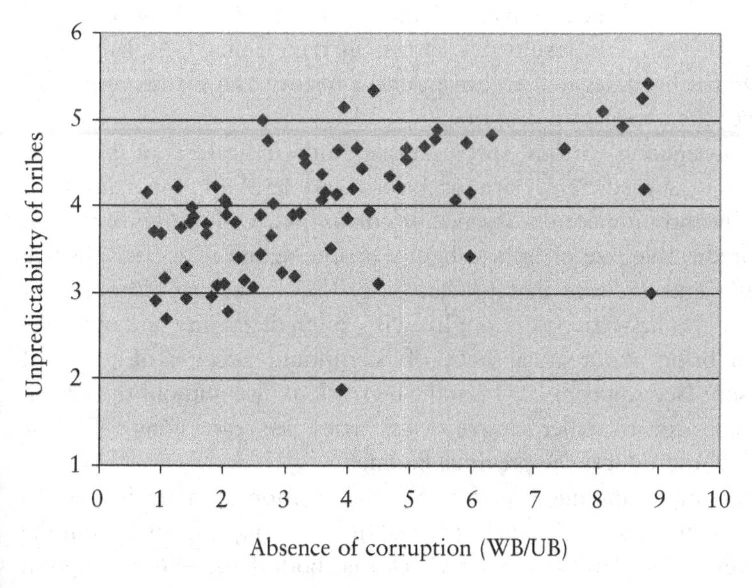

Figure 8.2. Unpredictability of bribes

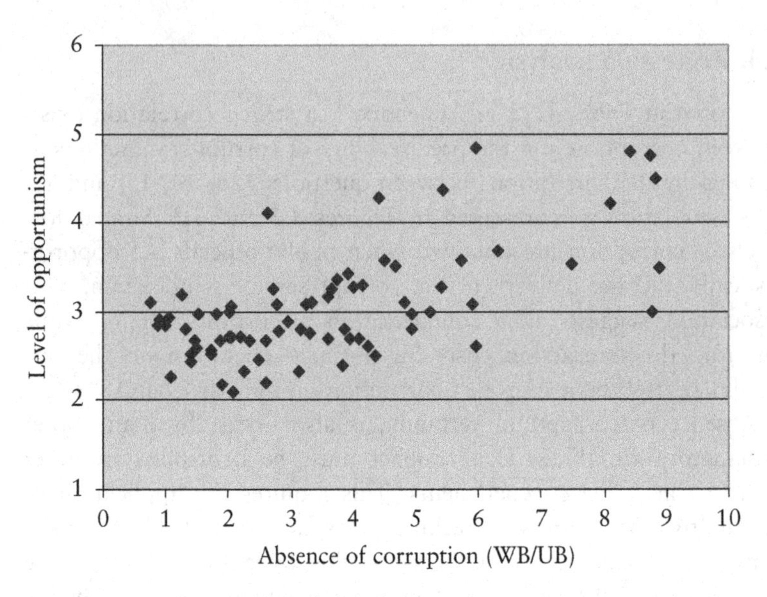

Figure 8.3. Opportunism and the absence of corruption

I test for income (GDP per head in logarithmic scale), whether a country has formerly been a British colony and whether respondents reported legal alternatives to the payment of corruption (legal alternatives). The results are shown in regressions 1–4, Table 8.1. GDP per head, legal alternatives, and a history as a British colony all lower the extent of corruption.

Throughout various specifications both indicators of predictability – unpredictable size of bribes and level of opportunism – significantly impact on absence of corruption. Only in regression 4, unpredictable size of bribes slightly misses significance. The positive coefficients indicate that predictability (low values to responses 15 and 17) enhances corruption; likewise, unpredictability and opportunism bring about an absence of corruption. Because of technical reasons (see Appendix 2) I run the regressions also without the British colonies for a smaller sample of countries; see regressions 5–7. This largely reproduces the previous findings.

An important question for the investigation at hand is how to determine a country's level of corruption. Picking responses from the survey by WB/UB has the drawback that both the level of corruption and its predictability are determined by the same sample of

Table 8.1 OLS, Dependent variable: absence of corruption, WB/UB

Independent variables	*1*	*2*	*3*	*4*	*5*	*6*	*7*
Constant	– 5.33	– 8.40	– 8.66	– 1.07	– 1.06	2.32	– 3.35
	(–4.8)	(–8.7)	(–9.5)	(–0.5)	(–0.4)	(1.2)	(–1.3)
Unpredictable size of bribes	0.87	1.09	0.87	0.42	0.65		1.33
	(2.5)	(4.0)	(3.3)	(1.6)	(2.1)		(5.2)
Level of opportunism	1.79	0.53	0.69	0.99	1.15	1.61	
	(4.7)	(1.5)	(2.1)	(3.2)	(3.5)	(6.2)	
GDP/head 1995		0.80	0.86	0.64	0.40	0.34	0.66
		(6.9)	(7.9)	(5.6)	(3.2)	(2.7)	(5.9)
Britishy colony			1.17	0.85			
			(3.3)	(2.6)			
Legal alternatives				– 1.29	– 1.20	– 1.64	– 0.89
				(–4.1)	(–3.2)	(–5.07)	(–2.2)
Observations	72	71	71	71	55	55	55
R^2	0.52	0.72	0.76	0.81	0.84	0.74	0.80
Jarque-Bera	16.9	3.0	0.5	0.3	1.9	1.2	0.9

respondents. One potential criticism is that these data are subjective assessments. The relationship thus reported may come about if respondents have subjectively anticipated what this chapter tries to prove. A notion among respondents that predictability increases corruption could influence their assessments. This may suggest that the results do not exhibit actual relationships between these variables, but merely how respondents consider this relationship to be.

Whether this objection is relevant can be tested by using another measure of corruption, the TI CPI, as described in Chapter 1 and the appendix on pages 236–255. I use the data from 1999 here, given that the other data is from a similar period in time. This composite index, however, also uses the data by WB/UB. It is thus not immune to the points raised above. I will therefore modify the CPI by determining each country's score only with data other than those by WB/UB. This

Table 8.2 OLS; Dependent variable: absence of corruption, Transparency International

Independent variables	*1*	*2*	*3*	*4*	*5*	*6*	*7*
Constant	– 2.22	– 5.43	– 5.72	0.89	– 1.56	2.23	– 2.59
	(–2.1)	(–6.0)	(6.3)	(0.4)	(–0.6)	(1.0)	(–1.0)
Unpredictable size of bribes	0.49	0.65	0.53	0.18	0.74		1.06
	(1.4)	(2.6)	(2.1)	(0.7)	(2.3)		(3.9)
Level of opportunism	1.48	0.35	0.41	0.65	0.57	1.03	
	(4.0)	(1.1)	(1.3)	(2.2)	(1.6)	(3.6)	
GDP/head 1995		0.78	0.84	0.62	0.47	0.44	0.60
		(6.9)	(7.2)	(4.9)	(3.1)	(2.7)	(4.5)
British colony			0.60	0.22			
			(1.6)	(0.6)			
Legal alternatives				– 1.11	– 0.64	– 1.18	– 0.52
				(–3.2)	(–1.5)	(–3.1)	(–1.2)
Observations	62	62	62	62	47	47	47
R^2	0.45	0.70	0.71	0.76	0.77	0.74	076
Jarque-Bera	7.2	2.1	2.0	0.9	0.5	1.0	0.4

is still a subjective indicator for actual levels of corruption, but in contrast to the data by WB/UB it relates to different respondents. If the observed relationship holds, we can be more confident that it does not result from subjective conjectures. I conduct the same regressions as before. The results are given in Table 8.2, with regressions 5–7 excluding British colonies. It can be observed that compared with Table 8.1, the coefficients for "unpredictable size of bribes" and "level of opportunism" are smaller and less significant. However, in most specifications they remain significant at conventional levels, particularly when their influence is tested separately, as in regressions 6 and 7. Appendix 2 of this chapter provides some further technical details, particularly with respect to causality, sample selection, and robustness.

8.5. Conclusion

Investors' confidence suffers from corruption. Fighting corruption and restoring investors' confidence will therefore typically go hand in hand. But a conflict between these two goals can arise when investors themselves have been paying bribes. Attempts to protect primarily investors' confidence in a corrupt environment are misplaced, because the confidence involved may itself be a source of further embedded corruption. This chapter presents evidence that the predictability of corruption causes further corruption. When businesspeople have confidence that after paying a bribe a return will be provided as promised, there is less motivation to seek legal alternatives. Thus, a predictable type of corruption that goes along with investors' confidence should not lead to complacency among policy-makers, because this type enhances the further spread of corruption.

To root out corruption, it may be necessary to risk destroying some of the confidence that goes along with it: the trust that corrupt favors are reciprocated. Reform strategies should be revised with regard to their repercussions on this type of trust. For example, encouraging whistle-blowing can help in destroying the confidence among corrupt partners. Making sure that courts do not enforce corrupt agreements is another fruitful consideration. Finally, as the two case studies discussed in the introduction to this chapter suggest, politicians must stop honoring corrupt agreements.

Appendix 1: Description of WB/UB-data

Table 8.A1 Distribution

	Q12N	*Q14*	*Q15*	*Q17*	*Q18*
Mean	4.14	3.79	4.04	3.06	3.81
Maximum	5.26	5.96	5.80	5.47	4.83
Minimum	1.56	2.36	2.70	2.10	2.37
Standard Deviation	0.88	0.90	0.71	0.65	0.51
Skewness	– 1.23	0.50	0.11	1.48	– 0.59
Kurtosis	3.89	2.33	2.43	5.35	2.96
Jarque-Bera	20.54	4.39	1.14	42.85	4.15

Table 8.A2 Correlation coefficients

	Q12N	*Q14*	*Q15*	*Q17*	*Q18*
Q12N high value = corruption	1	−0.80	−0.43	−0.62	0.60
Q14 low value = corruption	−0.80	1	0.74	0.70	−0.68
Q15 (Unpredictable size of bribes) low value = predictable	−0.43	0.74	1	0.66	−0.48
Q16 (No additional requests) high value = no requests	−0.67	0.86	0.73	0.63	−0.53
Q17 (Level of opportunism) low value = no opportunism	−0.62	0.70	0.66	1	−0.32
Q18 (Legal alternatives low value = effective legal alternatives)	0.60	−0.68	−0.48	−0.32	1

Appendix 2: Technical details to the regressions

Whether the relationships are actually linear, as assumed in the regressions, is certainly food for debate. Analyzing the impact of cross-terms on residuals revealed that the British colonies, in particular, are performing differently compared with other countries and that this difference is not captured well by a dummy variable. This motivated to rerun the regressions without British colonies.

Regressions on a cross section of countries can certainly be affected by the selected sample of countries. There is no perfect statistical approach to investigate the relevance of this problem because data on further countries is not available. A selection bias is particularly relevant when countries have not been picked at random but must meet certain criteria in order to qualify for inclusion. Knack and Azfar (2003) provide evidence that for some investigations the resulting limited sample can bias regression results, such as those that state a positive correlation between country size and corruption. This arises because data on governance are commonly collected in order to inform investors. However, investors are barely interested in countries that are small and corrupt. Regression analysis then reveals a significant and positive relationship between corruption and country size, simply because small and corrupt countries are disregarded by the institutions that provide data to investors. It is not clear whether the relationship between confidence and corruption would also be misrepresented if sample selection were biased. But, more important, the data by WB/UB were not gathered in order to inform investors and thus are less susceptible to the aforementioned type of selection bias. Instead, the data include largely World Bank debtor countries, in addition to some industrial countries that serve as a benchmark for the results. Consequently, there is no apparent bias toward clean and large countries. For example, while the countries in the WEF's Global Competitiveness Report (GCR) have on average 80 million inhabitants, those surveyed by WB/UB have 50 million. While countries in the GCR obtain a mean score of 6.1 in the CPI, those from WB/UB score 4.2 on the average, a value that largely resembles the world average. The selection of countries can thus be assumed to be representative of the world as a whole; no indicator exists hinting at a potential selection bias.

Any type of regression is certainly vulnerable to omitted variables bias. The omission of variables that would impact on both confidence and levels of corruption would bias the results. For example, high-income countries may simultaneously rely less on reciprocal exchange and contain levels of corruption. It was thus important to include GDP per head in the regressions. In countries where legal alternatives and complaint mechanisms are not available, confidence in corruption may be high while at the same time high levels of corruption are induced. It was thus important to control for the quality of legal alternatives. Another variable could be the existence of bothersome regulation. The resulting frequent encounter between private business and bureaucrats can help in establishing trusted relationships, but at the same time regulation creates opportunities for corruption. In order to test the relevance of this impact, an indicator of regulation was taken from WB/UB, measuring to what extent regulations (regarding foreign trade, foreign currency, labor, or new operations) and price controls are problematic for doing business. This variable was insignificant. Since it did not further alter the results, the regression is not reported here.[10] To the best of my knowledge there are no further crucial variables whose omission could have biased the results.

[10] Low-income countries exhibited higher levels of regulation. The effect of regulation on corruption may thus already be captured by GDP per head.

Predictability can smooth out and secure corrupt deals and become a cause for corruption. However, there is also reason to assume the reverse may occur. When large profits are at stake for those who engage in corruption, an environment may be designed that allows for these deals to become predictable. For example, prospects of future corrupt gains through repetitive exchange can help enforce current dealings (Lambsdorff 2002a; Chapter 6 of this book). Such reverse causality would bias results from ordinary least squares (OLS) regressions. The first task in dealing with this issue is to find instrumental variables. These should be well correlated with predictability, but not with the error term of the regressions. The instrument to be used here is the proportion of Protestants in a country. Data on the number of Protestants are from La Porta *et al.* (1999). Protestantism was linked by Treisman (2000), Paldam (2001) and (La Porta *et al.* 1997; 1999) to lower levels of corruption. Certainly, with regard to corrupt deals, religion may be effective in setting up ethical guidelines. Resulting intrinsic obstacles may motivate potential actors to reject a corrupt transaction because they also value its moral costs. But, compared with Protestantism, other religions are more hierarchical (La Porta *et al.* 1997). This is commonly considered to be the crucial reason that societies with large shares of Protestants exhibit lower levels of corruption. But the actual link between hierarchy and corruption needs further elaboration.

As argued previously, by sanctioning opportunism networks may make corrupt deals more secure and predictable.[11] But for this impact to occur, network members' ethical considerations that run counter to corruption must be effectively suppressed. A network that aims at advancing the material benefit of its members requires control mechanisms and, in particular, a hierarchical order. Protestants are less embedded in hierarchical structures, and they may be less easily involved in binding networks that disregard the negative externalities their actions impose on outsiders. On the average, they may face fewer extrinsic obstacles. Societies with a large share of Protestants cultivate attitudes in which individuals are less reliable toward their

[11] La Porta *et al.* (1997) emphasize that hierarchical forms of religion are detrimental to civic engagement, a factor that is seen to contain corruption. But civic engagement may also lead to corruption, particularly when it relates to the engagement of public servants. The impact of religion on the predictability of corruption may thus be the dominant argument.

kin and are less subject to the material interests of their immediate social environment. In these cases, individuals might even be willing to act opportunistically, particularly when the illegitimacy of a corrupt deal could provide an excuse for their behavior. Thus, our assumption is that Protestant Christianity tends to decrease corruption because it increases the transactional difficulties that accompany corrupt contracts.

The proportion of Protestants correlates at the 0.46 level with "unpredictable size of bribes," and at the 0.35 level with "level of opportunism," making this a good instrument. Other instruments that were considered are colonial history and ethnolinguistic fractionalization. Colonial history may have engendered covert transactions among the indigenous population and the use of reciprocal exchange as a means to avoid exploitative taxation and expropriation by the colonizer. These institutions may in turn provide fertile ground for securing corrupt transactions. As a result, opportunism among partners in a corrupt transaction may be less of a problem in former colonies. Ethnolinguistic fractionalization has been suggested by Mauro (1995) as a factor affecting levels of corruption. For more recent evidence on this link, see Box 2. A good deal of this impact can again be related to transactional considerations, because fractionalized societies may honor reciprocal exchange as a means of favoring their respective kin or ethnic group. This enables corrupt exchange to flourish and avoids opportunism among clansmen. But regressing "unpredictable size of bribes" and "level of opportunism" on the proportion of Protestants and these variables shows that their impact was insignificant. These instruments were therefore disregarded. Apart from its impact on opportunism and predictability, Protestantism may directly impact on corruption. This impact may arise if Protestant societies tend to establish more procedurally and legally oriented institutions, which in turn help in countering corruption. Whether this assumption holds may be food for debate. If it does, Protestant societies would develop legal alternatives available to those who reject getting involved in corruption. Since this variable is controlled for in the regression, this potential type of impact would not bias the regressions.

The results are in Table 8.A3. For all other variables (GDP per head, British colony, legal alternatives), problems with endogeneity were not considered relevant and the variables were also used as

Table 8.A3 TSLS; Dependent variable: Absence of Corruption, Transparency International; instrument: share of Protestants

Independent variables	*1*	*2*	*3*	*4*	*5*	*6*
Constant	– 5.02	– 8.05	– 21.55	– 0.48	– 4.17	0.20
	(–1.3)	(–4.7)	(–2.2)	(–0.2)	(–4.0)	(0.1)
Unpredictable size of bribes	1.32	3.16	4.10			
	(2.3)	(3.0)	(2.7)			
Level of opportunism				1.47	2.47	2.21
				(2.3)	(3.0)	(2.7)
GDP/head 1995	0.74	– 0.01	0.10	0.49	0.11	0.05
	(6.2)	(–0.0)	(0.4)	(2.7)	(0.3)	(0.2)
British colony	0.02			0.05		
	(0.4)			(1.2)		
Legal alternatives	– 0.47		2.30	– 0.98		– 0.82
	(–1.0)		(1.6)	(–2.9)		(–1.8)
Observations	63	47	47	63	47	47
R^2	0.72	0.64	0.72	0.72	0.64	0.72
Jarque-Bera	1.8	1.1	0.4	1.8	1.1	0.4

instruments. Regressions 1 and 4 include all countries, while British colonies are disregarded in the other regressions. In regression 2 and 3, the share of Protestants did not significantly impact on "unpredictable size of bribes" and the results should therefore not be overrated. For all other regressions the share of Protestants was significant, supporting its use as an instrument. The results confirm that the impact of "unpredictable size of bribes" and "level of opportunism" on absence of corruption remains significant and positive.

9 Corrupt relational contracting

9.1. Introduction

> "Why are so many politicians lawyers? – because everyone employs lawyers, so the congressman's firm is a suitable avenue of compensation, whereas a physician would have to be given bribes rather than patronage."
>
> Stigler (1971)

Corruption, no doubt, is regarded as one of the modern evils. It is carried out by those with a criminal intention and motivated by greed. Yet, if this simple explanation were valid, why would we have to face in reality some disturbing counterexamples? Why, in particular, do we face a significant pattern where corrupt people tend to be involved in a variety of charitable institutions? Why do many bribers and bribees engage in an assortment of regular business transactions and political initiatives where they are regarded as trustworthy and honest partners? Our viewpoint of them as criminals contradicts their social engagement. The trust they enjoy in their regular relations sounds rather controversial, given their misuse of entrusted power.

A straightforward argument would, certainly, point out that corrupt actors must be entrusted with power before misusing it. There must be opportunities for corrupt misbehavior. These opportunities commonly arise where public office holders are in a monopoly position, have discretion in interpreting, applying, or changing the law, and lack accountability (Klitgaard 1988: 75). This often takes place either in the area of public procurement or where excessive government regulation

A related version of this chapter was jointly written with Utku Teksoz and was originally published in *The New Institutional Economics of Corruption – Norms, Trust, and Reciprocity*, ed. by J. Graf Lambsdorff, M. Schramm, and M. Taube, (London: Routledge), 2004, 138–51.

interferes with market forces. Since elected politicians are entrusted with power whereas appointed bureaucrats have informational advantages over their superiors, they can also misuse their position for corrupt purposes. A certain level of trust is therefore a basic prerequisite to corruption. But what motivates corrupt people to misuse this power? One hypothesis would suggest that these are just hypocrites. They may seek to profit from a reputation for altruism and commitment whereas in reality self-seeking is all that guides them. Social engagement would simply serve to camouflage their true intentions. Their trustworthiness is based entirely on their capacity to disclose their true corrupt goals. Indeed, there is some truth to this explanation. Nonetheless, this chapter provides an alternative one: there hardly exists such a thing as a purely corrupt relationship. Corrupt deals are only commonly embedded in more complex relationships between different actors. More often than not, these relationships entail also a variety of legal transactions and even charitable ones.

This chapter aims to examine the link between completely legal relationships and illegal ones. This link, basically, relates to the fact that corrupt arrangements go along with high transaction costs. Corrupt relationships are unstable. They entail that sticking to one's word may be dominated by betrayal and fraud. Corrupt agreements may even end up in mutual denunciation. Preexisting legal relationships can lower these transaction costs and serve as a basis for the enforcement of corrupt arrangements.

In order to establish the link between corruption and legal exchange we will start with a brief review of the new institutional economics framework and apply it to corrupt deals (Section 6.2). How legal exchange can serve as a basis for sealing and enforcing corrupt deals will be illustrated on the basis of case studies (Section 6.3). A final section concludes and provides policy recommendations.

9.2. The contribution of the new institutional economics

Transaction cost analysis

Since Coase (1937) it is standard to assume that exchanging goods or services goes along with transaction costs. A crucial cause for the existence of these costs is that information is substantially incomplete. A good deal of time and material resources are therefore spent for searching the right contract partner, gathering enough background information about the market conditions, working out the details of the contracts, and seeking measures – legal or informal – to cover the parties against opportunistic behavior. Owing to these costs, people's information to assess market opportunities and to predict the future is necessarily incomplete. Another aspect of the transaction costs is that their level is negatively associated to the level of mutual trust among the contract partners (Furubotn and Richter 1998: 49). That is, the less trust among contractors, the more time, effort, and money must be spent to organize an exchange. This explains partly why, in the case of large transaction costs, contractual relationships tend to be sticky in that most transactions are carried out repeatedly with well-acquainted business partners rather than with anonymous market participants.

The limited information available to some business partners can be exploited by others who possess an informational advantage. This type of behavior is generally termed "opportunism," defined as self-interest seeking with guile (Williamson 1985). This includes intended forms of deceit such as lying, stealing, distorting, obfuscating, and disguising. Opportunism can only arise when information is distributed asymmetrically. Given the presence of *ex-ante* asymmetric information, the problem of adverse selection may arise depending on the contract design. A similar argument is viable for the case of *ex-post* asymmetric information and the problem of moral hazard. In order to cope with this situation, *ex-ante* screening efforts are made and *ex-post* safeguards are created (Williamson 1985: 64).

The problem of informational asymmetry is not only one between the contracting parties but also vis-à-vis outsiders. Even if both contracting parties are well informed about each other and the efforts exerted, they may not be able to communicate this to a third party. While an employer may know about the shirking of her employee, he may fail to prove this to a court. The issue of informational asymmetry therefore becomes even stronger, because deviations from contracts must not only be observed by partners but also be proven to outsiders. Some disputes are impossible to resolve in court because partners fail to prove an accusation to outsiders (Hart 1987: 168).

Relational contracting

Informational asymmetries and the risk or opportunism suggest that resources should be devoted to gathering as much information as possible. Yet, there are transaction costs involved for this purpose. Gathering information is particularly dear in the case of long-term contracts. Here it becomes difficult to anticipate the various eventualities that may occur during the life of a relationship. There arise costs of deciding and reaching an agreement about how to deal with such eventualities, as well as those of writing the contract in a sufficiently clear and unambiguous way so that the terms of contract can be enforced (Hart 1987: 166). Given these costs, it becomes preferable to live with limited information. Contracts will be incomplete because it might be either impossible, or simply uneconomic, to anticipate all contingencies in advance. As a matter of fact, the information that parties have on the agreed-upon process tends to increase during the contract execution stage compared with the outset (Nelson and Winter 1982: 96–139). Especially in long-term relationships, such as labor contracts, parties generally set off with an initially incomplete contract. When further information is obtained in the process of exchange, contracts can then be further specified. Consequently, leaving certain gaps in the contract design appears to be a perfectly rational approach to make the contracts flexible enough to fit any contingencies. This suggests a "relational" type of contract with the duration and the complexity of contracts increasing progressively (Macneil 1978: 890). Based on Macneil's work, Williamson (1985) recognizes that between the neoclassical and relational contracting schemes there is a shift of emphasis from the original agreements in the former to the entire relation as it evolves through time in the latter.

Contracts are relational to the extent that it is impossible to reduce the terms of agreement to well-defined obligations (Goetz and Scott 1981: 1091). Instead of well-defined obligations, partners now anticipate trouble as a normal outcome, seeking certain measures – apart from legal ones – for their resolution (Macneil 1974: 738–40). Defined as such, relational contracts are implicit, informal, and nonbinding transactions that are embedded in a structure of relations and long-term business associations (Furubotn and Richter 1998: 158). Owing to their incomplete nature, the contracts form part of a continuous relationship. The negotiation stage assumes a continuous character, since it is the implicitly or explicitly stated intention that settling new arrangements takes place by negotiating over future transactions. The term continuous is employed in the sense that there is no strictly defined and prespecified beginning and ending terms of the relations. The continuity of enforcement and renegotiations stabilizes the relationship (Macneil 1974: 753).

While a simple neoclassical analysis of exchange assumes anonymity of exchange partners, relational contracting suggests that the identity of the people engaged in transactions matters. Certain transactions are bound to remain within a closed group of associates. Such cost-minimizing transactions require an initial investment in transaction-specific resources. One refers to this as a specialization of identity. Identity matters because engaging in a certain transaction necessitates the negotiation of certain rules, norms, or codes of conduct among the related parties. Once the identity of the contracting parties change, the whole process starts over, implying new transaction costs. The identity-specific exchange relationships are themselves deterrent against opportunistic behavior, as cheating now would spare the parties from future benefits of the ongoing relation (Ben-Porath, 1980: 1–6). Individuals tend to conduct their relations within their own group not only because of the transaction costs of finding new partners but also because effective sanctions can be imposed more efficiently within a small group.[1] Accordingly, reliance on reciprocal business relationships and group-enforcement mechanisms are transaction cost-reducing mechanisms (Klein *et al.* 1978).

Contract-enforcement mechanisms can be purposefully designed with an aim to contain opportunistic behavior. However, the causality may also run in reverse direction, that is, relationships might be conducted exclusively among people with an already established degree of social embeddedness so as to ensure the honoring of contracts. Presence of social embeddedness, such as being colleagues in a certain institution or network, makes opportunism a less likely outcome. Being embedded in a social relationship facilitates containing opportunism

[1] See Schramm and Taube (2003) for an interesting discussion of the Chinese *Guanxi* networks and how the efficiency of the sanctions are jeopardized as the group size increases.

thanks to the presence of safeguarding mechanisms (Granovetter 1992). Social embeddedness, such as family and kinship ties, is a condition that outlives the duration of contracts. Furthermore, these cannot be changed easily. Therefore, an individual would have an interest in staying loyal to her group, even when the temptation for opportunism is great.

Corrupt contracting

In a variety of respects, an analysis of legal contracts can fruitfully be applied to corrupt contracts. There are apparent parallels: partners may cheat each other; there might be informational asymmetries; safeguards against opportunism must be supplied; trust might be instrumental to design a corrupt transaction; social embeddedness may facilitate corrupt deals. And because all these mechanisms go along with transaction costs, unresolved contractual problems between partners are likely.

But concerning transaction costs and enforcement mechanisms there are three major differences between corrupt and legal deals (Lambsdorff 2002a; Chapter 6 of this book). First, courts do not enforce corrupt deals. Therefore, private ordering must be perfected to such an extent that it completely substitutes for the lack of legal sanctions. The associated transaction costs are likely to increase considerably and the remaining loopholes are expected to be numerous. Second, corrupt deals are sealed in secrecy. This implies that transaction costs associated with sealing corrupt deals are substantially higher. Searches for partners as well as negotiations and enforcement of contracts have to be carried out away from the eyes of the public. Transparent means, such as advertising, are not available. Alternative forms, which are likely to be more expensive, have to be sought. Third, the corrupt deals have an aftermath, unlike the legal ones. The parties end up being mutually dependent on one another, because they hold secret information about the other party. Corrupt deals put the partners of such deals at the mercy of one another. Even long after the service in question is rendered, the partners remain in a binding relationship of mutual dependence, which can also serve as a basis for extortion or hush-money. Denunciation can be used as a threat when one of the parties has more to lose from a potential exposure of involvement in corrupt activities.

If there are prospects of negotiating further contracts with the same people over time, both the transaction costs and risks associated with the advertising, gaining trust, and forming a capital of common knowledge are substantially reduced. The process of seeking partners and of negotiating and enforcing contracts displays considerable risks of denunciation in each stage, which forces corrupt relationships to have a closed nature vis-à-vis the outsiders. Therefore, the very illegality of corruption makes it imperatively an identity-specific transaction. Trust becomes a crucial element in corrupt deals. In order to cover the parties against *ex-post* opportunistic behavior, corrupt deals are more often than not sealed between parties enjoying a considerable degree of mutual trust.

9.3. Linking corruption to legal exchange

Corrupt contracts go along with higher transactional difficulties than legal contracts. There exists a variety of mechanisms to lower these transaction costs (della Porta and Vanucci 1999; Husted 1994; Lambert-Mogiliansky 2002; Lambsdorff 1999; 2002a; 2002c; see Chapters 6 and 7; Rose-Ackerman 1999: 91–110; Vanucci 2000). Here we focus on one such mechanism: linking a corrupt deal to an established legal relationship. The presence of a perfectly legal relationship between two parties may set a fertile ground for corrupt deals to flourish. Corruption in this case is not a single act between anonymous partners. Rather, it is embedded into a complex relationship. Corruption comprises implicit, informal, and nonbinding agreements that are enforced by being rooted in long-term business or hierarchical associations.

In the context of carrying out legal deals, a variety of means is available to business partners to sanction each other. They can destroy each other's reputation, end profitable future exchange, penalize each other when provided with hierarchical control, or transform their existing friendship into a relationship with mutual accusations. Threatening such sanctions helps the enforcement of legal deals. In the presence of already established legal relationships, the parties might find it tempting to collude for proceeding with a corrupt deal. As their legal relationship provides the possibility to sanction each other, threatening sanctions can also be used to enforce a corrupt side-agreement. Above that, they can economize on search costs, because they already know each other and simply expand the range of exchange to include corrupt agreements also. For anonymous partners it is difficult to carry out a corrupt transaction. But for those with preexisting legal ties it will be much easier to link their corrupt transaction to the established legal relationship. Parties may initially start off with a legal relationship that later deteriorates into one where corrupt deals also are carried out. The presence of trust in this case facilitates the process. The core proposition of this chapter is therefore that corrupt transactions are often linked to legal ones. Corrupt transactions are often embedded in social relationships where a variety of legal transactions are also carried out. We will discuss some case studies in this section to show how the theory applies to real life.

Three case studies from Germany

Case 1

A recent corruption scandal in Germany involved Günter R., an ex-social democratic MP from Bielefeld.[2] The news that Günter R. was arrested on the charges of corruption fell like a bomb right into the heart of his hometown, Bielefeld. Had he not been an almost ideal example of a "good citizen" for years and years? His social commitment had been exemplary. He was engaged in a series of charity organizations, NGOs, and, nonprofit organizations with a particular emphasis on education. Nonetheless, he was accused of having abused these positions for his self-enrichment amounting to six-digit figures in German Marks during 1995–2000. One of the foundations, whose chair was held by Günter R., operated a nonprofit company for lifestyle and education projects in cooperation with the German youth hostel association. These projects involved a considerable activity of construction. In the mid-1990s, the acquaintance between Lutz-Peter B., the managing director of a construction enterprise, and Günter R. grew closer. This acquaintance pushed the nonprofit targets of the Bielefeld politician to the background. He clearly had a clean hand to mediate certain contracts to the former's enterprise. Overinvoicing was used to hide the crimes. Against these invoices, the nonprofit organizations led by Günter R. paid out

[2] *Süddeutsche Zeitung*, "Langjähriger Bundestagsabgeordneter in Haft" January 11, 2002.

exaggerated sums, the kickbacks being divided between him and the managers of the aforementioned enterprise. The illegal cash flow was also masked by the fact that Günter R. received wages for his alleged activity as a "construction supervisor."

What conclusions should one draw from this case and countless similar ones? One might suggest that these people simply disguise their true nature and use their position to camouflage their corrupt transactions. An alternative proposition is that social engagement, trusted relationships within firms, and a reputation for honesty are not at all in contrast to corrupt dealings. On the contrary, Günter R. needed his reputation so as to be trusted when it came to striking corrupt deals. Had he been regarded as purely self-seeking, he might not have been able to establish a trusted relationship with Lutz-Peter B.

Case 2

As of 1992, Leonard A., director of Bayerische Vereinsbank in Potsdam, was tired of working in hastily erected provisional accommodations – like most of his competitors who had rushed into former East Germany's banking market after reunification. Instead, he dreamt of a luxurious office in the best area of the city of Potsdam, on a site owned by the city where construction was still blocked by pending restitution claims. There was yet another problem. One of the major competitors of the Bayerische Vereinsbank also showed interest in the property, hence drawing attention to the area. In order to work around these impediments A. sought out his friend and tennis partner Detlef K., city official for construction and housing since 1990. He let their personal relations play a role in the quest for the site. Consequently, A. obtained a construction permit before ordinary procedures had been finalized and his bank was preferred to its competitor when the city sold the building site. In exchange, the bank gave K. a legally certified option for buying an exquisite mansion for a price considerably below the market prices. The contract was formulated such that K. did not participate directly as a buyer; instead he was only given an option to buy the aforementioned dwelling. The winds, however, changed for all participants. First, the city mayor Horst G. rotated the personnel in the city office for construction and housing. In the meantime, higher authorities from the Bayerische Vereinsbank declared the option for

K. void. This had an impact on the friendship between the two tennis partners. What other explanation could there be for the fact that years later two friends of K. accused A. of demanding personal gratification in exchange for giving out bank loans, providing taped evidence? A. fought back by denouncing the former illegal deal with K. While A. served a thirty-month prison term, K. was expelled from office in 1998.[3]

In this case, a regular relationship – in the legal sense – and friendship served as a basis to strike a corrupt deal. In A.'s case, seeking a city official with the sufficient criminal capability to deliver him the corrupt service would have been a costly and risky undertaking. Offering bribes in the open might as well have backfired. However, he had an established relation with the right official, which happened to be his tennis partner K. Therefore, he did not have to invest resources into seeking a partner or into inquiring about the partner's criminal capacities. Resources were spent into organizing a contract for K. to buy a mansion below market prices, a hidden agreement that would pass for the actual payment for the corrupt service under consideration. Here one sees clearly the inevitable need for secrecy, a distinguishing feature of corrupt deals. For whatever reasons G. decided to rotate his officials and K. ceased to hold this critical position. This ended the legal base that was needed to enforce the corrupt side-agreement. There was no scope for future legal transactions that could have limited opportunism. The Bayerische Vereinsbank was therefore induced to act opportunistically by revoking the option for buying the mansion. The former friendship deteriorated in a relationship with mutual accusations.

Case 3

A thirty-three-year old police officer, assigned to the monitoring of the drug scene at the main station of Frankfurt, Germany, initiated a personal relationship with a brothel manager as well as with a prostitute from Colombia. Apparently, there was a divergence of viewpoints between how the parties viewed one another. While the officer naively believed in the sincerity of the relationships, the brothel

[3] See *Der Tagesspiegel*, December 16, 1997, "Ex-Bankchef wegen Erpressung verurteilt"; November 29, 1997, "Staatsanwalt prüft Ermittlung gegen K.," Main-Echo, January 13, 1998, "Potsdams schillerndster Politiker lässt Stadtoberhaupt wanken," and Lambsdorff (1999: 56).

manager and the prostitute seemed to have valued him basically as a contracting party from the outset, valuable for the information that he could access and deliver. The officer shared the information about the warranted persons in the environment with the brothel manager, and passed on certain other tips, such as informing the brothel manager about an impending police raid. The officer first encountered the brothel manager when he searched the brothel for drugs and dealers in 1997 and developed a personal relationship with him from 1998 onward. Then he started showing up frequently at dinners and participating at some parties with the women from the brothel. The officer got involved in intimate relationships with three women from the environment. Upon the officer's arrest on May 28, 2000, the brothel manager is reported to have fled to Spain. As to the financial aspects of the relationship, the officer rented three dwellings. These were then sublet to double rent to prostitutes, supplied by the brothel manager. While this contract design should have provided the officer with extra income, in fact, it set him even more at the mercy of the brothel owner. In case the dwellings were not fully occupied, which indeed happened, the officer would even risk making losses. After his arrest, the officer regretted his relationship with the Colombian prostitute, declaring that she was nothing more than an ice-cold person who used him.[4]

Police officers can be in a strong bargaining position. The case suggests that if they are in charge of controlling a fixed area, such as the red-light district, they have ample possibilities to demand a bribe. Given the frequent contact with those they control, transaction costs can be lowered considerably. For example, Borner and Schwyzer (1999) argue that policemen can lower the transaction costs of corrupt agreements with criminals by regularly controlling the activities of such people. The idea would be that opportunism among the criminals could be avoided by threatening increased supervision or even harassment. There exists a legal relationship of control that can serve as a base for corrupt deals. While this may have been relevant for our case too, the friendship, as being felt by the officer, seems to have been already a sufficient condition for enforcing the corrupt agreement.

[4] *Frankfurter Neue Presse*, August 9, 2000, "Polizist ließ sich vom Rotlicht-Milieu bestechen."

The Philippine Jueteng

Another case study comes from the Philippines and is described in detail by Coronel (2000: 26–36). *Jueteng* was an illegal lottery, a variation of an old Chinese numbers game. Illegal as it was, the game was popular throughout the country thanks to various layers of protection. Officials and law enforcers from the village level to the national level protected the activities of the *jueteng* operators. Bet collectors (*cobradores*) reported to headmen (*cabos*), who were, in turn, supervised by a *jueteng* operator. It was the operator's task to ensure that influential officials protect the game. Of course, protection always comes at a price. According to estimates in 1995, every year some P2.5 billion (almost US$100 million) of *jueteng* money was going to bribes in return for toleration of the game.

Enjoying such protection, the game was hardly ever kept secret. The *jueteng* operators were well known both by the folk in their area and by government officials. In October 2000, Ilocos Sur Governor Luis 'Chavit' Singson charged President Joseph Estrada with having received more than P540 million (US$10.8 million) from the illegal gambling payoffs between November 1998 and October 2000. In the Philippines, daily politics and the *jueteng* network were so much intertwined that it is hard to draw a line between the two. It was not uncommon for a *jueteng* operator to be a member of a political clan, or even further, to hold an official position. Singson himself is no exception to the rule. He and his brother Jose "Bonito" Singson appeared frequently in police reports as *jueteng* operators. At the same time, *jueteng* money seems to have played some role in campaigns for the top administrative offices.

According to the story of Singson, Estrada invited him, Bong Pineda (another *jueteng* operator) and a close friend of his, Charlie "Atong" Ang, to his residence in August 1998. There, he appointed Pineda with the duty of collecting *jueteng* payoffs and handing them in to Ang. However, Singson was asked to take over the collection of *jueteng* payoffs two months later as a result of a problem between Estrada and Ang. Singson kept a ledger of the collections from twenty-two provinces and estimated the daily *jueteng* money collection at P50 million (US$1 million). Of this amount, 3 percent was the kickback to the President. Singson confessed that he collected the money and delivered it to Estrada either at his home or at Malacañang Palace.

Up to this point, everything seemed to be in perfect harmony. Yet, Estrada wanted a higher cut from the *jueteng* network. The means to achieve this end was to legalize *jueteng* under the name Bingo-2 Ball via the Philippine Amusement and Gaming Corporation (Pagcor). It was Atong Ang who was to supervise the operation of replacing the illegal *jueteng* game with the new legal alternative. Ang set out by appointing some of the existing *jueteng* operators as Bingo-2 Ball franchisees. However, he awarded an impressively high 27 percent share of the total collections to a private firm, headed by himself. In essence, this represents a form of embezzlement. According to Singson, he was merely fronting Estrada in the firm, and the whole scheme was not one of legalizing the business, but rather of grabbing a higher share from gambling. Interesting to note is that Ang proceeded without the permission of the Congress to legalize the game. The backing of the President furnished him with the due flexibility to do so. By legalizing the game, what was formerly given to the police as protection money (*intelihensiya*) would now belong to him. In the meantime, the police were reported to be negotiating with Pagcor to have a legal cut from these proceedings to make up for the *intelihensiya* money that they lost from legalizing the game.

The events then took a turn that rid Chavit Singson of the potential gambling profits from his region. The Bingo 2-Ball franchise was given to Bonito Singson, Chavit Singson's brother, but at the same time his rival as a *jueteng* operator. Chavit Singson was carelessly pushed out of the game. He struck back, exposing the hidden deals of the President. He later admitted that he made the whole story public because Estrada gave a gambling concession to someone else.[5]

The *jueteng* case demonstrates how an existing perfectly legal relationship, that of a local governor and a president, could be used as a means to seal a corrupt deal. Politics and *jueteng* were so much intertwined. Day-to-day political dealings provide affluent opportunities of building trusted relationships or of sanctioning one another. This provided a robust base for striking illegal deals. Singson, in particular, already depended on the benevolence of the president, because he was a public servant. This would put a check on the potential opportunism from his part. The political positions Singson

[5] See Coronel (2000: 26–36), and *Economist*, October 19, 2000, "The Philippines Turns on Its President."

and Estrada held enabled them to strike a corrupt deal behind closed doors. Therefore, they saved on transaction costs of seeking a partner and minimized the risk of raising some eyebrows through advertising for their corrupt intents. The deal enabled Estrada to claim his cut from the national collection of gambling proceeds in return for tolerance, or protection, of the illegal game. The end result is a striking case of centralized corruption. It was Estrada's strive for further acquisition that brought the stable relationship to an end. Singson was pushed aside instead of being retained as an insider that could have been handy in future corrupt prospects. As such deals are sealed within a closed group, it was surely a mistake for the corrupt parties to exclude an insider without providing him with an incentive to remain silent.

Such cases of highly organized and centralized corrupt practices are rare because the inevitable publicity commonly calls for counteractive measures. As shown, their organization was only possible because hierarchical government organizations, political parties, and clans were highly intertwined with *jueteng*. These legal relationships provided for sufficient mechanisms to sanction opportunism and to guarantee loyalty. Corrupt relationships could then be parasitically linked to these legal relations. While the corrupt relationships broke up, it remains to be seen whether the Philippine government organizations, political parties, and clans will manage to contain this effective base for corruption in the future.

9.4. Conclusion and policy recommendations

This chapter argues that corrupt deals require particularly high transaction costs because, (1) the deals necessitate secrecy, (2) court ordering, that is, legal enforcement mechanisms are not available and, (3) corrupt partners live at the mercy of one another after contract fulfillment. A variety of institutional mechanisms can be employed to seal and enforce corrupt agreements. Linking corrupt relationships to legal ones is a measure to economize on transaction costs. Corrupt relationships per se are not necessarily secure in and of themselves. What makes them more secure, or less vulnerable to opportunism is their embeddedness in a legal relationship. In this context, one can no longer talk about a corrupt relationship, but about a relationship that has legal aspects as well as corrupt ones. The presence of existing legal ties either in a political context or in that of friendship may create ripe opportunities to secure a corrupt deal. The case studies presented also support the hypothesis that sealing corrupt deals in an ongoing context of a legal relationship saves a considerable amount of transaction costs and reduces the related risks.

There is rarely ever a purely corrupt relationship in life; instead, corrupt deals are sealed in a framework of existing legal relationships, owing to transaction cost considerations. Corrupt partners often need a legal base on which, at a later stage, to build their corrupt side-dealings. The same ambivalence might also arise with people's motivations. There might not be such a thing as a purely corrupt intention. It is not (only) due to psychological reasons why a person's motivations are usually more complicated and more divert. Even those who are charged with the most unscrupulous and corrupt self-seeking behavior must pursue some further genuine goals and interests. They must find partners and friends to establish trusted relationships; they must find jobs and seal contracts where they are expected to honestly deliver what was promised. In sum, legal and illegal actions are not substitutes, where one is chosen and the other is omitted. Very often they are complements. Legal relationships can provide the basis for sealing and enforcing corrupt agreements.

This approach suggests various avenues for future research. First, while there is consensus about the negative welfare effects of corruption, it is plausible that some forms of corruption are more disruptive than others. One issue could relate to the legal base that is used for the enforcement. For example, where corruption is linked to otherwise fertile business relations, it may be less harmful than where it is embedded in less-productive political connections.

Reform commonly focuses on how to avoid corrupt opportunities by limiting bureaucratic discretion and increasing public servants' accountability. This chapter suggests one further important pillar of an anticorruption strategy. A public servant's office not only provides the opportunity for exacting a corrupt payoff, but may also supply mechanisms to enforce a corrupt deal, and to economize on transaction costs. Reform strategies should therefore focus on how to aggravate the enforcement of corrupt deals and how to impede a public office from being used for lowering the respective transaction costs.

Alongside the official duties, all other legally undertaken relationships of a public servant must equally form part of a reform strategy.

In cases where a conflict of interest arises, supervision and regulation is required. Based on our approach, such conflicts of interest arise particularly where such relationships, for example, long-term business relationships, can serve as a basis for the enforcement of corrupt deals. Regulation must, in this case, limit misusing a public office for the enforcement of corrupt deals. Friendship belongs to the private sphere of a public servant and should not overshadow his or her duties. This is not only true because a public servant might otherwise be tempted to favoritism but also because friendship allows to camouflage a bribe as a gift, obfuscate the quid pro quo, and allow reciprocity even years after a favor has been given. It thus helps in enforcing a corrupt agreement. As this chapter highlights, investigation of the potential of legal relationships to allow for corrupt spin-offs is an indispensable element of a successful reform strategy.

10 *Concluding thoughts*

ANTICORRUPTION is society's perpetual endeavor to discipline its public servants and politicians. It cannot be imagined that this goal will ever be reached solely by intellectual effort. Courage and commitment among civic-minded people will remain a prerequisite for low levels of corruption. But societies' ventures require some thorough guidance. Our knowledge on anticorruption is increasing at a remarkable speed. Reform ideas are tested throughout the world and experiences are rapidly exchanged so as to determine best practice. Yet, there is still no overarching framework available that helps in organizing our thinking. An inspiration for such a framework is suggested in this book: the principle of the invisible foot.

A first approach intended to inspire anticorruption related to *repression*: draconic penalties and higher probabilities of detecting malfeasance. While this approach has its merits, it is doubtful whether it can be the guiding principle for the future. Data on prosecutions related to bribery and fraud reveal that they are common particularly in some more developed countries but extremely rare in some less-developed countries (United Nations 2006). Whether conviction rates in many crucial countries would ever reach levels where they can represent an effective deterrence can therefore be put in question. Furthermore, if the effects follow an economic law of decreasing marginal gains and increasing marginal costs, the likely outcome would be that criminals are less deterred by higher penalties while the pursuit of absolute integrity becomes more and more expensive, bringing about unpleasant side effects. Law enforcement is costly and requires an honest judiciary. Administrative procedures are complex owing to enhanced monitoring and may adversely affect the intrinsic motivation of the bureaucracy. Even worse, sanctioning even minor malfeasance can backfire. If those guilty of negligible malfeasance have to fear severe prosecution, they may become entrapped in a corrupt career. Repression would become ineffective if it does not provide an emergency exit for the petty sinners. These drawbacks may increasingly materialize in the future and other guiding principles have to be sought that inspire anticorruption efforts.

Some prosecutors are fighting a devoted battle for integrity. They consider their strong stand to serve as an effective deterrent against corruption. But their treatment of insiders and whistle-blowers is sometimes unsatisfactory. It is essential to provide pardon to minor misbehavior so as to catch the big fish. A policy of zero tolerance that can be in contradiction to effective anticorruption. Also political commitments to absolute integrity can backfire badly. Take the following case. The Aerospace Engineering Design Corporation (AEDC), registered in Panama, is alleged to have arranged the sale of aircraft equipment worth British £20 billion from Rolls-Royce to the Saudi Arabian Air Force. Commissions of up to 15 percent had been agreed upon. In exchange, the Panamanian firm maintained "close relationships" with prominent Saudi Arabian nationals. Allegedly Rolls-Royce did not pay as negotiated. AEDC brought the case to the high court in Great Britain. Following a High Court writ, Rolls-Royce feared for its reputation, as did the British Government, which had always denied any bribery payments in connection with the deal. This induced Rolls-Royce to settle the case out of court, causing AEDC to withdraw the case.[1] The British Government, it seems, was unable to deliver on its promise of a perfectly honest deal. In order to avoid further investigation, they felt forced to opt for the worst option: the actual payment of the bribe.

Another approach to anticorruption focuses on *prevention*. This approach may likely be subject to similar limitations. These confines particularly relate to incentives and ethical training. Such training will certainly be an important issue for the years to come. It can help in communicating more clearly the conflicts of interest unique to specific sectors and countries. Furthermore, ethical training can help in developing an atmosphere of transparency and stewardship among a firm's and bureaucracy's employees. At the same time, it is costly and time consuming and it may sometimes serve to camouflage an organization's true interests. Private firms, for instance, might be in a prisoner's dilemma, paying lip service to anticorruption but at the

[1] See the *Financial Times*, December 20, 1997: "Rolls Royce: Silent on Saudi Talks."

same time profiting from a corrupt contract. Ethical training would be given to those supposed to stay clean, while the dirty work would be outsourced. In the end ethical training may simply provide firms with official excuses when their employees are caught, resulting, for instance, in exemption from corporate liability. Ethical training of bureaucrats is likely to face similar limitations.

Using incentives instead of ethical training for inducing honesty in the bureaucracy and in politics is arduous to implement. First, there is no measurable economic surplus that might serve as a yardstick for remuneration. Bureaucratic departments and political initiatives cannot be transformed into profit centers. Second, incentive schemes imply a variation of public servants' income, lowering the security equivalent of their pay and crowding out the risk-averse (and potentially less corrupt) from obtaining a public position. The consequence is that incentive schemes in the bureaucracy and in politics fall short of economists' prescriptions. Incentive theory, at best, helps us detect the variety of inconsistencies and disincentives that exist in the public sector. Yet incentives per se will hardly ever be sufficient to outbid the briber, as is sometimes suggested by formal principal–agent modeling. Realistically, incentive schemes can provide a helpful contribution that complements other factors such as public servants' intrinsic motivation, cultivation of professional ethics, and anticorruption norms in society.

Fostering *transparency* still seems to be an overarching principle with latent benefits. Its potential in reducing corruption is immense. The administrative costs of increasing transparency are limited, albeit often mentioned as an excuse for inactivity. Freedom of information in administration can effectively limit the arbitrariness required for corrupt transactions. A culture of corporate transparency inhibits the condoning of bribery. But this concept might, at least, be fine-tuned to some extent in the future. One concern is that transparency may support the monitoring of corrupt reciprocity (Pechlivanos 2004). Bribers may prefer a transparent environment if this allows them to avoid opportunism among public servants. Likewise, nontransparent bureaucracies may at times prevent corruption, because bribers would have a hard time (1) finding the right person to compromise, and (2) observing whether the bribee reciprocates honestly. In a similar spirit it is standard practice that public procurement requires some limits on transparency: bidders are not supposed to know the incoming bids of their competitors. Some secrecy must prevail until all bids are jointly opened. The reason is that bid-rigging would be facilitated if transparency is introduced at the wrong stage. The principle of transparency, therefore, will undergo a more fine-tuned interpretation. Instead of advocating unlimited disclosure of all information, comprehensive information management systems that provide key data to stakeholders would have to be put in place. Their design will remain an important issue for the years to come.

A recent experience in Beijing well illustrates the advantages and limitations of transparency in organizing public procurement. All local public contracts related to construction are organized by a so-called "tangible construction market." Tenders are announced and bids collected via Internet. The names of the firms are recorded separately, not in the incoming documents. A computer then randomly selects experts from its database and requests them to meet at the office without revealing for which project their expertise is sought. Experts pass a security check and meet in a video-supervised room where their mobile phones are not operated. There, the experts determine the best bid, which need not necessarily be the cheapest one. From my impression, the system is capable of seriously reducing corruption, if not making it impossible. At the same time, it becomes apparent that a mixture of transparency and obfuscation is fruitfully employed to minimize corruption.

Currently, anticorruption activities mostly embrace the testing of some best practice – without knowing to what extent such approaches can claim global validity. Integrity systems are often suggested that embrace aspects of accountability, monitoring, and reporting. But we know little whether criminals may seek loopholes within the newly established system and undermine the efforts. New initiatives, for example, aim at increasing revenue transparency for the extractive industries and the respective host governments where the extraction takes place. But crucial questions for the future will be whether bribery may continue in different form. Companies with a criminal intent may engage local agents, subsidiaries, or design joint-ventures so as to pass on advantages to local politicians. Any integrity system is quickly overburdened if these more sophisticated criminal methods are employed. Instead of avoiding corruption, the new systems may just force the criminals to reorganize their activities.

A more promising approach to fighting corruption requires a microanalysis of the criminal's activities. Instead of imagining benchmarks of integrity, diagnosis must focus on where corruption is most prevalent and how corrupt transactions are arranged. The particular institutional design that is employed for carrying out corrupt transactions must be at the core of analysis.

Given the limitations of some principles for anticorruption, this book expounded that an understanding of the criminal's calculus can provide us with a vivid starting point for future reform approaches. The *principle of the invisible foot*, as developed here, utilized some thought by the New Institutional Economics. It stated that corrupt actors can neither commit to honestly serve the public nor credibly promise reciprocity to their corrupt counterparts. This implies that their willingness to take bribes leaves them in uncertainty. Strengthening this principle ascertains that even self-seeking public servants refrain from corruption. The general approach for reform would be to make those willing to take bribes untrustworthy for public positions, to encourage betrayal among corrupt parties, to destabilize corrupt agreements, to disallow contracts to be legally enforced, to hinder the operation of corrupt intermediaries, and to find clearer ways of regulating conflicts of interest.

Box 28 Fighting corruption with asymmetric penalties, jointly written with Mathias Nell[2]

Corrupt actors must be deterred from their criminal actions. But deterrence involves more than just the threat of suffering from legal sanctions. It encompasses the possibility of being cheated by one's counterpart; besides, deterrence also increases with the risk of being reported. These uncertainties can be amplified by designing legal sanctions in a strategic way, aimed at enhancing opportunism.[3]

In essence there are four actions in a corrupt deal that can be subject to legal sanctions. A bribe-taker (public official) may, first, be punished for accepting bribes and, second, for illicitly reciprocating the bribes by supplying favorable treatment, such as a

[2] Mathias Nell has a degree in economics and holds a research assistant position at the Chair for Economic Theory at the University of Passau, Germany. His doctoral thesis focuses on corruption, law, and compliance.

[3] A more detailed analysis of the effect of asymmetric penalties is provided in Lambsdorff and Nell (2005).

Box 28 (*Cont.*)

government contract or permit. On the bribe-giver (businessperson) sanctions may be levied, first, for paying bribes and, second, for accepting the contract or permit. These (expected) sanctions can be fine-tuned in order to shatter some of the confidence that corrupt favors will be reciprocated and to foster whistle-blowing. We propose the following asymmetric design: sanctions for accepting bribes should be low and those for illicitly reciprocating bribes high; in turn, penalties for paying bribes should be severe, while those for accepting illicit reciprocity (contracts, permits, etc.) mild.

Because it paves the way for reciprocity, any type of bribe-giving to public servants should be avoided (if these bribes are likely to be aimed at exerting influence). Prosecutors have a hard time proving irregularities in the conduct of public servants, particularly if there is repeated exchange with a private party. In this context, the exchange of gifts and monetary inducements may be the clearest indicator for misbehavior, which must be subject to legal sanctions. Yet, rigorously penalizing public servants for accepting bribes may backfire as corrupt partners may be squeezed into a pact of silence because officials are placed at the mercy of businesspeople: reneging on the promise to provide a contract or license after taking a bribe may invoke "negative reciprocity" on the part of the businessperson. The businessperson may retaliate for the tricks played by the public servant and blow the whistle. If mild sanctions are imposed on the public servant for taking bribes, however, the official has ample scope for reneging on his promises without fearing such retribution. We therefore propose sanctions to be imposed for giving bribes but less for bribe-taking.

The largest harm placed on society arises if public servants' decisions are distorted, for example, by placing a contract or granting a permit to an unqualified bidder. Sanctions should in this case be imposed on public servants rather than on businesspeople who accept illicit reciprocity (contracts, permits, etc.). A public servant who accepts bribes may be effectively deterred from returning the favor if precisely this action is severely penalized.

Opportunism would be enhanced owing to the uncomfortable choice arising for public servants after taking bribes.

Punishing businesspeople for accepting reciprocal favors, however, would backfire. Their willingness to blow the whistle would arise only if they were cheated, and be reduced if they faced severe penalties for accepting the illicit reciprocity. Yet, businesspeople should retain their readiness to report a deal even if they accepted the favorable treatment. Public servants, on the other hand, should not be able to lower the risk of whistle-blowing by awarding a public contract or granting a permit, because this would stabilize corrupt agreements.

In this regard, granting businesspeople unconditional immunity from prosecution for bribe-giving may equally backfire – because this option could be misused to threaten public servants who renege. In order to avoid this effect, immunity from prosecution must be granted to the bribe-giver only in case the public servant has already supplied the favorable treatment. By this it would become impossible for public servants to lower the risk of whistle-blowing by awarding a contract or a license.

Because of its potential to shatter corrupt actors' trust in reciprocity and in mutual silence, an asymmetric design of sanctions might unleash higher deterrent effects of anticorruption laws. Yet in most countries sanctions for bribery tend to be symmetric. In Germany, as in many other countries,[4] symmetry prevails under §§331–335 of the penal code, because law scholars treat the integrity and the public's trust in the immaculateness of the administrative authorities as well as the objectivity of governmental decisions as the laws' subject of protection (Bannenberg 2002: 18–19; Kargl 2002: 782–3).[5] It is argued that both parties in a corrupt deal jeopardize the subject of protection similarly and should thus be punished equally. Such symmetry also follows from Article 3 of the German basic law. Put simply, Article 3 implies that equal facts of a case have to be tied to equal legal consequences and unequal facts of a case have to be tied to different legal consequences.

[4] One notable exception is Taiwan, where only those taking bribes are penalized (Hepkema and Booysen 1997).

[5] The subject of protection is designed similarly in §§299–300 (corruption in commerce).

Box 28 (*Cont.*)

As we see it, however, reasoning that both parties equally interfere with the subject of protection of §§331–335 is not indisputable. Indeed, the solicitation or the acceptance of a bribe by a public official may give the impression of venality but does not imply the actual supply of reciprocity. Yet, only reciprocating bribes in reality may violate official duties, harm the integrity of the administrative authorities, and may reduce the public's trust. Moreover, from an economic perspective, it is only to a minor extent that soliciting or accepting bribes leads to economic losses. In fact, the acceptance of a bribe merely constitutes a redistribution of resources from the private to the public sector. Thus, it may rather be the act of reciprocating bribes that offends the integrity of public office, runs contrary to the notion of governmental objectivity, distorts allocative efficiency, and annuls fair competition. In this respect, we perform a shift of the subject of protection's emphasis from venality toward the act of reciprocating bribes. Likewise, it may not be businesspeople's willingness to accept illicit reciprocity that distorts decisions in public office but the initiative to sidestep competition by offering bribes and other advantages. Already from this perspective, symmetry may not be the self-evident and logical consequence.

Interestingly, some legal provisions are likely to inhibit opportunism rather than encourage it. Former Article 215 (2) of the Turkish penal code granted immunity from prosecution to the briber only if the public official had not yet reciprocated the bribe (Tellenbach 1997: 642). Remarkably, according to Article 215 (2), the bribe-giver was entitled to reclaim the bribe in case of blowing the whistle. Such provisions run contrary to our recommendations, because they strengthen the briber in requesting illegal reciprocity. Subject to this legislation, bribe-givers could credibly threaten public servants who failed to reciprocate. The design of the legal system may have thus forced public servants to deliver on their corrupt promises.[6]

[6] The Turkish penal code was revised in 2005, with new but equally disputable clauses taking effect.

Also adjudication relating to §§299–300 (corruption in commerce) and §§331–335 of the German penal code does not conform with our recommendations, as highlighted by the Bavarian district court's final judgment concerning the conviction of Karl-Heinz Wildmoser, a prominent football manager ensnarled in a corruption scam related to the building of Munich's new football stadium, the Allianz Arena. The district court emphasized that the subject of protection of §§299–300 and §§331–335 is already violated (and thus the provisions take effect) if a public official (or commissary) accepted a bribe but did not intend to deliver the reciprocal service (Bavarian Criminal Division 2005). If high sanctions are already imposed for accepting bribes, bribe-takers are no longer deterred from reciprocating and, thus, from taking the next step in their criminal career.

Asymmetric sanctions and immunity from prosecution might bring about higher deterrent effects of anticorruption laws, if deterrence is understood in the broader sense of reducing potential perpetrators' willingness to participate in illegal acts. In order to clamp down more vigorously on corruption, legislators should seriously consider the benefits of asymmetric sanctions and immunity from prosecution in their (re-)formulation of anticorruption laws.

Corrupt actors must be deterred from their criminal actions. But deterrence is more than just the threat of suffering from legal sanctions. It embraces also the risk of being cheated by one's counterpart. It includes the threat of being denounced. Deterrence imposed with utmost rigor can backfire where it forces corrupt partners into a cartel of silence. Penalizing public servants already for the taking of bribes and gifts may increase rather than decrease corruption. Such penalties place officials at the mercy of business-people after a minor malfeasance – and open the door to worse types of misbehavior. Take the example provided on p. 158. A public official felt being at the mercy of the briber after taking DM2000. Although he had done little to favor the briber, he was entrapped in corrupt relationship afterward. A plethora of practical methods for anticorruption emanate from this approach. To name but a few, fostering whistleblowing by help of crown witness regulation, making life hard for intermediaries in corrupt transactions, and immunity and monetary incentives to informants provide a fruitful approach to deterring bribery. One concept emanating from this concept relates to the design of legal penalties, as explained in Box 28. Penalties must be stopped from stabilizing corrupt relationships. Instead of marking the starting point of a corrupt career they must be designed so as to encourage opportunism and whistle-blowing.

Anticorruption activists often start their campaigns by trying to form broader coalitions and seeking collaborators. But where are these found? Is it only the civil society activist, the moralists, idealists, or the priests who can be trusted? As emphasized in this book, the willingness to engage in corrupt transactions can turn against the actors themselves. Consequently, nobody can upfront be excluded when forming coalitions against corruption. Public servants, even when tempted to take bribes, can have an interest in committing to honesty, as explained in Chapter 3. An engagement against corruption can provide them with avenues for committing to honesty; their service may increase in value and provide them with promising perspectives for their career. As shown in Chapter 7, businesspeople may like to join an anticorruption initiative. Not only might this help them in overcoming a prisoner's dilemma, it may also be an individually profit-maximizing strategy because a visible commitment to anticorruption may drive down the solicitation of bribes and businesspeople's subordinates would no longer be induced to betray their own firm. Lobbyists may dislike corruption because it limits their capacity to find popular support for the interests of their clients and constrains them in broadening the base of supporters. Also intermediaries may like to seek binding rules that disallow their engagement in bribery, so as to ascertain honest firms that these are not liable for any criminal activities, as shown in Box 27. Even kleptocratic rulers may have an (apparently very limited) interest to engage in anticorruption and they would be willing to curb their own corrupt opportunities. This is somewhat comparable with Mafia bosses who attempt to legalize their business in a strategy to avoid the hazards for their offspring. Totalitarian rulers must seek ways to commit themselves to their announced policies, which is in contrast to a reputation for constant misuse of power. In sum, anticorruption crusaders can find support among many in society.

Combating corruption is like judo. Instead of bluntly resisting the criminal forces, one must redirect the enemy's energy to his own decay. Instead of proclaiming a policy of zero tolerance one must recognize that the imperfections of human behavior will endure. Instead of demanding a world of absolute integrity, fighting corruption foremost is the art of exploiting these imperfections for our battle.

The power of economic thinking started with the notion of the invisible hand: competition substituted for benevolence by guiding self-seeking actors to serve the public. Individual morality lost relevance as a guiding principle for directing behavior in private markets. May this also be true for politics and administration? Can anticorruption flourish without good intentions? Will anticorruption come to a standstill if it focuses on moral sanctions that may be detrimental to civil liberties? With respect to fighting corruption we may not have a mechanism as powerful as the invisible hand. If something comes close to it, it is the corrupt actor's failure to make credible promises. The risk of betrayal may operate like an invisible foot, making life hard for those who fail to commit to honesty. This principle can motivate even the self-seeking actors to abstain from corruption and reconcile civil liberties with good governance.

Appendix: Technical details to the Transparency International Corruption Perceptions Index

In an attempt to determine the causes and consequences of corruption, academics have focused lately on cross-country analyses. These require assessments of the extent of corruption in various countries. Such assessments are sometimes compiled by agencies to determine country risks, and the data gathered are sold to investors. Other sources are surveys of elite businesspeople or the general public. While perceptions should never be confused with reality, the given consensus provides some confidence that the perceptions gathered are informative on actual levels of corruption. Most prominent in recent years has been the TI CPI.

Objective versus subjective data

Instead of using perceptions data, Goel and Nelson (1998), Fisman and Gatti (2002) and Glaeser and Saks (2006) employ objective data: the number of public officials convicted for abuse of public office in various states of the United States. They assume that high conviction rates are an indicator of actual high levels of corruption. Certainly, conviction rates may not well depict levels of corruption but rather the quality of the judiciary. But Glaeser and Saks (2006) defend the data on the grounds that they refer to central government prosecutor's charges and convictions, not those by the local judiciary. Glaeser and Saks (2006) report that conviction rates decrease with income and education. Goel and Nelson (1998) significantly relate conviction rates to the real per capita total expenditures of the local government, arguing that state intervention and public spending give rise to rent-seeking activities and thereby corruption. Still, if federal prosecutors are in need of local assistance, the data would be biased by the quality of local institutions. Given such concern, most researchers rely on subjective indicators.

With respect to cross-country data, unbiased, hard data on corruption is difficult to obtain and usually raises even more serious questions with respect to validity. One such set of data has been assembled by the United Nations Office on Drugs and Crime (United Nations 2006). This is a survey of national agencies in a large variety of countries called the United Nations Survey of Crime Trends and Operations of Criminal Justice Systems. The major goal of this investigation has been to collect cross-national and comparative data on the incidence of reported crime. The questionnaire consists of a series of questions to collect primarily statistical data on the main components of the criminal justice system. The latest version of this survey relates to the years 1998–2000. All national data are derived from the official national criminal statistics.[1] However, the precise legal definition of corruption offences can be different in each national context; the differences drawn between bribery, embezzlement, and fraud may be troublesome; and the statistical methodology of counting and aggregating used in each national agency can differ considerably from that used elsewhere. Apart from this, countries such as Germany, New Zealand and Finland have extremely high per capita conviction rates for fraud. This lends itself to the conclusion that the data are to a large extent determined by the effectiveness and capacity of a country's judiciary in prosecuting corruption. High levels in this case indicate the success of anticorruption initiatives rather than high levels of actual corruption. Such problems commonly arise with objective data. Therefore, international surveys on perceptions are more credible for comparing the extent of corruption from one country to another.

Sources in 2005

Before selecting sources, guidelines have been set up that organize the underlying decision-making process. These include the necessary criteria that a source needs to meet in order to qualify for inclusion as well as organizational guidelines on how the final decision is reached with the help of the Transparency International Steering Committee.

[1] A full description of the methodology and the complete data can be obtained via Internet at www.uncjin.org/Statistics/WCTS/wcts.html.

This process aims at making the final decision as transparent and robust as possible. A list of sources that enter the index is provided in Box 5 on p. 21–22. This list also provides the various abbreviations used here in the text.

An essential condition for inclusion is that a source must provide a ranking of nations. This condition is not met if a source conducts surveys in a variety of countries but with varying methodologies. Comparison from one country to another is not feasible in this case and a ranking cannot be produced. Another condition is that sources must measure the overall extent of corruption. This is violated if aspects of corruption are mixed with issues other than corruption such as political instability or nationalism, or if changes are measured instead of levels of corruption.

For example, the index "Corruption in Government" from the ICRG conducted by the PRS does not meet these requirements, in spite of its widespread use in research as a measure of levels of corruption. This index does not determine a country's level of corruption but the political risk involved in corruption. As pointed out to us by Tom Sealy, the ICRG-editor, these two issues can differ considerably, depending on whether there exists a high or low public tolerance toward corruption. In a personal correspondence he explained that the

"Corruption Index is an attempt to provide a comparable measure of corruption (under the standard international definition), while our Corruption Risk is an attempt to provide a comparable measure of the political risk involved in corruption . . . this produces some apparently odd assessments with countries with reportedly high levels of corruption being assessed by us as having a lower corruption risk than countries with reportedly low levels of corruption. The reason for this is that, in general terms, countries with low measurable corruption often have a high degree of democratic accountability and a low tolerance of corruption. Because of this an instance of corruption that would hardly raise an eyebrow in some countries could contribute to a government's fall. . . . So, although the measurable corruption in such countries is low, the political risk might be high. On the other hand countries with reportedly widespread corruption often have low levels of democratic accountability and a high tolerance of corruption. Such a country could end up with a lower Corruption Risk rating under our system than would be the case if we were taking account of measurable corruption."

Corruption leads to political instability if it is not tolerated. PRS also assumes that political instability as caused by corruption increases with the length a government has been in power continuously. The lowest ratings are usually given to one-party states and autarchies. Quite clearly, the data by PRS/ICRG does not depict levels of corruption, contrary to widespread belief. Considering this, PRS's good scores for Greece (5 points out of a clean score of 6), Nicaragua (4) and the Republic of Congo (4) are understandable – as well as the bad scores for Ireland (2) and Hong Kong (3).

The 2005 CPI combines assessments from the past three years to reduce abrupt variations in scoring that might arise because of random effects. Some of the sources entering the index, such as II und UNECA, provided only one recent survey. Others such as WEF, IMD, and PERC conducted annual surveys between 2003 and 2005. It was decided that all these annual surveys should be included, not only the most topical ones. More recent data is averaged with data that is up to two years old.

While this averaging is valuable when including surveys, it is inappropriate for application to the data compiled by professional risk agencies. Such assessments as compiled by EIU, CU, FH, MIG, and WMRC are conducted by a small number of country experts who regularly analyze a country's performance, counterchecking their conclusions with peer discussions. Following this systematic evaluation, they then consider a potential upgrading or downgrading. As a result, a country's score changes rather seldom, and the data shows little year-to-year variation. Changing scores in this case are the result of a considered judgment by the organization in question. To then go back and average the assessments over a period of time would be inappropriate. On the other hand, in the case of surveys of elite businesspeople an averaging over various years produces a useful smoothing effect. While some annual data may contain random errors, these do not necessarily carry over to the next year.

In an approach related to the CPI, Kaufmann *et al.* (1999a) have similarly determined the extent of corruption as a composite index. They have updated their data on a regular basis and determine further governance indicators, along with corruption. They do not use the data by II and have in the past been more reluctant to incorporate surveys that are conducted only once. However, unlike the CPI, they use the data by PRS, some surveys of the general public, and two further expert assessments by Business Environment Risk Intelligence

(BERI) and Global Insight (formerly Standard and Poors / DRI). The data by PRS is problematic, as explained above. BERI is a private firm, founded in 1966 and is headquartered in Geneva, Switzerland. In their Political Risk Index, one of eight causal criteria is called "Mentality – Including Xenophobia, Nationalism, Corruption, Nepotism, and Willingness to Compromise." The source may not be a helpful contribution to a composite index on corruption because of its untidy definition. Global Insight is an economic consulting company that provides data and expert advice to business and policy-makers. However, it does not assess the extent of corruption but the risk of a one-point increase of corruption, given its level on a scale from 0 to 10. In personal correspondence they discouraged the usage of their data for cross-country comparisons of levels of corruption. Owing to the inclusion of these additional sources, Kaufmann *et al.* were able to cover a larger set of countries in their index. This advantage, however, seems to come at the cost of losing validity.

Year-to-year comparisons

Comparisons to the results from previous years should be based on a country's score, not its rank. A country's rank can change simply because new countries enter the index and others drop out. A higher score is an indicator that respondents provided better ratings, whereas a lower score suggests that respondents revised their perception downward. However, year-to-year comparisons of a country's score do not only result from a changing perception of a country's performance but also from a changing sample and methodology. Old sources drop out of the index and new sources enter, disturbing the consistency of the assessment. The index primarily provides a snapshot of the views of businesspeople and country analysts, with less of a focus on year-to-year trends.

However, to the extent that changes can be traced to a change in the assessments provided by individual sources, trends can be identified. Comparing older data (that is, data that was used for the 2004 CPI) with topical data from the same sources for 2005 allows us to identify such changes in perceptions during the last three years. Countries whose CPI score decreased relative to the 2004 CPI and where this deterioration is not the result of technical factors are Barbados, Belarus, Costa Rica, Gabon, Nepal, Papua New Guinea,

Russia, Seychelles, Sri Lanka, Suriname, Trinidad and Tobago, and Uruguay. The considerable decline in their scores of at least 0.3 does not result from technical factors – actual changes in perceptions are therefore likely.

With the same caveats applied, on the basis of data from sources that have been consistently used for the index, improvements of at least 0.3 can be observed for Argentina, Austria, Bolivia, Estonia, France, Guatemala, Honduras, Hong Kong, Japan, Jordan, Kazakhstan, Lebanon, Moldova, Nigeria, Qatar, Slovakia, South Korea, Taiwan, Turkey, Ukraine, and Yemen.

Trends relating to developments between 1995 and 2005 have recently been determined in a comprehensive investigation, (Lambsdorff 2005b; 2006). The studies reveal that significant improvements between 1995 and 2005 occurred (in descending order of significance) in Estonia, Italy, Spain, Colombia, Finland, Bulgaria, Hong Kong, Australia, Taiwan, Iceland, Austria, Mexico, New Zealand, and Germany. This is in contrast to a reduction in the score as perceived (in descending order of significance) in Poland, Argentina, Philippines, Zimbabwe, Canada, Indonesia, Ireland, Malaysia, Israel, Slovenia, Czech Republic, United Kingdom, and Venezuela.

Validity

All sources generally apply a definition of corruption such as the misuse of public power for private benefit, for example bribing public officials, kickbacks in public procurement, or embezzlement of public funds. Each of the sources also assesses the "extent" of corruption among public officials and politicians in the countries in question:

- CU asks its panel of experts to rate the severity of overall corruption within the state on the following scale: Low; Low/Modest; Modest; Modest/Severe; Severe.
- EIU asks its panel of experts to assess the incidence of corruption and defines corruption as the misuse of public office for personal (or party political) financial gain. Integers between 0 (denoting a "very low" incidence of corruption) and 4 (denoting a "very high" incidence) are provided.

- FH asks its panel of experts to assess the implementation of anticorruption initiatives; the government's freedom from excessive bureaucratic regulations and other controls that increase opportunities for corruption; public perceptions of corruption; the business interests of top policy makers; laws on financial disclosure and conflict of interest; audit and investigative rules for executive and legislative bodies; protections for whistle-blowers, anticorruption activists, and others who report corruption; and the media's coverage of corruption.
- II asks "which are the countries, besides this one, with which you have had the most business experience in the last 3–5 years? Please name up to five countries.

  a. In [country 1], how common are payments like bribes, hidden, illegitimate, or additional personal payments to obtain business or other improper advantages to senior public officials, like politicians, senior civil servants, and judges?
  b. In [country 1], how significant of an obstacle are the costs associated with such payments for doing business?
  c. In [country 1], how frequently are public contracts awarded to business associates, friends, and relatives rather than on a competitive bidding basis?
  Continue with countries 2–5. Scale for answers is from "Very Common" [01] to "Very Uncommon / Never"[04]. Don't know [88].

- IMD surveys elite businesspeople and asks them to assess whether "bribing and corruption prevail or do not prevail in the economy."
- MIG asks its panel of correspondents to assess levels of corruption. Corruption in their definition ranges from bribery of government ministers to inducements payable to the "humblest clerk."
- PERC asks expatriate businessmen to rate on a scale of 0 to 10 how bad they considered the problem of corruption to be in the country in which they are working as well as in their home country.
- United Nations Economic Commission for Africa, African Governance Report (UNECA) determines the control of corruption as determined by its local expert panel. This variable includes aspects related to corruption in the legislature, judiciary, at the executive level, and in tax collection. Aspects of access to justice and government services are also involved.

- WEF asks: "In your industry, how commonly would you estimate that firms make undocumented extra payments or bribes connected with:"

  1 – exports and imports
  Common |1|2|3|4|5|6|7| Never occur
  2 – public utilities (e.g. telephone or electricity)
  Common |1|2|3|4|5|6|7| Never occur
  3 – annual tax payments
  Common |1|2|3|4|5|6|7| Never occur
  4 – public contracts
  Common |1|2|3|4|5|6|7| Never occur
  5 – loan applications
  Common |1|2|3|4|5|6|7| Never occur
  6 – influencing laws and policies, regulations, or decrees to favor selected business interests
  Common |1|2|3|4|5|6|7| Never occur
  7 – getting favorable judicial decisions
  Common |1|2|3|4|5|6|7| Never occur
  From these questions the simple average has been determined.

- WMRC provides an assessment of the likelihood of encountering corrupt officials. Corruption can range from petty bureaucratic corruption (such as the paying of bribes to low-level officials) right through to grand political corruption (such as the paying of large kickbacks in return for the awarding of contracts). Scores take the following values: 1, 1.5, 2, 2.5, 3, 3.5, 4, 4.5, 5. They have the following meaning:

  1. This country will have an excellent business environment and corruption will be virtually unknown.
  2. This country will have a good and transparent business environment. Corruption – official and otherwise – may occur occasionally, but most businesses will not encounter this.
  3. This country will have some significant operational obstacles, including corruption. However, whilst official corruption may be relatively common, it should not affect business in an overly negative manner.
  4. This country will have a poor business environment. Corruption is likely to be endemic in the business world and officialdom, and

it will not be uncommon for kickbacks or bribes to be demanded in return for the awarding of contracts.

5. This country will have severe operational obstacles, which in practice make business impossible. Corruption will be pervasive and will reach the highest levels of government.

The various terms used by the sources, that is, "prevalence," "commonness," "frequency," "likelihood," "problematic," and "severity" are closely related. They all refer to some kind of extent of corruption, which is also the aim of the CPI. This common feature of the various sources is particularly important in view of the fact that corruption comes in different forms. It has been suggested in numerous publications that distinctions should be made between these forms of corruption, for example between nepotism and corruption in the form of monetary transfers. Yet, none of the data included in the CPI emphasize one form of corruption at the expense of other forms. The sources can be said to aim at measuring the same broad phenomenon. The sources do not distinguish between administrative and political corruption, nor between petty and grand corruption. In 2006 TI commissioned the WEF to ask respondents to its annual survey to assess the extent of facilitating extra payments or bribes (1) to lower-level public servants and, (2) to high ranking politicians, political parties and senior public servants. As revealed by respondents, the two forms of corruption are strongly correlated with a correlation coefficient across 125 countries of 0.956. This emphasizes that the overall level of corruption is the most important piece of information, providing justification for the CPI to report only one single figure.

The term "extent of corruption" may imply different things (Rose-Ackerman 1999: 4). In particular, it may relate to the frequency of bribes or the size of bribes in firms' deals with the government. But we know from the results of our sources that frequency and the size of bribes tend to correlate. In countries where corruption is frequent, it is also costly. In sum, the term "extent of corruption" seems to equally reflect the two aspects, frequency of corruption and the total value of bribes paid in firms' dealings with the government. Interestingly, the CPI shows no correlation to the size of the government; see Box 1 for related evidence. Thus, even where firms tend to deal much more with the government, this does not per se increase their assessment of levels of corruption. It is rather the likelihood and price of bribes in an average contact with public servants that is assessed by the CPI.

Critics raised concern that the CPI might reproduce what it has in the past been propagating. The CPI's prominence might introduce a problem of circularity. Respondents might "go with the herd" instead of submitting their experienced judgment. This hypothesis was tested. In 2006 respondents to the WEF-survey were asked how well they know the CPI. Two different corruption indices have been determined, one by those who know the CPI well and another one by those who less well know the CPI. The sample familiar with the CPI produced an index that correlates slightly less (0.89) with the CPI 2005 than the sample that does not know the CPI (0.90). This indicates that knowledge of the CPI does not induce respondents to "go with the herd". Knowledge of the CPI may equally motivate respondents to determine their own position more clearly. This is a strong indicator that currently there is no circularity in our approach.

Standardization

Each of the sources uses its own scaling system, requiring that the data be standardized before each country's mean value can be determined. This standardization is carried out in two steps.

Older sources that were already standardized for the CPI of a previous year enter the 2005 CPI with the same values. New sources are standardized using matching percentiles. The *ranks* (and not the scores) of countries is the only information processed from each source. For this technique the common subsamples of a new source and the previous year's CPI are determined, meaning that countries that appear *only in either* the new source *or* the old CPI are disregarded. Then, the largest value in the CPI is taken as the standardized value for the country ranked best by the new source. The second largest value is given to the country ranked second best, and so forth.[2] Imagine that a

[2] If two countries share the same rank, their standardized value is the simple mean of the two respective scores in the CPI. The scores for countries where no CPI value was available are determined by referring to neighbor countries in the source's ranking. Linear interpolation is applied to their scores, suggesting that if a source assigns such a country a score close to the upper neighbor, also its standardized value is closer to that of this neighbor. If such a country is ranked best (or worst) by a source it would have only one neighbor and not two. The second neighbor is constructed by using the highest (or lowest) attainable score by the source and the CPI value 10 (or 0). This approach guarantees that all values remain within the range between 10 and 0.

new source ranks only five countries: United Kingdom (4.2), Singapore (3.9), China (2.8), Malaysia (2.7), and India (2.4). In the 2004 CPI these countries obtained the scores 8.6, 9.3, 3.4, 5.0, and 2.8, respectively. Matching percentiles would now assign the United Kingdom the best score of 9.3, Singapore second best with 8.6, China 5.0, Malaysia 3.4, and India 2.8.

Matching percentiles are superior in combining indices that have different distributions. Only the ordinal information by a source, and not the cardinal information, is processed. Many of the alternative parametric standardization methods, on the other hand, would require a multitude of assumptions – some of which may not be realistic. But, as matching percentiles make use of the ranks and not the scores of sources, this method loses some of the information inherent in the sources. What tips the balance in favor of this technique is its capacity to keep all reported values within the bounds from 0 to 10. This results because any standardized value is taken from the previous year's CPI, which by definition is restricted to the aforementioned range. Such a characteristic is not obtained by various alternative techniques, for example one that standardizes the mean and standard deviation of the joint subsamples of countries.

Having obtained standardized values that are all within the reported range, a simple average from these standardized values can be determined. However, the resulting index has a standard deviation that is smaller than that of the CPI of previous years. Without a second adjustment there would be a trend toward a continuously smaller diversity of scores. If, for example Finland were to repeat its score from the previous year, it would have to score best in all sources. If it scores second best in any source, the standardized value it obtains after using matching percentiles and aggregation would be lower than its current score. Thus, given some heterogeneity among sources, it seems inevitable that Finland's score would deteriorate over time. The opposite would be true of Bangladesh, which would obtain a better score if it is not consistently rated worst by all its sources. A second standardization is required in order to avoid a continuous trend to less diversity among scores.

However, simply stretching the scores (by applying a simple mean and standard deviation technique) might bring about values that are beyond our range from 0 to 10. A more complicated standardization is required for the second step: a beta-transformation. The idea behind this monotonous transformation is to increase the standard

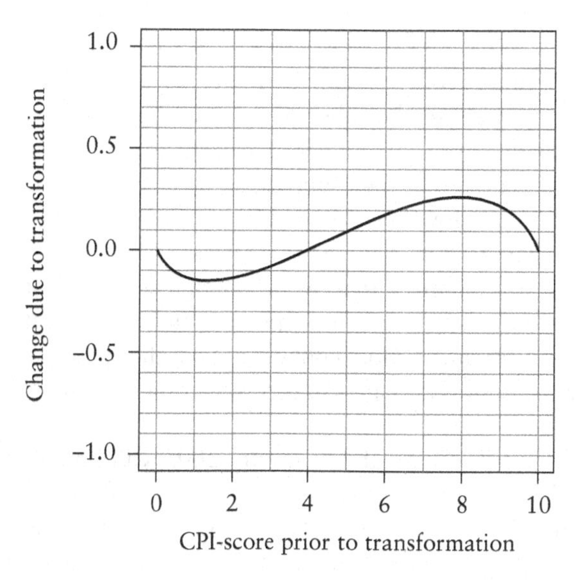

Figure A.1. Beta transformation

deviation to the previous year's value, while preserving the range from 0 to 10. Each value (X) is therefore transformed according to the following function:

$$10 \times \int_0^1 (X/10)^{\alpha-1} (1 - X/10)^{\beta-1} \, dX$$

This beta-transformation is available in standard statistics programs. The crucial task is to find the parameters α and β so that the resulting mean and standard deviation of the index have the desired values, that is, values that are equal to that of the 2004 CPI for a joint subsample of countries. An algorithm has been determined that carries out this task. Applying this approach to the 2005 CPI, the change in the scores is depicted by Figure A.1. The parameters are $\alpha = 1.135$ and $\beta = 1.165$. As shown in the figure, scores between 4.0 and 10 are increased slightly, while those between 0 and 4.0 are lowered.

Reliability and precision

A ranking of countries may easily be misunderstood as measuring the performance of a country with absolute precision. This is certainly not true. Since its start in 1995 TI has provided data on the standard deviation and the amount of sources contributing to the index. This data already serves to illustrate the inherent imprecision. Also the high–low range is provided in the main table. This depicts the highest and the lowest values provided by our sources, so as to portray the whole range of assessments. However, no quick conclusions should be derived from this range to the underlying precision with which countries are measured. Countries that were assessed by three or twelve sources can have the same minimum and maximum values, but in the latter case we can feel much more confident about the country's score. In order to arrive at such measures of precision, other statistical methods are required.

An indicator for the overall reliability of the 2005 CPI can be drawn from the high correlation between the sources. This can be depicted from the standard Pearson correlation and Kendall's rank correlation, provided in Tables A.1 and A.2.[3] The correlations on average are 0.87 for the Pearson correlation and 0.72 for Kendall's rank correlation. This suggests that the sources do not differ considerably in their assessment of levels of corruption.

Confidence range

We have been providing the public with information on the confidence range for some years now. Up to 2001 these were based on the determination of the standard error for a country's average score and a resulting parametric assessment of a ninety-five percent confidence range. This approach required the assumption that there is no imprecision associated with the source's values and that these values are independent of each other. Another strong assumption required is that errors are normally distributed. While it is statistically difficult to relax the first two assumptions, one can relax the assumption of a normal distribution and apply tests that are valid for any type of distribution. Another drawback of the older confidence ranges was, again, that they sometimes violated the given range from 0 to 10. For example, while in 2001 Bangladesh had a score of 0.4, its ninety-five percent confidence range was between −3.6 and 4.4. For Finland, on

[3] The correlations refer to all countries, even those not included in the CPI. Abbreviations are explained in Box 5, p. 21–22.

Table A.1 Pearson Correlation

	CU 2003	EIU 2005	FH 2005	II 2003	IMD 2003	IMD 2004	IMD 2005	PERC 2003	PERC 2004	PERC 2005	MIG 2005	UNECA 2005	WEF 2003	WEF 2004	WEF 2005	WMRC 2005
CU 2003	1.00	0.84	0.77	0.69	0.85	0.86	0.84	0.87	0.85	0.90	0.82	0.59	0.79	0.84	0.85	0.81
EIU 2005	0.84	1.00	0.87	0.74	0.91	0.93	0.93	0.92	0.90	0.90	0.86	0.60	0.90	0.88	0.87	0.92
FH 2005	0.77	0.87	1.00	—	0.87	0.83	0.86	—	—	—	0.82	—	0.82	0.83	0.77	0.83
II 2003	0.69	0.74	—	1.00	0.79	0.76	0.77	0.69	0.57	—	0.75	—	0.82	0.76	0.77	0.78
IMD 2003	0.85	0.91	0.87	0.79	1.00	0.98	0.98	0.95	0.94	0.97	0.88	—	0.95	0.95	0.94	0.88
IMD 2004	0.86	0.93	0.83	0.76	0.98	1.00	0.98	0.93	0.94	0.96	0.90	—	0.95	0.95	0.94	0.89
IMD 2005	0.84	0.93	0.86	0.77	0.98	0.98	1.00	0.95	0.96	0.97	0.89	—	0.95	0.95	0.93	0.90
PERC2003	0.87	0.92	—	0.69	0.95	0.93	0.95	1.00	0.96	0.97	0.90	—	0.89	0.88	0.91	0.95
PERC2004	0.85	0.90	—	0.57	0.94	0.94	0.96	0.96	1.00	0.99	0.94	—	0.93	0.93	0.97	0.93
PERC2005	0.90	0.90	—	—	0.97	0.96	0.97	0.97	0.99	1.00	0.96	—	0.94	0.94	0.96	0.97
MIG 2005	0.82	0.86	0.82	0.75	0.88	0.90	0.89	0.90	0.94	0.96	1.00	0.52	0.88	0.86	0.85	0.83
UNECA 2005	0.59	0.60	—	—	—	—	—	—	—	—	0.52	1.00	0.63	0.70	0.63	0.60
WEF 2003	0.79	0.90	0.82	0.82	0.95	0.95	0.95	0.89	0.93	0.94	0.88	0.63	1.00	0.95	0.94	0.89
WEF 2004	0.84	0.88	0.83	0.76	0.95	0.95	0.95	0.88	0.93	0.94	0.86	0.70	0.95	1.00	0.96	0.89
WEF 2005	0.85	0.87	0.77	0.77	0.94	0.94	0.93	0.91	0.97	0.96	0.85	0.63	0.94	0.96	1.00	0.90
WMRC 2005	0.81	0.92	0.83	0.78	0.88	0.89	0.90	0.95	0.93	0.97	0.83	0.60	0.89	0.89	0.90	1.00

Note: Only correlations that relate to at least six countries are reported.

Table A.2 Kendall's Rank Correlation

	CU 2003	EIU 2005	FH 2005	II 2003	IMD 2003	IMD 2004	IMD 2005	PERC 2003	PERC 2004	PERC 2005	MIG 2005	UNECA 2005	WEF 2003	WEF 2004	WEF 2005	WMRC 2005
CU 2003	1.00	0.67	0.60	0.53	0.72	0.72	0.70	0.69	0.67	0.76	0.63	0.48	0.58	0.63	0.62	0.56
EIU 2005	0.67	1.00	0.78	0.59	0.78	0.81	0.81	0.76	0.75	0.76	0.68	0.58	0.72	0.71	0.69	0.80
FH 2005	0.60	0.78	1.00	—	0.67	0.62	0.74	—	—	—	0.55	—	0.55	0.72	0.49	0.77
II 2003	0.53	0.59	—	1.00	0.67	0.60	0.62	0.68	0.55	—	0.56	—	0.63	0.62	0.65	0.66
IMD 2003	0.72	0.78	0.67	0.67	1.00	0.92	0.88	0.81	0.85	0.92	0.74	—	0.84	0.85	0.81	0.76
IMD 2004	0.72	0.81	0.62	0.60	0.92	1.00	0.90	0.75	0.82	0.87	0.76	—	0.84	0.84	0.82	0.78
IMD 2005	0.70	0.81	0.74	0.62	0.88	0.90	1.00	0.74	0.82	0.92	0.75	—	0.83	0.84	0.78	0.78
PERC2003	0.69	0.76	—	0.68	0.81	0.75	0.74	1.00	0.86	0.73	0.77	—	0.76	0.66	0.68	0.82
PERC2004	0.67	0.75	—	0.55	0.85	0.82	0.82	0.86	1.00	0.88	0.86	—	0.84	0.72	0.80	0.83
PERC2005	0.76	0.76	—	—	0.92	0.87	0.92	0.73	0.88	1.00	0.93	—	0.90	0.83	0.87	0.91
MIG 2005	0.63	0.68	0.55	0.56	0.74	0.76	0.75	0.77	0.86	0.93	1.00	0.47	0.66	0.66	0.63	0.65
UNECA 2005	0.48	0.58	—	—	—	—	—	—	—	—	0.47	1.00	0.52	0.54	0.43	0.44
WEF 2003	0.58	0.72	0.55	0.63	0.84	0.84	0.83	0.76	0.84	0.90	0.66	0.52	1.00	0.81	0.79	0.70
WEF 2004	0.63	0.71	0.72	0.62	0.85	0.84	0.84	0.66	0.72	0.83	0.66	0.54	0.81	1.00	0.81	0.69
WEF 2005	0.62	0.69	0.49	0.65	0.81	0.82	0.78	0.68	0.80	0.87	0.63	0.43	0.79	0.81	1.00	0.70
WMRC 2005	0.56	0.80	0.77	0.66	0.76	0.78	0.78	0.82	0.83	0.91	0.65	0.44	0.70	0.69	0.70	1.00

Note: Only correlations that relate to at least six countries are reported.

the other hand, the upper limit was as high as 10.4. This type of a range is confusing even to an expert. Since it is in contradiction to the official range reported, the public is equally disoriented.

In order to restrict the confidence range to our prespecified limits we now apply a different methodology: a nonparametric approach applying the bootstrap methodology. The principal idea of such a bootstrap confidence range is to resample the sources of a country with replacement. Imagine a country with five source values (3.0, 5.0, 3.9, 4.4, 4.2). An example of such a sample with replacement would be (5.0, 5.0, 4.2, 4.4, 4.4). Whereas the mean value of the original data is 4.1, that of our sample with replacement is 4.6. This value portrays how diverse the mean could have been if a different random selection of values from the original pool of data occurred.

A sufficiently large number of such samples (in our case 10,000) are drawn from the available vector of sources and the sample mean is determined in each case. Based on the distribution of the resulting means, inferences on the underlying precision can be drawn. The lower (upper) bound of a ninety percent confidence range is then determined as the value where five percent of the sample's means are below (above) this critical value.[4] There are two interesting characteristics of the resulting confidence range.[5]

[4] There may come up boundary effects when only three or four sources exist. Only ten different combinations are possible in the case of three sources, suggesting that a five percent confidence point can "hit" the boundary. If this is the case, the BC-approach could produce at random two different values for the upper (or the lower) confidence point. These boundary effects have been identified and, if existent, the more conservative range is reported in the table.

[5] In addition to the "percentile" method just described, more complicated approaches exist. First, the confidence levels can be adjusted if (on average) the mean of a bootstrap sample is smaller than the observed mean. The relevant parameter is called z_0. Another adjustment is to assume the standard deviation also to be dependent on the mean of the bootstrap sample. The relevant parameter is *a*. If both these adjustments are considered, the resulting approach is called a bootstrap-BC_a-method (bias-corrected-accelerated). A description of this approach can be obtained from Efron, B. and R. Tibshirani (1993); Chapters 14.3, 22.4, and 22.5. One concern with the BC_a-approach is that it throws a lot of machinery at very few observations. Owing to statistical considerations, a simple method might prove superior. Brad Efron had therefore suggested the use of a (bias-corrected) BC-approach for our purpose. In this case, z_0 is determined endogenously from the bootstrap sample but *a* is set equal to zero.

(1) When requiring a ninety percent confidence range (that allows with five percent probability that the true value is below and with five percent probability that the value is above the determined confidence range) the upper (lower) bound will not be higher (lower) than the highest (lowest) value provided by a source. This implies that our range from 0 to 10 will never be violated.
(2) The confidence range remains valid even if the data (i.e. the standardized values for a given country) are not normally distributed. The range is even free of assumptions with regard to the distribution of these data.

However, with only few sources being used, there is a downward bias in the confidence range thus reported. When only few sources are available these do not fully capture the whole range of possible values. This misrepresentation becomes larger, the fewer the sources available. This issue is part of a general statistical problem that is not specific to our application: one simply cannot expect accurate estimates of a confidence interval from few observations.

In order to determine the size of this bias Walter Zucchini and Florian Hoffmann from the Institute for Statistics and Econometrics, University of Göttingen, wrote a short unpublished research paper. Given that the data are approximately beta distributed, various simulation tests were required. They found that the unbiased coverage probability is lower than its nominal value of ninety percent. The accuracy of the confidence interval estimates increases with a growing number of sources (n). The mean coverage probability is 65.3 percent for $n=3$; 73.6 percent for $n=4$; 78.4 percent for $n=5$; 80.2 percent for $n=6$ and 81.8 percent for $n=7$. While the confidence range nominally relates to a ninety percent level, an unbiased estimate of the confidence level is lower.

In order to contrast the current standardization technique with different approaches, research at the University of Passau is carried out relating to a completely nonparametric approach (Kleinschmidt *et al.* 2005). This approach does not require a master list, as it is currently necessary. It employs a linear-ordering model that attempts to minimize the contradictions that a composite index imposes on the ranking provided by individual sources. The idea of such an approach can be visualized by imagining all our sources being assembled in a room to judge on the composite ranking. A moderator would propose a sequence of two countries – for example France being better than the United States. If sources have both these countries in their list, they are entitled to vote on this sequence. For the current case, six sources would object, three would be indifferent, and only one would agree that France performs better than the United States. Apparently, this sequence would not win approval. The task of the moderator would be to determine a sequence for the 159 countries that minimizes disagreement for all pairwise comparisons, meaning, for example, that France is also compared with all other 157 countries. Integer linear programming is employed to determine such a sequence. The resulting ranking of countries correlates 0.98 with that of the CPI. This high correlation provides another justification for the current approach – suggesting that our results are to a large extent invariant to the chosen methodology.

The strength of the CPI is based on the concept that a combination of data sources combined into a single index increases the reliability of each individual figure. As in previous years, the 2005 CPI includes all countries for which at least three sources had been available. The idea of combining data is that the nonperformance of one source can be balanced out by the inclusion of at least two other sources.[6] This way, the probability of misrepresenting a country is seriously lowered. Overall, the CPI is a solid assessment of perceived levels of corruption, helping our understanding of real levels of corruption. Figure 1.4 on page 25 portrays the confidence ranges alongside with the scores.

Weighting

Given that our various sources have some differences with respect to sample and date, a number of ideas can be considered for weighting the sources before aggregating them. We decided at the outset in favor of a simple approach of assigning equal weights to all the sources, which met the criteria of reliability and professionalism. Other procedures may have their merits, but this averaging system is simple and transparent.

[6] This argument is valid even in case the sources are not totally independent of each other. Such partial dependency may arise if some respondents are aware of other people's perception of the level of corruption or of other sources contributing to the CPI.

It was suggested in this context that data from various years provided by the same source should not obtain the same weight as other data. One may adhere to the viewpoint that the data provided by an institution is independent to that from another institution, but the same independence may not prevail for surveys originating from the same institution. But this argument may push a hard-to-assess issue too far, since an institution may also be likely to lean on the data produced by others in reaching a conclusion. Since the matter of independence is therefore difficult to quantify, there was no clear argument in changing the methodology used so far. As a result of giving each survey an equal weight, some institutions obtain a larger weight than others. While other approaches can certainly be justified there is also some rationale to this. It reflects previous recommendations by the Transparency International Steering Committee that continuous annual surveys are superior for our purposes than one-off surveys: they may have gathered more expertise in providing their service and their inclusion helps in avoiding abrupt year-to-year changes in the CPI. In addition to that, continuous annual surveys may be seen to be superior to expert assessments because the methodology of producing data is more transparent and subject to a clear procedure.

Another approach to weighting sources was adopted by Kaufmann *et al.* (1999a). They assume that each source is a noisy indicator for actual levels of corruption, which is the "unobservable component" they seek to determine. Since the error term varies with the sources, an approach must be presented that determines for each source how precisely it measures corruption, that is, the quality of the source. Included in their approach is the assumption that those sources that correlate better with the resulting aggregate index are of higher quality (and receive a higher weight), whereas those that correlate less well are considered to be of lower quality. The quality of sources is therefore determined endogenously and is not an expert's opinion on a source's validity and reliability. There might be some truth behind this idea, but it can also be misleading. If a source's assessment is based on hearsay or prejudice, it may correlate well with other sources. On the contrary, if a source engages in discovering original insights it may end up with results differing from other's perceptions. The first source would obtain a higher weight because it tends to say what all the others say, whereas the second one would be punished for its original research. The weighting system would then be in contrast to experts' viewpoints regarding the quality of sources. Whereas sources may certainly differ in quality, application of statistical methods for determining such differences is a thorny issue.

Another problem with the weighting used by Kaufmann *et al.* is the host of assumptions on which their approach is based. They assume all sources to be normally distributed but have claimed in personal correspondence that this assumption can be relaxed without changing the results. Still, the assumption that all sources are distributed equally is certainly problematic and counterfactual. The nonparametric approach taken here avoids such strong assumptions. Still, the results by Kaufmann *et al.* correlate well with the TI-data, giving us confidence that the findings are largely invariant to the particular aggregation method.

References

Abbink, K. (2004), "Staff Rotation as an Anti-corruption Policy: An Experimental Study," *European Journal of Political Economy*, Vol. 20 (4): 887–906.

Abbink, K., B. Irlenbusch, and E. Renner (2000), "The Moonlighting Game," *Journal of Economic Behavior and Organization*, Vol. 22: 265–77.

Abed, G. T. and H. R. Davoodi (2002), "Corruption, Structural Reforms, and Economic Performance," *Governance, Corruption & Economic Performance*, ed. by G. T. Abed and S. Gupta, Washington, DC: International Monetary Fund 489–537.

Aburish, S. (1985), *Pay-Off: Wheeling and Dealing in the Arab World* (New York: Harper Collins Publishers).

Acemoglu, D. and T. Verdier (1998), "Property Rights, Corruption and the Allocation of Talent: A General Equilibrium Approach," *The Economic Journal*, Vol. 108: 1381–1403.

Acemoglu, D. and T. Verdier (2000), "The Choice Between Market Failures and Corruption," *The American Economic Review*, Vol. 90: 194–211.

Ades, A. and R. Di Tella (1995), "Competition and Corruption," Draft Paper, Oxford: Keble College, Oxford University.

Ades, A. and R. Di Tella (1996), "The Causes and Consequences of Corruption: A Review of Recent Empirical Contributions," *Liberali zation and the New Corruption*, ed. by B. Harris White and G. White (Brighton: Institute of Development Studies Bulletin, 27): 6–12.

Ades, A. and R. Di Tella (1997), "National Champions and Corruption: Some Unpleasant Interventionist Arithmetic," *The Economic Journal*, Vol. 107: 1023–42.

Ades, A. and R. Di Tella (1999), "Rents, Competition, and Corruption," *The American Economic Review*, Vol. 89: 982–94.

Adsera, A., C. Boix, and M. Payne (2000), "Are You Being Served? Political Accountability and Quality of Government," *Inter-American Development Bank Research Department* Working Paper 438, Washington, DC.

Aidt, Toke S. (2003), "Economic Analysis of Corruption: A Survey," *The Economic Journal*, Vol. 113: 632–52.

Aizenman, J. and M. Spiegel (2003), "Institutional Efficiency, Monitoring Costs, and the Investment Share of FDI," Federal Reserve Bank of San Francisco Working Paper 2003–06.

Alam, S. M. (1990), "Some Economic Costs of Corruption in LDC's," *Journal of Development Studies*, Vol. 27: 89–97.

Alesina, A. and B. Weder (1999), "Do Corrupt Governments Receive Less Foreign Aid?," *NBER Working Paper* 7108, Cambridge, MA.

Alesina, A. and B. Weder (2002), "Do Corrupt Governments Receive Less Foreign Aid?," *American Economic Review*, Vol. 92 (4): 1126–37.

Alesina, A., A. Devleeschauwer, W. Easterly, S. Kurlat, and R. Wacziarg (2003), "Fractionalization," *Journal of Economic Growth*, Vol. 8: 155–94.

Ali, A. M. and H. S. Isse (2003), "Determinants of Economic Corruption: A Cross-Country Comparison," *Cato Journal*, Vol. 22 (3): 445–66.

Al-Marhubi, F. A. (2000), "Corruption and Inflation," *Economics Letters*, Vol. 66 (2): 199–202.

Anderson, A. (1995), "Organized Crime, Mafia and Governments," *The Economics of Organized Crime*, ed. by G. Fiorentini and S. Peltzman (Cambridge: Cambridge University Press): 33–54.

Anderson, C. J. and Y. V. Tverdova (2003), "Corruption, Political Allegiances, and Attitudes toward Government in Contemporary Democracies," *American Journal of Political Sciences*, Vol. 47 (1): 91–109.

Andvig, J. (1995), "Corruption in the North Sea Oil Industry: Issues and Assessments," *Crime, Law and Social Change*, Vol. 23: 289–313.

Andvig, J. C. (1991), "The Economics of Corruption: A Survey," *Studi Economici*, Vol. 43: 57–94.

Andvig, J. C. and O. H. Fjeldstadt (2000), "Research on Corruption. A Policy Oriented Survey," Chr. Michelsen Institute and Norwegian Institute for International Affairs. Online version at: www.icgg.org/downloads/contribution07_andrig.pdf

Andvig, J. C. and K. Moene (1990), "How Corruption May Corrupt," *Journal of Economic Behavior and Organization*, Vol. 13: 63–76.

Anoruo, E. and H. Braha (2005), "Corruption and Economic Growth: The African Experience," *Journal of Sustainable Development in Africa*, Vol. 7 (1).

Appelbaum, E. and E. Katz (1987), "Seeking Rents by Setting Rents: The Political Economy of Rent Seeking," *The Economic Journal*, Vol. 97: 685–99.

Arikan, G. (2004), "Fiscal Decentralization: A Remedy for Corruption?," *International Tax and Public Finance*, Vol. 11: 175–95.

Arlen, J. (1994), "The Potentially Perverse Effects of Corporate Criminal Liability," *Journal of Legal Studies*, Vol. 23: 833–67.

Axelrod, R. (1984), *The Evolution of Cooperation* (New York: Basic Books).

Bannenberg, B. (2002), *Korruption in Deutschland und ihre strafrechtliche Kontrolle: Eine kriminologisch-strafrechtliche Analyse* (Neuwied/Kriftel, Germany: Luchterhand).

Bardhan, P. (1997), "Corruption and Development: A Review of Issues," *Journal of Economic Literature*, Vol. 35: 1320–46.

Bartsch, E. and I. Thomas (1993), "Spieltheoretische Ansätze in der Rent-Seeking Theorie: Ein Literaturüberblick," *Kieler Arbeitspapiere*, Institut für Weltwirtschaft, Kiel, Germany, No. 564.

Bartsch, E. and I. Thomas (1995), "Rent-Seeking, Umverteilung und soziale Kosten," *WiSt –wirtschaftswissenschaftliches Studium*, Vol. 24: 174–9.

Bates, R. (1981), *Markets and States in Tropical Africa* (Berkeley, CA: University of California Press).

Bavarian Criminal Division (2005), unpublished conviction, 4th Criminal Division of the Munich District Court.

Bayley, D.H. (1966), "The Effects of Corruption in a Developing Nation," *The Western Political Quartely*, Vol. 19 (4): 719–32. Reprinted in A. Heidenheimer, M. Johnston and V. LeVine (1989), *Political Corruption – A Handbook* (New Brunswick, NJ: Transaction Publishers): 935–52.

Beck, P.J. and M. Maher (1986), "A Comparison of Bribery and Bidding in Thin Markets," *Economics Letters*, Vol. 20: 1–5.

Beck, P.J., M.W. Maher and A.E. Tschoegl (1991), "The Impact of the Foreign Corrupt Practices Act on US Exports," *Managerial and Decision Economics*, Vol. 12: 295–303.

Becker, G.S. (1968), "Crime and Punishment: An Economic Approach," *Journal of Political Economy*, Vol. 76: 169–217.

Becker, G.S. (1994), "To Root Out Corruption, Boot Out Big Government," *Business Week*, January 31: 18.

Becker, G.S. and G.J. Stigler (1974), "Law Enforcement, Malfeasance, and Compensation of Enforcers," *Journal of Legal Studies*, Vol. 3: 1–19.

Ben-Porath, Y. (1980), "The F-Connection: Families, Friends, and Firms and the Organization of Exchange," *Population and Development Review*, Vol. 6 (1): 1–30.

Besley, T. and J. McLaren (1993), "Taxes and Bribery: The Role of Wage Incentives," *The Economic Journal*, Vol. 103: 119–41.

Besley, T. and A. Prat (2006), "Handcuffs for the Grabbing Hand? Media Capture and Government Accountability," *American Economic Review*, Vol. 96(3): 720–736.

Bhagwati, J.N. (1982), "Directly Unproductive, Profit Seeking (DUP) Activities," *Journal of Political Economy*, Vol. 90: 998–1002.

Bhagwati, J.N. and T.N. Srinivasan (1980), "Revenue Seeking: A Generalization of the Theory of tariffs," *Journal of Political Economy*, Vol. 87: 1069–87.

Bhagwati, J.N., R.A. Brecher, and T.N. Srinivasan (1984), "DUP activities and Economic Theory," *Neoclassical Political Economy. The Analysis of Rent-Seeking and DUP Activities*, ed. by D.C. Colander (Cambridge, MA: Ballinger Publishing Company): 17–32.

Björnskov, C. and M. Paldam (2004), "Corruption Trends," *The New Institutional Economics of Corruption – Norms, Trust, and Reciprocity*, ed. by J. Graf Lambsdorff, M. Schramm and M. Taube (London: Routledge): 59–75.

Borner, S. and C. Schwyzer (1999), "Bekämpfung der Bestechung im Lichte der Neuen Politischen Ökonomie," *Korruption im internationalen Geschäftsverkehr, Bestandsaufnahme, Bekämpfung, Prävention*, ed. by M. Pieth and P. Eigen (Basel, Frankfurt am Main: Luchterhand): 17–39.

Boycko, M., A. Shleifer, and R. Vishny (1995), *Privatizing Russia* (Cambridge, MA and London: MIT Press).

Boyko, M., A. Shleifer, and R. Vishny (1996), "A Theory of Privatization," *Economic Journal*, Vol. 106 (435): 309–19.

Braun, M. and R. Di Tella (2000), "Inflation and Corruption," *Harvard Business School,* Division of Research Working Paper 00–053.

Bray, J. (1999), "Beyond Compliance: Corruption as a Business Risk," Conference on Fighting Corruption in Developing Countries and Emerging Countries: The Role of the Private Sector, Organisation for Economic Co-operation (OECD) Development Centre, Washington, DC, February.

Bray, J. (2004), "The Use of Intermediaries and other 'Alternatives' to Bribery," *The New Institutional Economics of Corruption – Norms, Trust, and Reciprocity*, ed. by J. Graf Lambsdorff, M. Schramm, and M. Taube (London: Routledge): 112–37.

Bray, J. (2006), International Business Attitudes to Corruption-Survey 2006. Report (London: Control Risks Group). Online version at www.control-risks.com/pdf/corruption_survey_2006_v3.pdf

Breton, A. and R. Wintrobe (1975), "The Equilibrium Size of a Budget-maximizing Bureau: A Note on Niskanen's Theory of Bureaucracy (in Communications)," *The Journal of Political Economy*, Vol. 83 (1): 195–208.

Broadman, H.G. and F. Recanatini (1999), "Seeds of Corruption – Do Market Institutions Matter?," World Bank Policy Research Working Paper 2368, Washington, DC.

Brock, W. A. and St. P. Magee (1978), "The Economics of Special Interest Politics: The Case of the Tariff," *The American Economic Review, Papers and Proceedings*, Vol. 68: 246–50.

Brock, W. A. and St. P. Magee (1984), "The Invisible Foot and the Waste of Nations," *Neoclassical Political Economy. The Analysis of Rent-Seeking and DUP Activities*, ed. by D. C. Colander (Cambridge, MA: Ballinger Publishing Company): 177–86.

Browning, E. K. (1974), "On the Welfare Costs of Transfers," *Kyklos*, Vol. 27: 374–7.

Brunetti, A. and B. Weder (1998), "Investment and Institutional Uncertainty: A Comparative Study of Different Uncertainty Measures," *Weltwirtschaftliches Archiv*, Vol. 134: 513–33.

Brunetti, A. and B. Weder (2003), "A Free Press is Bad News for Corruption," *Journal of Public Economics*, Vol. 87 (7–8): 1801–24.

Brunetti, A., G. Kisunko, and B. Weder (1997), "Institutional Obstacles for Doing Business. Data Description and Methodology of a Worldwide Private Sector Survey," Background Paper for the World Development Report 1997, Washington, DC: The World Bank.

Brunetti, A., G. Kisunko, and B. Weder (1998), "Credibility of Rules and Economic Growth: Evidence from a World Wide Private Sector Survey," *The World Bank Economic Review*, Vol. 12 (3): 353–84.

Brunner, K. and W. H. Meckling (1977), "The Perception of Man and the Conception of Government," *Journal of Money, Credit and Banking*, Vol. 9 (1): 70–85.

Buchanan, J. M. (1980), "Rent-Seeking and Profit-Seeking," *Toward a Theory of the Rent-Seeking Society*, ed. by J. M. Buchanan, R. D. Tollison, and G. Tullock (College Station, TX: Texas A&M University Press): 3–15.

Buchanan, J. M. (1993), "Public Choice after Socialism," *Public Choice*, Vol. 72: 67–74.

Buchanan, J. M. and G. Tullock (1962), *The Calculus of Consent. Logical Foundations of Constitutional Democracy* (Ann Arbor, MI: University of Michigan Press).

Bundeskriminalamt (2004), "Lagebild Korruption Bundesrepublik Deutschland 2003," August. Online version at www.bka.de/lageberichte/ko/blkorruption2003.pdf, retreived July, 2005

Button, K. J. and T. G. Weyman-Jones (1994), "X-Efficiency and Technical Efficiency," *Public Choice*, Vol. 80: 83–104.

Campos, J. E., D. Lien, and S. Pradhan (1999), "The Impact of Corruption on Investment: Predictability Matters," *World Development*, Vol. 27 (6): 1059–67.

Cartier-Bresson, J. (1997), "The Economics of Corruption," *Democracy and Corruption in Europe*, ed. by D. Della Porta and Y. Mény (London: Pinter): 148–65.

Center for the Study of Democracy (1998), "Relations between Citizens and Public Administration and Public Opinion on Corruption in Bulgaria," *Draft Paper*, Sofia, Bulgaria.

Chang, E. and M. Golden (2004), "Electoral Systems, District Magnitude and Corruption," mimeo, Departments of Political Science, Michigan State University and the University of California at Los Angeles, CA.

Choi, J. P. and M. Thum (2005), "Corruption and the Shadow Economy," *International Economic Review*, Vol. 46 (3): 817–36.

Ciocchini, F., E. Durbin, and D. T. C. Ng (2003), "Does Corruption Increase Emerging Market Bond Spreads?," *Journal of Economics and Business*, Vol. 55: 503–28.

Coase, R. H. (1937), "The Nature of the Firm," *Economica*, Vol. 4: 386–405.

Colombo, G. (1995), "Korruption als Flächenbrand. Bekämpfungsstrategien in Italien," *Korruption in Deutschland – Ursachen, Erscheinungsformen, Bekämpfungsstrategien*, (Berlin: Friedrich Ebert Stiftung): 37–44.

Congleton, R. (1980), "Competitive Process, Competitive Waste, and Institutions," *Toward a Theory of the Rent-Seeking Society*, ed. by J. M. Buchanan, R. D. Tollison, and G. Tullock (College Station, TX: Texas A&M University Press): 153–79.

Coolidge, J. and S. Rose-Ackerman (1997), "High-Level Rent-Seeking and Corruption in African Regimes: Theory and Cases," Policy Research Working Paper 1780, Washington, DC: World Bank.

Coronel, S. S. (2000), "The Jueteng Republic," *Investigating Estrada: Millions, Mansions and Mistresses*, ed. by Sheila S. Coroner (Manila: PCIJ) 26–36.

Crain, W. M. and R. D. Tollison (1979), "The Executive Branch in an Interest-Group Perspective," *Journal of Legal Studies*, Vol. 8: 555–67.

Damania, R., P. G. Fredriksson, and M. Mani (2004), The Persistence of Corruption and Regulatory Compliance Failures: Theory and Evidence," *Public Choice*, Vol. 121: 363–90.

Darroch, Fiona (2004), Lesotho – "A sheep or a springbock? The herd boy tackles Goliath," commissioned case study, Anti-Corruption Strategies Programme, Three Strikes Against Graft, Assessing the Impact of Groundbreaking Corruption Cases in Lesotho, Mozambique and South Africa; The Implications for Countering Corruption in Southern Africa, 2004. www.iss.co.za/SEMINARS/2004/1503graft/lesotho.pdf

Davidson, S. (1999), "Okeahalam and Bah on Corruption: A Comment," *South African Journal of Economics*, Vol. 67 (1) March: 157–65.

De Soto, H. (1989), *The Other Path* (New York: Harper and Row).

della Porta, D. and A. Vanucci (1999), *Corrupt Exchanges, Actors, Resources and Mechanisms of Political Corruption* (New York: de Gruyter).

Dick, A. R. (1995), "When does Organized Crime Pay? A Transaction Cost Analysis," *International Review of Law and Economics*, Vol. 15: 25–45.

Di Tella, R. and E. Schargrodsky, (2003) "The Role of Wages and Auditing during a Crackdown on Corruption in the City of Buenos Aires." *Journal of Law and Economics*, Vol. 46(1): 269–92.

Djankov, S., R. La Porta, F. Lopez-de-Silanes, and A. Shleifer (2002), "The Regulation of Entry," *Quarterly Journal of Economics*, Vol. 117 (1): 1–37.

Doh, J. and H. Teegen (2003), "Private Telecommunications Investment in Emerging Economies – Comparing the Latin American and Asian Experience," *Management Research*, Vol. 1 (1): 9–26.

Dollar, D., R. Fisman, and R. Gatti (2001), "Are Women Really the 'Fairer' Sex? Corruption and Women in Government," *Journal of Economic Behavior and Organization*, Vol. 46 (4): 423–9.

Downs, A. (1957), *An Economic Theory of Democracy* (New York: Harper and Row).

Drew, E. (1983), *Politics and Money. The New Road to Corruption* (New York: Macmillan).

Dušek, L., A. Ortmann, and L. Lízal (2005), "Understanding Corruption and Corruptibility through Experiments: A Primer, Prague Economic Papers 2. University of Economics, Prague, Czech Republic.

Efron, B. and R. Tibshirani (1993), *An Introduction to the Bootstrap*, New York and London: Chapman & Hall.

EIRIS (2005), "Corporate Codes of Business Ethics: An International Survey of Bribery and Ethical Standards in Companies." Publication of the Ethical Investment Research Services, London. Online version at www.eiris.org/files/research%20publications/corporatecodesofbusinessethicsep05. pdf, retrieved December 2006.

Elliott, K. A. (1997), "Corruption as an International Policy Problem: Overview and Recommendations," *Corruption and the Global Economy*, ed. by K. A. Elliott (Washington, DC: Institute for International Economics): 175–233.

Esty, D. and M. Porter (2002), "National Environmental Performance Measurement and Determinants," in ed. by D. Esty and P. Cornelius, *Environmental Performance Measurement: The Global Report 2001–2002*, (New York: Oxford University Press): 24–43.

Evans, P. B. and J. E. Rauch (2000), "Bureaucratic Structures and Economic Performance in Less Developed Countries," *Journal of Public Economics*, Vol. 75: 49–71.

Faccio, M. and D. C. Parsley (2006), "Sudden Deaths: Taking Stock of Political Connections," ECGI – Finance Working Paper 113/2006.
Fikentscher, W. (1987), "Ersatz im Ausland gezahlter Bestechungsgelder," *Praxis des internationalen Privat- und Verfahrensrechts*, (2): 86–90.
Findlay, R. and St. Wellisz (1984), "Toward a Model of Endogenous Rent-Seeking," *Neoclassical Political Economy. The Analysis of Rent-Seeking and DUP Activities*, D. C. Colander (ed.) (Cambridge, MA: Ballinger Publishing Company): 89–100.
Fisman, R. and R. Gatti (2002), "Decentralization and Corruption: Evidence Across Countries," *Journal of Public Economics*, Vol. 83 (3): 325–45.
Fjeldstad, O.-H. and B. Tungodden (2001), "Skatteunndragelse og korrupsjon i Tanzania. En studie av Tanzania Revenue Authority," *Den Ny Verden*, Vol. 34 (3): 55–79.
Flowers, M. R. (1987), "Rent-Seeking and Rent Dissipation: A Critical View," *Cato Journal*, Vol. 7: 431–40.
Fons, J. (1999), "Improving Transparency in Asian Banking Systems," *Internet Center for Corruption Research*, Contribution No. 4. Online version at www.icgg.org/downloads/contribution04_fons.pdf
Foreign Policy (2001), "Measuring Globalization," *Foreign Policy*. Online at www.foreignpolicy.com/story/cms.php?story_id=2493, accessed December 2006.
Friedman, E., S. Johnson, D. Kaufmann, and P. Zoido-Lobaton (2000), "Dodging the Grabbing Hand: The Determinants of Unofficial Activity in 69 Countries," *Journal of Public Economics*, Vol. 76: 459–93.
Friedman, M. (1970), "The Social Responsibility of Business Is to Increase Its Profits," *New York Times Magazine*, September 13. Reprint, L. P. Hartmann, Business Ethics (Chicago, IL: Irwin/McGraw-Hill): 246–51.
Frisch, D. (1999), "Entwicklungspolitische Gesichtspunkte der Korruption," *Korruption im internationalen Geschäftsverkehr: Bestandsaufnahme, Bekämpfung, Prävention*, ed. by M. Pieth and P. Eigen (Basel, Frankfurt am Main: Luchterhand): 89–100.
Furubotn, E. G. and R. Richter (1998), *Institutions and Economic Theory: The Contribution of New Institutional Economics* (Ann Arbor, MI: University of Michigan Press).
Galeotti, G. and A. Merlo (1994), "Political Collusion and Corruption in a Representative Democracy," Unpublished manuscript. Universita'di Roma "La Sapienza" and University of Minnesota, Minneapolis, MN.
Galtung, F. (1999), "BPI Framework Document," Transparency International Background Paper. Online version at www.transparency.org/cpi/1999/bpi_framework.html, retrieved March, 2004.

Gambetta, D. (1998), "Comment on 'Corruption and Development,' by Susan Rose-Ackerman," *Annual World Bank Conference on Development Economics* 1997, ed. by. B. Pleskovic and J. E. Stiglitz (Washington D.C.: The World Bank): 58–61.

Gardiner, J. A. and D. J. Olson (1974), *Theft of the City* (Bloomington, IN: Indiana University Press).

Gastil, R. D. (1986), *Freedom in the World. Political Rights and Civil Liberties 1985–86* (New York: Greenwood Press).

Gatti, R. (1999), "Corruption and Trade Tariffs, or a Case for Uniform Tariffs," *World Bank Policy Research Working Paper* 2216.

Gerring, J. and S. Thacker (2004), "Political Institutions and Governance: Pluralism versus Centralism," *British Journal of Political Science*, Vol. 34 (2): 295–3.

Gerring, J. and S. Thacker (2005), "Do Neoliberal Policies Deter Political Corruption?," *International Organization*, Vol. 59: 233–54.

Ghura, D. (2002), "Tax Revenue in Sub-Saharan Africa: Effects of Economic Policies and Corruption," *Governance, Corruption & Economic Performance*, ed. by G. T. Abed and S. Gupta, Washington, DC: International Monetary Fund, 369–95.

Githongo, J. (1997), "Independency, Investigation and Denunciation of Corruption from the Press – The Case of Kenya," 8th *International Anti-Corruption Conference*, Lima, Peru, September.

Glaeser, E. and R. E. Saks (2006), "Corruption in America," *Journal of Public Economics* Vol. 90(6–7): 1053–72.

Goel, R. K. and M. A. Nelson (1998), "Corruption and Government Size: A Disaggregated Analysis," *Public Choice*, Vol. 97 (1): 107–20.

Goel, R. K. and M. A. Nelson (2005), "Economic Freedom versus Political Freedom: Cross-Country Influences on Corruption," *Australian Economic Papers*, Vol. 44: 121–33.

Goetz, C. J. and R. E. Scott (1981), "Principles of Relational Contracts," *Virginia Law Review*, Vol. 67: 1089–150.

Goldsmith, A. A. (1999), "Slapping the Grasping Hand: Correlates of Political Corruption in Emerging Markets," *The American Journal of Economics and Sociology*, Vol. 58 (4): 866–83.

Graeff, P. and G. Mehlkop (2003), "The Impact of Economic Freedom on Corruption: Different Patterns for Rich and Poor Countries," *European Journal of Political Economy*, Vol. 19: 605–20.

Granovetter, M. (1992), "Economic Action and Social Structure: The Problem of Embeddedness," *The Sociology of Economic Life*, ed. by M. Granovetter and R. Swedberg (Boulder, CO: Westview Press): 53–81.

Grossman, H. I. (1995), "Rival Kleptocrats: The Mafia versus the State," *The Economics of Organized Crime*, ed. by G. Fiorentini and S. Peltzman (Cambridge: Cambridge University Press): 143–56.

Gupta, M. R. and S. Chaudhuri (1997), "Formal Credit, Corruption and the Informal Credit Market in Agriculture: A Theoretical Analysis," *Economica*, 64: 331–43.

Gupta, S., L.de Mello, and R. Sharan (2001a), "Corruption and Military Spending," *European Journal of Political Economy*, Vol. 17 (4): 749–77.

Gupta, S., H. Davoodi, and E. R. Tiongson (2001b), "Corruption and the Provision of Health Care and Education Services," *The Political Economy of Corruption*, ed. by A. K. Jain (London: Routledge): 111–41.

Gupta, S., H. Davoodi, and R. Alonso-Terme (2002), "Does Corruption Affect Income Inequality and Poverty?," *Economics of Governance*, Vol. 3: 23–45.

Gylfason, T. (2001), "Nature, Power and Growth," *Scottish Journal of Political Economy*, Vol. 48: 558–88.

Gymiah-Brempong, K. (2002), "Corruption, Economic Growth, and Income Inequality in Africa," *Economics of Governance*, Vol. 3: 183–209.

Gwartney, J. and R. Lawson (2000), "*Economic Freedom of the World: 2000 Annual Report*," (Vancouver, BC): Fraser Institute.

Habib, M. and L. Zurawicki (2001), "Country-Level Investments and the Effect of Corruption: Some Empirical Evidence," *International Business Review*, Vol. 10 (6): 687–700.

Habib, M. and L. Zurawicki (2002), "Corruption and Foreign Direct Investment," *Journal of International Business Studies*, Vol. 33 (2): 291–307.

Hall, R. and C. Jones (1999), "Why Do Some Countries Produce So Much More Output Per Worker than Others," *Quarterly Journal of Economics*, Vol. 114: 83–116.

Hall, T. and G. Yago (2000), "Estimating the Cost of Opacity Using Sovereign Bond Spreads," unpublished manuscript, Milken Institute, Santa Monica, CA.

Harden, B. (1993), *Africa. Dispatches from a Fragile Continent* (London: Harper Collins Publishers, paperback edition).

Hart, A. G. (1970), "Fiscal Policy in Latin America," Part 2: Key Problems of Economic Policy in Latin America, *The Journal of Political Economy*, Vol. 78 (4): 857–89.

Hart, O. D. (1987), "Incomplete Contracts," *The New Palgrave-Allocation, Information and Markets*, Vol. 2, ed. by J. Eatwell, M. Milgate, and P. Newman, (London: Macmillan): 752–9.

Hart, O. D. (1991), "Incomplete Contracts and the Theory of the Firm," *The Nature of the Firm: Origins, Evolution, and Development*, ed. by

O. D. Williamson and S. G. Winter (New York: Oxford University Press): 138–58.

Hasker, K. and C. Okten (2004), Intermediaries and Corruption, unpublished working paper, Ankara, Turkey: Bilkent University. Forthcoming in *Journal of Economic Behavior and Organization.*

Heidenheimer, A., M. Johnston and V. LeVine (1989), *Political Corrup tion – A Handbook*, 2nd ed. (New Brunswick, NJ: Transaction Publishers).

Henderson, D. R. (1999), "Power Corrupts – Editorial Comment," *The Wall Street Journal*, April 19.

Henisz, W. (2000), "The institutional environment for multinational investment," *Journal of Law, Economics and Organization*, Vol. 16 (2): 334–64.

Hepkema, S. and Booysen, W. (1997), "The Bribery of Public Officials: An IBA Survey," *International Business Lawyer*, Vol. 25 (9): 415–16, 422.

Herrera, A. and P. Rodriguez (2003), "*Bribery and the Nature of Corruption*,"unpublished manuscript, Michigan State University, East Lansing, MI and The Darden School, University of Virginia, Charlottesville, VA, July.

Herzfeld, T. and C. Weiss (2003), "Corruption and legal (in)effectiveness: an empirical investigation," *European Journal of Political Economy*, Vol. 19: 621–32.

Heymann, P. B. (1995), "Korruption in den USA. Rechtliche, wirtschaftliche und ethische Aspekte," *Korruption in Deutschland – Ursachen, Erscheinungsformen, Bekämpfungsstrategien*, (Berlin: Friedrich Ebert Stiftung): 49–56.

Hillman, A. L. and E. Katz (1984), "Risk Averse Rent Seekers and the Social Cost of Monopoly Power," *Economic Journal*, Vol. 94: 104–10.

Hines, J. R. (1995), "Forbidden Payment: Foreign Bribery and American Business after 1977," *NBER Working Paper* 5266, Cambridge, MA.

Hirshleifer, J. (1976), "Toward a More General Theory of Regulation: Comment," *Journal of Law and Economics*, Vol. 19: 241–4.

Hofstede, G. (1997), *Cultures and Organizations: Software of the Mind* (New York: McGraw Hill).

Huntington, S. P. (1968), "Modernization and Corruption," *Political Order in Changing Societies* (New Haven, CT: Yale University Press): 59–71. Reprinted in A. Heidenheimer, M. Johnston, and V. LeVine (1989), *Political Corruption – A Handbook* (New Brunswick, NJ: Transaction Publishers): 377–88.

Husted, B. (1999), "Wealth, Culture, and Corruption," *Journal of International Business Studies*, Vol. 30 (2): 339–60.

Husted, B.W. (1994), "Honor Among Thieves: A Transaction-Cost Interpretation of Corruption in Third World Countries," *Business Ethics Quarterly*, Vol. 4: 17–27.

Huther, J. and A. Shah, (1998), "A Simple Measure of Good Governance and its Application to the Debate on the Appropriate Level of Fiscal Decentralization," World Bank Working Paper, 1894, Washington, DC.

Hwang, J. (2002), "A Note on the Relationship between Corruption and Government," *Journal of Development Economics*, Vol. 27 (2): 161–77.

Isham, J. and D. Kaufmann (1999), "The Forgotten Rationale for Policy Reform: The Productivity of Investment Projects," *Quarterly Journal of Economics*, Vol. 114: 149–84.

Jagannathan, N.V. (1986), "Corruption, Delivery Systems, and Property Rights," *World Development*, Vol. 14: 127–32.

Jain, A.K. (1998), "Models of Corruption," *Economics of Corruption*, ed. by A.K. Jain (Boston, London, and Dordrecht): 13–34.

Jarvin, S. (1986), "Aus der Praxis des ICC Schiedgerichtshofes," *Recht und Praxis der Schiedsgerichtsbarkeit der Internationalen Handelskammer. Schriftenreihe des Deutschen Instituts für Schiedsgerichtsverfahren*, ed. by K.-H. Böckstiegel (Köln: Heymann): 7–51.

Johnson, S., D. Kaufmann, and P. Zoido-Lobaton (1998), "Regulatory Discretion and the Unofficial Economy," *The American Economic Review, Papers and Proceedings*, Vol. 88: 387–92.

Kapstein, E. (2001), "Five Basic Principles for a Worldwide Code of Business Ethics," *International Herald Tribune*, January 24.

Kargl, W. (2002), "Über die Bekämpfung des Anscheins der Kriminalität bei der Vorteilsannahme (§ 331 StGB)," *Zeitschrift für die gesamte Strafrechtswissenschaft (ZStW)*, Vol. 114 (4): 763–81.

Kaufmann, D. and S.-J. Wei (1999), "Does 'Grease Money' Speed up the Wheels of Commerce?," NBER Working Paper 7093, Cambridge, MA.

Kaufmann, D., A. Kraay, and P. Zoido-Lobaton (1999a), "Aggregating Governance Indicators," World Bank Policy Research Working Paper 2195, Washington, DC: The World Bank.

Kaufmann, D., A. Kraay, and P. Zoido-Lobaton (1999b), "Governance Matters," *World Bank Policy Research Working Paper* 2196, October, Washington, DC: The World Bank.

Khalil, F. and J. Lawarree (1995), "Collusive Auditors," *The American Economic Review Papers and Proceedings*, Vol. 85 (2): 442–6.

Klein, B. (1996), "Why Hold-Ups Occur: The Self-Enforcing Range of Contractual Relationships," *Economic Inquiry*, Vol. 34: 444–63.

Klein, B., R. G. Crawford, and A. A. Alchian (1978), "Vertical Integration, Appropriable Rents, and the Competitive Contracting Process," *Journal of Law and Economics*, Vol. 21: 297–326.

Kleinschmidt, P., H. Achatz, and J. Graf Lambsdorff (2005), "The Corruption Perceptions Index and the Linear Ordering Problem," presented at the Annual International Conference of the German Operations Research Society (GOR), September 9, 2005.

Klitgaard, R. (1988), *Controlling Corruption* (Berkeley, CA: University of California Press).

Knack, S. and O. Azfar (2003), "Trade Intensity, Country Size and Corruption," *Economics of Governance*, Vol. 4 (1): 1–18.

Knack, S. and P. Keefer (1995), "Institutions and Economic Performance: Cross-Country Tests Using Alternative Institutional Measures," *Economics and Politics*, Vol. 7: 207–27.

Knapp, W. (1986), "Sittenwidrige Vermittlung von Regierungsaufträgen durch Bestechungsgelder," *RIW – Recht der Internationalen Wirtschaft*: 999–1001.

Kofman, F. and J. Lawarree (1996), "On the Optimality of Allowing Collusion," *Journal of Public Economics*, Vol. 61: 383–407.

Kranton, R. E. (1996), "Reciprocal Exchange: A Self-Sustaining System," *The American Economic Review*, Vol. 86 (4): 830–51.

Kreps, D. M. (1990), "Corporate Culture and Economic Theory," *Perspectives on Positive Political Economy*, ed. by J. Alt and K. Shepsle (Cambridge: Cambridge University Press): 90–143.

Kreps, D. M. and R. Wilson (1982), "Reputation and Imperfect Information," *Journal of Economic Theory*, Vol. 27: 253–79.

Krueger, A. (1974), "The Political Economy of the Rent Seeking Society," *American Economic Review*, Vol. 64: 291–303.

Krueger, A. (1990), "Government Failures in Development," *Journal of Economic Perspectives*, Vol. 4: 9–23.

Kunicova, J. (2005), *"Are Presidential Systems More Susceptible to Political Corruption?,"* mimeo, Department of Political Science, Yale University, New Haven, CT.

Kunicova, J. (2002), *"When Are Opposition's Lips Sealed? Comparative Political Corruption in Democracies,"* mimeo, Department of Political Science, Yale University, New Haven, CT.

Kunicova, J. and S. Rose-Ackerman (2005), "Electoral Rules and Constitutional Structures as Constraints on Corruption," *British Journal of Political Science*, Vol. 35 (4): 573–606.

La Porta, R., F. Lopez-De-Silanes, A. Shleifer, and R. W. Vishny (1997), "Trust in Large Organizations," *The American Economic Review, Papers and Proceedings*, Vol. 137 (2): 333–8.

La Porta, R., F. Lopez-De-Silanes, A. Shleifer, and R.W. Vishny (1999), "The Quality of Government," *The Journal of Law, Economics and Organization*, Vol. 15 (1): 222–79.

Laffont, J.-J. and J. Tirole (1993), *A Theory of Incentives in Procurement and Regulation* (Cambridge, MA: MIT Press).

Lambert-Mogiliansky, A. (2002), "Why Firms Pay Occasional Bribes: The Connection Economy," *European Journal of Political Economy*, Vol. 18: 47–60.

Lambsdorff, J. Graf (1998a), "An Empirical Investigation of Bribery in International Trade," *European Journal for Development Research*, Vol. 10: 40–59. Reprinted in *Corruption and Development*, ed. by M. Robinson (London: Frank Cass Publishers): 40–59.

Lambsdorff, J. Graf (1999), "Korruption im internationalen Geschäftsverkehr. Bestandsaufnahme, Bekämpfung, Prävention," *Korruption als mühseliges Geschäft –eine Transaktionskostenanalyse*, ed. by M. Pieth and P. Eigen (Basel, Frankfurt am Main: Luchterhand): 56–88.

Lambsdorff, J. Graf (2000), "De la propension des exportateurs à verser des pots-de-vin –l'impact sur les échanges," *Revue Tiers Monde*, Vol. 41 (161): 89–116.

Lambsdorff, J. Graf (2002a), "Making Corrupt Deals – Contracting in the Shadow of Law," *Journal of Economic Behavior and Organization*, Vol. 48 (3): 221–41.

Lambsdorff, J. Graf (2002b), "Corruption and Rent-Seeking," *Public Choice*, Vol. 113 (1/2): 97–125.

Lambsdorff, J. Graf (2002c), "How Confidence facilitates illegal Transactions," *American Journal of Economics and Sociology*, Vol. 61 (4): 829–54.

Lambsdorff, J. Graf (2003a), "How Corruption Affects Productivity," *Kyklos*, Vol. 56 (4): 459–76.

Lambsdorff, J. Graf (2003b), "How Corruption Affects Persistent Capital Flows," *Economics of Governance*, Vol. 4 (3): 229–44.

Lambsdorff, J. Graf (2005a), "Between Two Evils – Investors Prefer Grand Corruption!," University of Passau, Discussion Paper V-31–05, January.

Lambsdorff, J. Graf (2005b), "Determining Trends for Perceived Levels of Corruption," Passau University, Discussion Paper V-38–06.

Lambsdorff, J. Graf (2006), "Ten Years of the CPI: Determining trends," Global Corruption Report 2006, Transparency International.

Lambsdorff, J. Graf and M. Nell (2005), "Let Them Take Gifts, and Cheat Those Who Seek Influence," Economics Faculty of Passau University, Discussion Paper 41–05, December 2005.

Lambsdorff, J. Graf and P. Cornelius (2000), "Corruption, Foreign Investment and Growth," *The Africa Competitiveness Report 2000/*

2001, ed. by K. Schwab, L. Cook, P. Cornelius, J.D. Sachs, S. Sievers, and A. Warner joint publication of the World Economic Forum and the Institute for International Development, (Cambridge, MA: Harvard University and Oxford: Oxford University Press: 70–78.

Lambsdorff, J. Graf, M. Schramm, and M. Taube (2004), *The New Institutional Economics of Corruption – Norms, Trust, and Reciprocity*, (London: Routledge).

Landes, W.M. and R.A. Posner (1975), "The Independent Judiciary in an Interest-Group Perspective," *Journal of Law and Economics*, Vol. 18: 875–901.

LaPalombara, J. (1994), "Structural and Institutional Aspects of Corruption," *Social Research*, Vol. 61: 325–50.

Lederman, D., N. Loayza, and R. Reis Soares (2001), "Accountability and Corruption. Political Institutions Matter," The World Bank Working Paper 2708.

Lee, C.M. and D. Ng (2004), "Corruption and International Valuation. Does Virtue Pay?," unpublished manuscript, Cornell University, Ithaca, NY.

Leff, N.H. (1964), "Economic Development Through Bureaucratic Corruption," *American Behavioral Scientist*, Vol. 8 (3): 8–14. Reprinted in A. Heidenheimer, M. Johnston, and V. LeVine (1989), *Political Corruption – A Handbook* (New Brunswick, NJ: Transaction Publishers) 389–403.

Leite, C. and J. Weidemann (1999), "Does Mother Nature Corrupt? Natural Resources, Corruption, and Economic Growth," International Monetary Fund Working Paper 99/85, July.

Li, H., L.C. Xu, and H.-F. Zou (2000), "Corruption, Income Distribution, and Growth," *Economics and Politics*, Vol. 12 (2): 155–82.

Lien, D.H.D. (1986), "A Note on Competitive Bribery Games," *Economics Letters*, Vol. 22: 337–41.

Lindstedt, C. and D. Naurin (2005), "Transparency and Corruption. A Cross-Country Study of the Significance of a Free Press," paper prepared for the 3rd ECPR Conference, *The Quality of Democracy*, Budapest, September.

Lipset, S.M. and G.S. Lenz (2000), "Corruption, Culture, and Markets," *In Culture Matters: How Values Shape Human Progress*, ed. by L.E. Harrison and S.P. Huntington (New York: Basic Books): 112–24.

Lui, F.T. (1985), "An Equilibrium Queuing Model of Bribery," *Journal of Political Economy*, Vol. 93: 760–81.

MacGuire, M.C. and M. Olson (1996), "The Economics of Autocracy and Majority Rule: The Invisible Hand and the Use of Force," *Journal of Economic Literature*, Vol. 34: 72–96.

Macneil, I. R. (1974), "The Many Futures of Contracts," *Southern California Law Review*, Vol. 47: 691–816.

Macneil, I. R. (1978), "Contracts: Adjustment of Long Term Economic Relations under Classical, Neoclassical and Relational Contract Law," *Northwestern University Law Review*, Vol. 72: 854–905.

Magee, St. P. (1984), "Endogenous Tariff Theory," *Neoclassical Political Economy. The Analysis of Rent-Seeking and DUP Activities*, ed. by D. C. Colander (Cambridge, MA: Ballinger Publishing Company): 41–54.

Mankiw, N. G. (2000), *Principles of Economics*, 2nd ed. (Fort Worth, TX, Harcourt College Publishers).

Manow, P. (2005), "Politische Korruption und politischer Wettbewerb: Probleme der quantitativen Analyse," *Dimensionen politischer Korruption*, ed. by U. von Alemann, PVS – Politische Vierteljahresschrift, VS – Verlag für Sozialwissenschaften: Wiesbaden, Sonderheft 35: 249–66.

Marcoullier, D. and L. Young (1995), "The Black Hole of Graft: The Predatory State and the Informal Economy," *The American Economic Review*, Vol. 85 (3): 630–46.

Marshall, A. (1897), "The Old Generation of Economists and the New," *Quarterly Journal of Economics*, Vol. 11 (2): 115–35.

Mauro, P. (1995), "Corruption and Growth," *Quarterly Journal of Economics*, Vol. 110 (3): 681–712.

Mauro, P. (1997a), "The Effects of Corruption on Growth, Investment, and Government Expenditure: A Cross-Country Analysis," *Corruption and the Global Economy*, ed. by K. Elliott (Washington, DC: Institute for International Economics): 83–107.

Mauro, P. (1997b), "Why Worry about Corruption?," *Economic Issues No. 6* (Washington, DC: International Monetary Fund).

Mauro, P. (1998), "Corruption and the Composition of Government Expenditure," *Journal of Public Economics*, Vol. 69: 263–79.

Mbaku, J. M. (1992), "Bureaucratic Corruption as Rent-Seeking Behavior," *Konjunkturpolitik*, Vol. 38: 247–65.

Mbaku, J. M. (1998), "Corruption and Rent-Seeking," *The Political Dimension of Economic Growth*, ed. by S. Borner and M. Paldam (London and New York: Macmillan Press and St. Martins Press): 193–211.

McChesney, F. S. (1987), "Rent Extraction and Rent Creation in the Economic Theory of Regulation," *Journal of Legal Studies*, Vol. 16: 101–18.

McChesney, F. S. (1997), *Money for Nothing. Politicians, Rent Extraction, and Political Extortion* (Cambridge, MA: Harvard University Press).

McGuire, M. C. and M. Olson (1996), "The Economics of Autocracy and Majority Rule: The Invisible Hand and the Use of Force," *Journal of Economic Literature*, Vol. 34: 72–96.

Méon, P.-G. and K. Sekkat (2004), "Does the Quality of Institutions Limit the MENA's Integration in the World Economy?," *The World Economy*, Vol. 27 (9): 1475–98.

Méon, P.-G. and K. Sekkat (2005), "Does Corruption Grease or Sand the Wheels of Growth?," *Public Choice*, Vol. 122: 69–97.

Miller, W. L., Å. GrØdeland, and T. Y. Koshechkina (2001), *A Culture of Corruption – Coping with Government in Post-communist Europe* (Budapest: Central European University Press).

Mo, P. H. (2001), "Corruption and Economic Growth," *Journal of Comparative Economics*, Vol. 29: 66–79.

Mocan, N. (2004), "What Determines Corruption? International Evidence from Micro Data," NBER Working Paper 10460.

Moe, T. M. (1984), "The New Economics of Organization," *American Journal of Political Science*, Vol. 28 (4): 739–77.

Montinola, G. and R. W. Jackman (2002), "Sources of Corruption: A Cross-Country Study," *British Journal of Political Science*, Vol. 32: 147–70.

Moody-Stuart, G. (1994), "Grand Corruption in Third World Development," Transparency International (TI) Working Paper, Berlin: Transparency International.

Moody-Stuart, George (1997), *Grand Corruption. How Business Bribes Damage Developing Countries* (Oxford, UK: WorldView Publishing).

Mookherjee, D. and I. P. L. Png (1995), "Corruptible Law Enforcers: How should they be compensated?," *The Economic Journal*, Vol. 105: 145–59.

Moran, Th. (2006), "How Multinational Investors Evade Developed Country Laws," Center for Global Development Working Paper 79. online version at www.cgdev.org/content/publications/detail/6113

Morgan, Th. (1964), "The Theory of Error in Centrally-Directed Economic Systems," *Quarterly Journal of Economics*, Vol. 78 (3): 395–419.

Moselle, B. and B. Polak (2001), "A Model of a Predatory State," *Journal of Law Economics and Organization*, Vol. 17 (1): 1–33.

Murphy, K. M., A. Shleifer, and R. W. Vishny (1993), "Why is Rent-Seeking so Costly to Growth?," *The American Economic Review Papers and Proceedings*, Vol. 82 (2): 409–14.

Myrdal, G. (1956), *An International Economy* (New York: Harper and Bros.).

Myrdal, G. (1968), *Asian Drama. Vol. II* (New York: Random House).

Neeman, Z., M. Paserman, and A. Simhon (2003), "Corruption and Openness," CEPR Discussion Paper 4057. London: Centre for Economic Policy Research.

Nelson, W. and S.G. Winter (1982), *An Evolutionary Theory of Economic Change* (Cambridge, MA: Belknap Press of Harvard University Press).

Neugebauer, G. (1978), *Grundzüge einer ökonomischen Theorie der Korruption. Eine Studie über die Bestechung*. Basler sozialökonomische Studien (Zürich: Schulthess Polygraphischer Verlag).

Niskanen, W. (1971), *Bureaucracy and Representative Government* (Chicago, IL: Aldine Press).

Niskanen, W. (1975), "Bureaucrats and Politicians," *Journal of Law and Economics*, Vol. 18: 617–43.

North, D. C. (1981), *Structure and Change in Economic History* (New York and London: Norton).

North, D.C. (1984), "Three Approaches to the Study of Institutions," *Neoclassical Political Economy. The Analysis of Rent-Seeking and DUP Activities*, ed. by D.C. Colander (Cambridge, MA: Ballinger Publishing Company): 33–40.

North, D. C. (1993), "Institutions and Credible Commitment," *Journal of Institutional and Theoretical Economics*, Vol. 149: 11–23.

North, D.C. and B.R. Weingast (1989), "The Evolution of Institutions Governing Public Choice in Seventeenth Century England," *Journal of Economic History*, Vol. 49: 803–32.

Nye, J.S. (1967), "Corruption and Political Development: A Cost Benefit Analysis," *American Political Science Review*, Vol. 61 (2): 417–27. Reprinted in A. Heidenheimer, M. Johnston, and V. LeVine (1989), *Political Corruption – A Handbook* (New Brunswick, NJ: Transaction Publishers): 963–83.

OECD (2003), *Business Approaches to Combating Corrupt Practices*, Study prepared by the Capital Movements, International Investment and Services Division, OECD Directorate for Financial, Fiscal and Enterprise Affairs, September.

Okeahalam, C. C. and I. Bah (1998), "Perceived Corruption and Investment in Sub-Saharan African," *South African Journal of Economics*, Vol. 67 (1), March: 386.

Oldenburg, P. (1987), "Middlemen in Third-World Corruption: Implications of an Indian Case," *World Politics*, Vol. 39: 508–35.

Olsen, T. and G. Torsvik (1998), "Collusion and Renegotiation in Hierarchies: A Case of Beneficial Corruption," *International Economic Review*, Vol. 39 (2), May: 413–38.

Olson, M. (1965), *The Logic of Collective Action: Public Goods and the Theory of Groups* (Cambridge, MA: Harvard University Press).

Olson, M. (1982), *The Rise and Decline of Nations* (New Haven, CT: Yale University Press).

Orchard, L. and Stretton, H. (1997), "Public Choice," *Cambridge Journal of Economics*, Vol. 21 (3): 409–30.

Paldam, M. (2001), "Corruption and Religion. Adding to the Economic Model," *Kyklos*, Vol. 54 (2/3): 383–414.

Paldam, M. (2002), "The Big Pattern of Corruption. Economics, Culture and the Seesaw Dynamics," *European Journal of Political Economy*, Vol. 18: 215–40.

Panizza, U. (2001), "Electoral Rules, Political Systems, and Institutional Quality," *Economics and Politics*, Vol. 13 (3): 311–42.

Pechlivanos, L. (1998), "Self-Enforcing Corruption and Optimal Deterrence," unpublished manuscript, Université des Sciences Sociales, Toulouse, France.

Pechlivanos, L. (2004), "Self-Enforcing Corruption: Information Transmission and Organizational Response," *The New Institutional Economics of Corruption – Norms, Trust, and Reciprocity*, ed. by J. Graf Lambsdorff, M. Schramm, and M. Taube London: Routledge: 93–111.

Pellegrini, L. and R. Gerlagh (2004), "Corruption's Effect on Growth and its Transmission Channels," *Kyklos*, Vol. 57 (3): 429–56.

Pellegrini, L. and S. Vujic (2003), "*Corruption, Economic Development and Environmental Policy*," Political Economy of the Environment, Institute for Environmental Studies, IVM, Working Paper, the Netherlands.

Peltzman, S. (1976), "Towards a More General Theory of Regulation," *Journal of Law and Economics*, Vol. 20: 322–40.

Peltzman, S. (1989), "The Economic Theory of Regulation after a Decade of Deregulation," *Brooking Papers of Economic Activity: Microeconomics*, ed. by M. N. Baily and C. Winston (Washington, DC: Brookings Institution): 1–41.

Persson, T., G. Tabellini, and F. Trebbi (2003), "Electoral Rules and Corruption," *Journal of the European Economic Association*, Vol. 1 (4): 958–89, formerly published in: *NBER* Working Paper 8154, March 2001.

Poirson, H. (1998), "Economic Security, Private Investment, and Growth in Developing Countries," International Monetary Fund Working Paper 98/4, January.

Pope, J. (2000), *The Transparency International Source Book 2000 – Confronting Corruption: The Elements of a National Integrity System* (Berlin: Transparency International). Online version at www.transparency.org/sourcebook/, retrieved December 2006.

Posner, R. A. (1974), "Theories of Economic Regulation," *Bell Journal of Economics and Management*, Vol. 5 (2): 335–58.

Posner, R. A. (1975), "The Social Cost of Monopoly and Regulation," *Journal of Political Economy*, Vol. 83: 807–27.

Pritzl, R. F. J. (1995), "La Corrupción pública: una forma dinámica e ilegal de rentismo o *rent-seeking* en la lucha distributiva de los grupos de interés organizados," *Corrupción. Contribuciones*. Publication Trimestral 4 (Buenos Aires: *Konrad Adenauer Stiftung and* CIEDLA).

Pryor, F. L. (1984), "Rent-Seeking and the Growth and Fluctuations of Nations. Empirical Tests of Some Recent Hypothesis," *Neoclassical Political Economy. The Analysis of Rent-Seeking and DUP Activities*, ed. by D. C. Colande (Cambridge, MA: Ballinger Publishing Company): 155–75.

Putnam, R. D. (1993), *Making Democracy Work. Civic Traditions in Modern Italy* (Princeton, NJ: Princeton University Press).

Rasmusen, E. and J. M. Ramseyer (1994), "Cheap Bribes and the Corruption Ban: A Coordination Game among Rational Legislators," *Public Choice*, Vol. 74: 305–27.

Robertson, C. J. and A. Watson (2004), "Corruption and Change: The Impact of Foreign Direct Investment," *Strategic Management Journal*, Vol. 25 (4): 385–96.

Rock, M. T. and Bonnett, H. (2004), "The comparative politics of corruption: Accounting for the East Asian paradox in empirical studies of corruption growth and investment," *World Development*, 32 (6): 999–1017.

Root, H. (1999), "The Importance of Being Small," Center for International Studies Working Paper 99–13, Los Angeles, CA: University of Southern California.

Rose-Ackerman, S. (1975), "The Economics of Corruption," *Journal of Public Economics*, Vol. 4: 187–203.

Rose-Ackerman, S. (1978), *Corruption – A Study in Political Economy* (New Haven, CT: Academic Press).

Rose-Ackerman, S. (1998), "The Role of the World Bank in Controlling Corruption," *Law and Policy in International Business*, Vol. 29: 93–114.

Rose-Ackerman, Susan (1999), *Corruption and Government. Causes, Consequences and Reform* (Cambridge: Cambridge University Press).

Rose-Ackerman, Susan (2005), *From Elections to Democracy. Building Accountable Government in Hungary and Poland* (Cambridge: Cambridge University Press).

Sachs, J. and A. Warner (1995), "Economic Reform and the Process of Global Integration," *Brookings Papers on Economic Activity*, Vol. 25 (1): 1–118.

Sandholtz, W. and M. Gray (2003), "International Integration and National Corruption," *International Organization*, Vol. 57 (4): 761–800.

Sandholtz, W. and W. Koetzle (2000), "Accounting for Corruption: Economic Structure, Democracy, and Trade," *Industrial Studies Quarterly*, Vol. 44: 31–50.

Sandholtz, W. and R. Taagepera (2005), "Corruption, Culture, and Communism," *International Review of Sociology*, Vol. 15 (1): 109–131.

Sayed, A. (2004): *Corruption in International Trade and Commercial Arbitration* (The Hague.: Kluwer Law International).

Schrag, J. and S. Scotchmer (1997), "The Self-Reinforcing Nature of Crime," *International Review of Law and Economics*, Vol. 17: 325–35.

Schramm, M. and M. Taube (2003), "The Institutional Economics of Legal Institutions, Guanxi, and Corruption in the PR China," *Fighting Corruption in Asia. Causes, Effects and Remedies* ed. by J. Kidd and J. Richter, New Jersey, London, Singapore, and Hong Kong): 271–96.

Schulze, G. and B. Frank (2003), "Deterrence versus Intrinsic Motivation: Experimental Evidence on the Determinants of Corruptibility," *Economics of Governance*, Vol. 4 (2): 143–60.

Schumpeter, J. A. (1942), Capitalism, Socialism and Democracy (New York: Harper & Bros.).

Scott, J. C. (1972), *Comparative Political Corruption* (Englewood Cliffs, NJ: Prentice Hall).

Shleifer, A. and R. W. Vishny (1993), "Corruption," *Quarterly Journal of Economics*, Vol. 108: 599–617.

Shleifer, A. and R. W. Vishny (1998), *The Grabbing Hand – Government Pathologies and their Cures*. Cambridge, MA: (Harvard University Press): 1–17.

Shugart, M. S. (1999), "Presidentialism, Parliamentarism, and the Provision of Collective Goods in Less-Developed Countries," *Constitutional Political Economy*, Vol. 10: 53–88.

Smarzynska, B. K. and S. Wei (2000), "Corruption and the Composition of Foreign Direct Investment: Firm-Level Evidence," World Bank Discussion Paper 2360, Washington, DC: World Bank.

Smith, R. J., R. D. J. Muir, M. J. Walpole, A. Balmford and N. Leader-Williams (2003), "Governance and the loss of biodiversity," *Nature*, Vol. 426: 67–70.

Soskice, D. (1999), "Divergent Production Regimes: Coordinated and Uncoordinated Market Economies in the 1990s," *Continuity and Change in Contemporary Capitalism*, ed. by Kitschelt, H., P. Lange, G. Marks, and J. Stephens (New York: Cambridge University Press).

Stansbury, N. (2004), Anti-corruption Initiative in the Construction and Engineering Industry, Report Five: The Prevention of Bribery Through Agency Commissions, Transparency International (UK).

Stigler, G. J. (1971), "The Theory of Economic Regulation," *Bell Journal of Economics and Management Science*, Vol. 2: 3–21.

Stiglitz, J. (1998a), "Redefining the Role of the State – What Should it do? How Should it do it? And How Should these Decisions be Made?," Paper presented on the Tenth Anniversary of MITI Research Institute, Tokyo. Online version at www.worldbank.org/html/extdr/extme/redefine.pdf, retrieved December 2006.

Stiglitz, J. (1998b), "Distinguished Lecture on Economics in Government: The Private Uses of Public Interests: Incentives and Institutions," *The Journal of Economic Perspectives*, Vol. 12 (2): 3–22.

Stratmann, T. (2003), "Do Strict Electoral Campaign Finance Rules Limit Corruption?," CESifo DICE Report 1: 24–27.

Straub, S. (2003), "Opportunism, Corruption and the Multinational Firm's Mode of Entry," Edinburgh School of Economics, Discussion Paper 102.

Strausz, R. (1995), "Collusion and Renegotiation in a Principal – Supervisior – Agent Relationship," *Center for Economic Research, Discussion Paper* 9548, Netherlands: Tilburg University.

Sung, H.-E. (2002), "A Convergence Approach to the Analysis of Political Corruption: A Cross-National Study," *Crime, Law and Social Change*, Vol. 38 (2): 137–160.

Sung, H.-E. (2003), "Fairer Sex or Fairer System? Gender and Corruption Revisited," *Social Forces*, Vol. 82 (2): 703–23.

Sung, H.-E. (2004), "Democracy and Political Corruption: A Cross-National Comparison," *Crime, Law and Social Change*, Vol. 41 (2): 179–93.

Sung, H.-E. and D. Chu (2003), "Does Participation in the Global Economy Reduce Political Corruption? An Empirical Inquiry," *International Journal of Comparative Criminology*, Vol. 3 (2): 94–118.

Svensson, J. (2003), "Who Must Pay Bribes and How Much? Evidence from a Cross Section of Firms," *The Quarterly Journal of Economics*, Vol. 118 (1): 207–30.

Svensson, J. (2005), "Eight Questions about Corruption," *The Journal of Economic Perspectives*, Vol. 19 (3): 19–42.

Swamy, A., St. Knack, Y. Lee, and O. Azfar (2001), "Gender and Corruption," *Journal of Development Economics*, Vol. 64: 25–55.

Tanzi, V. (1995), "Corruption: Arm's–length Relationships and Markets," *The Economics of Organized Crime*, ed. by G. Fiorentini and S. Peltzman (Cambridge: Cambridge University Press): 161–180.

Tanzi, V. and H. Davoodi (1997), "Corruption, Public Investment, and Growth," International Monetary Fund Working Paper 97/139.

Tanzi, V. and H. Davoodi (2001), "Corruption, Growth, and Public Finances," *Political Economy of Corruption*, ed. by A.K. Jain (London: Routledge): 89–110.

Tavares, S. (2005), "Does Rapid Trade Liberalization Increase Corruption?," paper presented at the European Public Choice Society Conference 2005.

Tellenbach, S. (1997), "Türkei," *Korruptionsbekämpfung durch Strafrecht*, ed. by A. Eser, M. Überhofen, and B. Huber. Freiburg, Germany: Max-Planck-Institut für ausländisches und internationales Strafrecht.

Testa, C. (2003), "Government Corruption and Legislative Procedures: Is One Chamber Better than Two?," mimeo, Royal Holloway College, University of London.

Thompson, D.F. (1993), "Mediated Corruption: The Case of the Keating Five," *American Political Science Review*, Vol. 87: 369–381.

Tollison, R.D. (1982), "Rent Seeking: A Survey," *Kyklos*, Vol. 35: 575–602.

Tonoyan, V. (2004), "The Bright and Dark Sides of Trust: Corruption and Entrepreneurship," Trust and Entrepreneurship: A West-East-Perspective, ed. by H. Höhmann and F. Welter (Cheltenham: Edward Elgar). Online version at: www.icgg.org/downloads/contribution11_tonoyan.pdf

Transparency International, (1999), Newsletter. Berlin: Transparency International, September.

Treisman, D. (1999), "Decentralization and Corruption: Why are Federal States Perceived to be More Corrupt," paper prepared for the presentation at the *Annual Meeting of the American Political Science Association*, Atlanta, September.

Treisman, D. (2000), "The Causes of Corruption: A Cross-National Study," *Journal of Public Economics*, Vol. 76: 399–457.

Tullock, G. (1967), "The Welfare Costs of Tariffs, Monopolies, and Theft," *Western Economic Journal*, Vol. 5 (3): 224–32.

Tullock, G. (1971), "The Cost of Transfers," *Kyklos*, Vol. 24: 629–43.

Tullock, G. (1975), "Competing for Aid," *Public Choice*, Vol. 21: 41–52.

Tullock, G. (1980a), "Rent Seeking as a Negative-Sum Game," *Toward a Theory of the Rent-Seeking Society*, ed. by J.M. Buchanan, R.D. Tollison, and G. Tullock (College Station, TX: Texas A&M University Press): 16–36.

Tullock, G. (1980b), "Efficient Rent Seeking," *Toward a Theory of the Rent-Seeking Society*, ed. by J.M. Buchanan, R.D. Tollison, and G. Tullock (College Station, TX: Texas A&M University Press): 97–112.

Tullock, G. (1989), "Klitgaard, Robert, Controlling Corruption," *The Journal of Economic Literature*, Vol. 27: 658–9.

Tullock, G. (1993), *Rent Seeking*, The Shaftesbury Papers 2, Cambridge: Cambridge University Press.

Uhlenbruck, K., P. Rodriguez, J. Doh, and L. Eden (2006), "The Impact of Corruption on Entry Strategy: Evidence from Telecommunication Projects in Emerging Economies," Organization Science, Vol. 17(3): 402–14.

United Nations (2006), "Seventh United Nations Survey of Crime Trends and Operations of Criminal Justice Systems, covering the period 1998–2000" *Report by the United Nations Office on Drugs and Crime.* Retrieved in December 2006 from: www.unodc.org/unodc/crime_cicp_survey_seventh.html

Uslaner, E. (2004), "Trust and Corruption," *The New Institutional Economics of Corruption – Norms, Trust, and Reciprocity*, ed. by J. Graf Lambsdorff, M. Schramm, and M. Taube (London: Routledge): 76–92.

van Rijckeghem, C. and B. Weder (2001), "Bureaucratic Corruption and the Rate of Temptation: Do Wages in the Civil Service affect Corruption, and by How Much?," *Journal of Development Economics*, Vol. 65 (2): 307–31.

Vanucci, A. (2000), "Corruption, Political Parties and Political Protection," European University Institute Economics Department, Working Paper 62, Badia Fiesolana: San Domenico.

Voigt, S., L. Feld, and A. van Aaken (2004), "Power over Prosecutors Corrupts Politicians: Cross Country Evidence Using a New Indicator," *Draft Version, Economics Faculty*, University of Kassel, Germany.

Weber, M. (1920), *Gesammelte Aufsätze zur Religionssoziologie* (Tübingen, Germany: Mohr & Siebeck). Reprinted 1988.

Wedeman, A. (1997), "Looters, Rent-scrapers, and Dividend–Collectors: Corruption and Growth in Zaire, South Korea, and the Philippines," *The Journal of Developing Areas*, Vol. 31: 457–78.

Wei, S.-J. (1997), "Why is Corruption so Much More Taxing than Tax? Arbitrariness Kills," *NBER Working Paper* 6255, Cambridge, MA.

Wei, S.-J. (2000a), "Natural Openness and Good Government," World Bank Poliy Research Working Paper 2411 and NBER Working Paper 7765.

Wei, S.-J. (2000b), "How Taxing is Corruption on International Investors," *Review of Economics and Statistics*, Vol. 82 (1): 1–11.

Wei, S.-J. (2000c), "Corruption, Composition of Capital Flows, and Currency Crises," World Bank Working Paper 2429.

Wei, S.-J. and S. Sievers (1999), "The Cost of Crony Capitalism," *The Asian Competitiveness Report 1999*. Geneva: World Economic Forum, 50–55.

Wei, S.-J. and Y. Wu (2001), "Negative Alchemy? Corruption, Composition of Capital Flows, and Currency Crises," NBER Working Paper 8187, March.

Weingast, B. R. (1993), "Constitutions as Governance Structures: The Political Foundations of Secure Markets," *Journal of Institutional and Theoretical Economics*, Vol. 149: 286–311.

Wellisz, St. and R. Findlay (1984), "Protection and Rent-Seeking in Developing Countries," *Neoclassical Political Economy. The Analysis of Rent-Seeking and DUP Activities*, ed. by D. C. Colander (Cambridge, MA: Ballinger Publishing Company): 141–54.

Welsch, H. (2004), "Corruption, Growth, and the Environment: A Cross-Country Analysis," *Environment and Development Economics*, Vol. 9: 663–93.

Wheeler, D. and A. Mody (1992), "International Investment Location Decisions: The Case of U.S. Firms," *Journal of International Economics*, Vol. 33: 57–76.

Wiehen, M. (1996), "OECD Recommendations and Enquiry," *Uganda International Conference on Good Governance in Africa* (Berlin: Transparency International): 115–22.

Wiggins, S. (1991), "The Economics of the Firm and Contracts: A Selective Survey," *Journal of Institutional and Theoretical Economics*, Vol. 147: 603–61.

Williamson, J. (1993), "Exchange Rate Management," *The Economic Journal*, Vol. 103: 188–97.

Williamson, O. E. (1983), "Credible Commitments: The Use of Hostages to Support Exchange," *American Economic Review*, Vol. 83: 519–40.

Williamson, O. E. (1985), *The Economic Institutions of Capitalism: Firms, Markets, Relational Contracting* (New York: The Free Press).

Winston, G. C. (1979), "The Appeal of Inappropriate Technologies: Self-Inflicted Wages, Ethnic Price and Corruption," *World Development*, Vol. 7 (8/9): 835–45.

Wintrobe, R. (1998a), "Some Lessons on the Efficiency of Democracy from a Study of Dictatorship," *The Political Dimension of Economic Growth*, ed. by S. Borner and M. Paldam (London and New York: Macmillan Press and St. Martin Press): 20–37.

Wintrobe, R. (1998b), *The Political Economy of Dictatorship* (Cambridge: Cambridge University Press).

Wintrobe, R. and A. Breton (1986), "Organizational Structure and Productivity," *The American Economic Review*, Vol. 76 (3): 530–8.

World Bank (1997), *World Development Report 1997* (Washington, DC: World Bank).

Wyatt, G. (2002), "Corruption, Productivity and Transition," Centre for Economic Reform and Transformation, (CERT) Discussion Paper 205, Heriot Watt University, Edinburgh, United Kingdom.

You, J.-S. and S. Khagram (2005), "Inequality and Corruption," *American Sociological Review*, Vol. 70 (1): 136–57.

Index